Bt
5.85

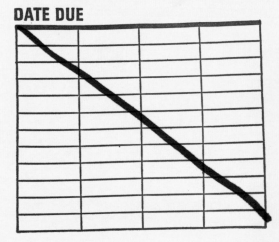

Under the editorship of

DAYTON D. McKEAN

University of Colorado

❖

OTHER TITLES IN THE SERIES

The Mexican

Political System

L. VINCENT PADGETT

SAN DIEGO STATE COLLEGE

HOUGHTON MIFFLIN COMPANY · BOSTON

To

EDNA

PREFACE

In 1920 a Mexican president, Venustiano Carranza, was killed while fleeing from a rebellion led by his former trusted lieutenant, Alvaro Obregón. These men had been heroes and collaborators in the Revolution, 1910–1917, but the problem of the presidential succession only a few years later shattered their relationship. In 1964 the presidential succession was resolved peacefully, as it had been for over three decades, and the foremost opposition candidate, instead of threatening armed revolt over the electoral count, expressed his satisfaction with the way the victorious candidate had conducted the campaign. The difference between these two situations involving the presidential succession is great. What are the political patterns and structures which have made such change possible?

This is a book about several keys to the political nature of the Mexican system. It is a system which has undergone remarkable change in the direction of political stability. Basic to this change is a pantheon of heroes and events which legitimize the system; a dominant, "official" party which provides a mechanism by which diverse groups can coalesce; a number of interest groups which operate channels for communicating the wishes of their rank and file to appropriate officials; an inordinately strong chief executive who is replaced every six years; and a series of policies for bringing greater material and psychic rewards to the population.

Unlike the underdeveloped country that it clearly was in the early 1930's, Mexico of today has modern transportation, modern communication, rising steel production, self-sufficiency in many foodstuffs, and modern merchandising techniques. However, Mexico also has poverty-stricken rural and urban masses, illiteracy, and a shortage of technicians and mechanics to maintain the industrial plant. Mexico is, therefore, a country not yet developed in the sense of the older industrial countries of the West, but one undergoing rapid change. The politics of the country are carried on within this transitional milieu.

There are two difficult problems that stand out in writing about the Mexicans. The first is substantive, the second technical. In the first case the problem is twofold. Mexican scholars and commentators spend relatively little time writing about present-day politics. There is a substantial body of writing on agricultural policy, but even that is thin compared with the magnitude of the subject. Another matter which also has to do with access to information is connected with the basic feeling which all Mexicans seem to have toward outsiders

viii PREFACE

— especially if they come from the United States. Mexican politicians are not easily cultivated. They are particularly reticent when asked about the basic political factors. The Mexican politician must know the observer very well before silence is broken. Most scholarly observers have neither the time nor the inclination to invest in such enterprises. Much about Mexican politics goes unknown for these reasons.

It is also difficult to write about Mexico because of the problem in the use of the words *Revolution* and *revolutionary*. When should these words be quoted, when capitalized? I have sought uniformity in these matters, but there is no clear-cut model to follow. Writers handle the problem differently. For purposes of this book a capital "R" is used when referring to the Revolution of 1910. The "r" is small and quoted with an adjective referring to the 1910–17 period or tradition springing directly from it. Finally, neither capitals nor quotation marks are used when speaking of a tradition of revolution that reaches back to independence.

I am indebted to a number of persons who have helped to make this book possible. I should like to mention, first of all, a few who have greatly aided my research efforts in Mexico — Lic. Manuel M. Moreno, Lic. Gilberto Loyo, Lic. Gregorio Delint Alarcón, Lic. Rómulo Sánchez Mireles, and Mr. Robert C. Jones. I am grateful for the encouragement and aid of some of my colleagues in the political science department at San Diego State College, particularly Ivo K. Feierabend, Richard C. Gripp, Henry L. Janssen, and Ned V. Joy. Kenneth F. Johnson and Marjorie Janssen provided helpful suggestions of both substantive and technical nature. Sergio Noriega was an outstanding student assistant. Mrs. Veva Link and Mrs. Yvonne Walker were most faithful in furthering the preparation of the manuscript. My wife, Edna Padgett, proved indispensable in editing and handling innumerable other details. Dayton D. McKean, editorial adviser to Houghton Mifflin Company, read the entire manuscript and offered many helpful suggestions. Richard N. Clark of Houghton Mifflin Company presided over all stages leading to publication with great care and patience. None of the people above is responsible for the inevitable inadequacies of this book.

Mexico City
July, 1965

L. VINCENT PADGETT

CONTENTS

1

The Bases of Legitimacy

Politics and Political Culture

The chairman had offered me a place beside his desk with the promise that I would learn more observing what happened in that office than he could possibly tell me about politics in the state of Puebla. This was the headquarters of the state committee of Mexico's dominant political party, the *Partido Revolucionario Institucional* (PRI). It was an old two-story building close to the center of the city. On the first floor were offices for the state chapter (*liga*) of the National Peasants Confederation (CNC). There was also a medical center for the needy supported by the PRI committee and a room at the back of the omnipresent courtyard where corn acquired at special prices through government cooperation was sold to the poor.

On this particular day the headquarters were much livelier than during my earlier visits, for this was the last day before the party municipal nominating assemblies scheduled throughout the state. The chairman of the state committee had been out of town making arrangements for these conventions and now was perpetually in demand. His outer office was crowded to capacity with long lines of peasants and workers waiting to see him. Party employees scurried in all directions through the throng, and self-important looking men in business suits pushed past the patient queues of people in work clothes in order to gain a word with the "chief." These were smaller scale political bosses, *jefes políticos,* from the surrounding regions. In a single hour between eleven and twelve o'clock Ignacio Morales, the chairman of the committee, was confronted with groups from four *municipios* in each of which two or more lists for town council posts had been proposed by

1

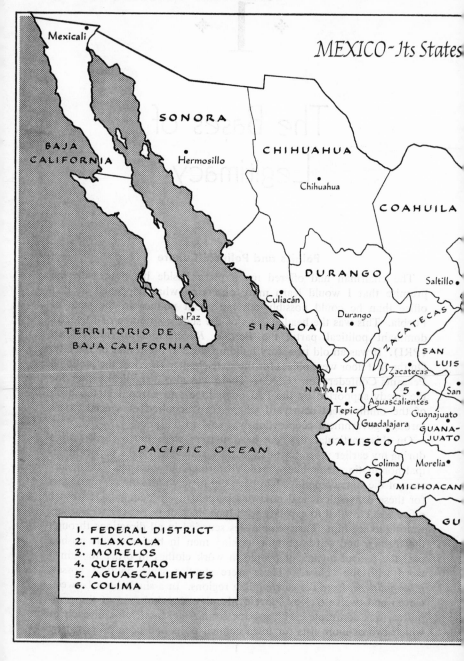

MEXICO~Its States

Mexicali

SONORA

BAJA CALIFORNIA

Hermosillo

CHIHUAHUA

Chihuahua

COAHUILA

Saltillo

DURANGO

Culiacán

Durango

ZACATECAS

SAN LUIS

La Paz

TERRITORIO DE BAJA CALIFORNIA

SINALOA

Zacatecas

San

NAVARIT

5

Aguascalientes

Guanajuato

Tepic

GUANA-JUATO

PACIFIC OCEAN

Guadalajara

JALISCO

Colima

Morelia

6

MICHOACAN

GU

1. FEDERAL DISTRICT
2. TLAXCALA
3. MORELOS
4. QUERETARO
5. AGUASCALIENTES
6. COLIMA

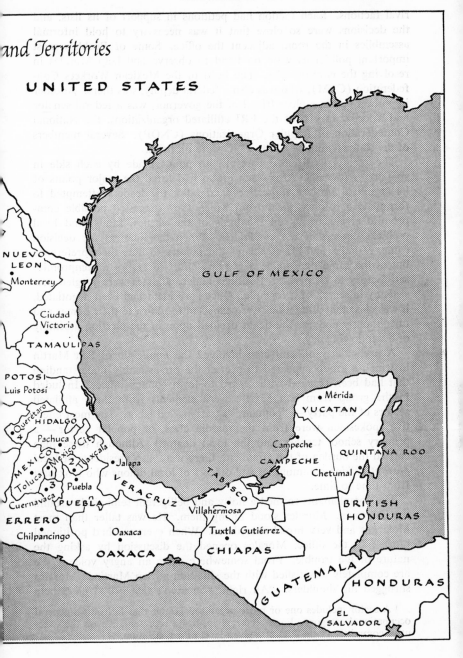

and Territories

UNITED STATES

NUEVO
LEON
• Monterrey

• Ciudad
  Victoria

TAMAULIPAS

POTOSI
Luis Potosí

Querétaro
HIDALGO
• Pachuca
MEXICO Mexico City
Toluca 2 Tlaxcala • Jalapa
3 • Puebla
Cuernavaca PUEBLA
VERACRUZ

ERRERO
• Chilpancingo • Oaxaca

OAXACA • Tuxtla Gutiérrez

CHIAPAS

GULF OF MEXICO

• Mérida
YUCATAN

Campeche
CAMPECHE QUINTANA ROO
• Chetumal

TABASCO
• Villahermosa

BRITISH
HONDURAS

GUATEMALA HONDURAS

EL
SALVADOR

rival factions. Each faction had petitions in support of its lists, and the decisions were so close that it was necessary to hold informal assemblies in the room adjacent the office. Some of Puebla's most important politicians were on hand to observe and help Morales in resolving the controversies. The head of the Mexican Workers Confederation (CTM), who was also a federal deputy, was there. Another important figure, a close friend of the governor, was a federal senator and a leader in one of the PRI affiliated organizations, the National Confederation of Popular Organizations (CNOP). Several members of the state committee of the CNC were on hand.

The politicians listened carefully to points made by each side in support of its case. After each group had listed the major points of its argument for the respective candidates, the leaders attempted to formulate a balance sheet from which they suggested possible compromise arrangements on the basis of the virtues, faults, and local political support of the candidates. When the moment for decision came, Morales and his associates did not try to hide their preference but at the same time made a genuine effort to secure a compromise satisfactory to all parties. Positions and candidates were juggled persistently in search of a formula. Once agreement had been negotiated, it was clear that all factions were expected to return to their homes and unanimously endorse the ticket decided upon in the election assembly of the following day.

A particularly difficult case involved the *municipio* of San Martín in which a group appeared to protest the pre-assembly understanding that had been reached with regard to town council offices. Included in the group from San Martín were elements from three affiliated sectors of the party — "popular," agrarian, and labor. The most effective spokesmen were from the middle class, or popular sector — a primary school teacher and the local doctor.[1] Although these men carried the burden of the argument, there were also presidents of local peasant (*ejido*) communities and officers of local unions who took part from time to time.

The complainants formed a noisy and belligerent semi-circle around the chairman. Morales stood facing them. He was taller than most Mexicans and very broad shouldered. When everyone had positioned himself in the office, Morales opened the discussion by asking the nature of the trouble. From somewhere came an angry voice. "We are completely dissatisfied with the situation at San Martín." Morales shrugged his shoulders. "All right, you aren't satisfied. I can't help

---

[1] A sector includes one or more organized groups that fall into a general occupational category. Each sector, then, has a representative on the executive committee of the PRI at a given level of organization.

that. This is no way to further your case." The group became quiet, and the school teacher, the doctor, several union officials and some of the *ejido* presidents spoke in turn for their people. They outlined a situation in which the municipal president was the prime offender. He had arranged a convention of the popular sector in which he had used outside help to win the endorsement of the assembly for his chosen successor. Neither the peasant leaders nor the union officials had been notified of the assembly. Despite these procedural irregularities the municipal president with his chosen group had proceeded to form the entire list of PRI candidates for municipal office. The list had then been presented to Morales who had given his approval since the minutes of the assembly had made it appear that all was in order. The result was that both labor and agrarian sectors were incensed because of the manner in which their strength had been ignored while the majority of the popular sector also felt cheated.

Morales argued that on the basis of the convening order for municipal assemblies he could not receive complaints until after the official assembly had been held on the morrow. His general secretary spoke up. "Look here! There are many factors involved in this situation. If you don't like the man your municipal president has selected as his successor, remember at least that he is a well-known businessman and well prepared to talk with government officials about the financial problems of your *municipio*. Moreover, the present nominee has close ties of friendship with various people in the federal government. It is necessary at least to give such a man a place on the ticket." In reply, the spokesmen for the delegation from San Martín pointed out that they clearly had an "absolute" majority and invited the party officials to come to the *municipio* and see this for themselves. "Don't tell us the party has to wait until after the municipal convention to act on a complaint!" they said. "You can act now if you want to! If you don't we will not have nearly so good a chance." Those from San Martín then pointed out that if the party persisted in the arrangement it would be responsible for putting an undesirable man in the municipal presidency, a man disliked throughout the *municipio*. One spokesman said with conviction, "The *municipio* will be seething with discontent. Do you like that kind of picture? Do you want to be a party to such an arrangement?" Several of the San Martín leaders pointed to sections of the party statutes which supported their argument.

When the delegation showed no signs of leaving until satisfaction had been obtained, Morales capitulated. He gave the following instructions. "Doctor, professor, and other members of the popular sector, hold your convention at eight o'clock this evening. I shall be there or shall send a trusted representative. The agrarian and labor sectors will meet beforehand to select nominees for the municipal ticket and delegates to attend the popular sector convention."

After the San Martín episode the excitement became less intense, and the number of people waiting grew steadily smaller. Finally, at four o'clock Morales left the office and took me along with some of his associates for refreshments at a nearby cafe. There it was decided that the candidate for the state legislature from San Martín should preside over the assemblies that evening. The outcome, as I later discovered, was a victory for the delegation which had visited Morales.

Mexico is a country of great contrasts and deep emotional involvements with a political history characterized by shattering revolutions and much bloodshed. Paternalism and personalism have been much in evidence. Until recently these tendencies existed in a milieu of backward economic institutions and an underdeveloped social stratification arrangement, i.e., one in which discernible strata are few and the distance between them great. All these patterns are evident or implied in the political behavior observed at Puebla. Their roots are ancient.

Bloodshed and paternalism were evident at the beginning of colonial times with the arrival of the Spanish, although these characteristics were also part and parcel of the native principalities and aboriginal empires which the Spanish overcame. The period of colonial rule was marked by an effort to transfer European institutions and adapt them to Mexican conditions under the sponsorship of a Crown which claimed to be omnipotent in all matters. Royal representatives were at first conquerors who shed the blood of Indian warriors and later viceroys who symbolized the paternalism of the Crown. All was accomplished through an emissary of the monarch. For some the emissary was the viceroy; for others, less highly placed, it was the viceroy's agent or some lesser official. Everything was done through personal contact with the paternalistic representative of a paternalistic power.

The concept of rebellion was not unknown in colonial times, but with the advent of the independence spirit revolution became endemic to Mexico. Independence replaced the Crown and the viceroy with the successful military leader as the paternalistic symbol of personal rule. The paternalistic pattern of the Crown's agent and his intimate personal way of dealing with the problems of the people, a pattern of centuries, is reflected in the political style of Ignacio Morales, the party committee chairman in Puebla, in his role as representative of the viceregal presidential power in Mexico City.

A tradition of revolution accompanied by an intense sense of personal pride exists in company with the tradition of paternalistic rule.

For this reason the personalistic interpretation of the existing system of rule must be "just," or the politician will be confronted with dangerous dissatisfaction among those he would govern. This is reflected in the Mexican politicians' admonition to each other that the Mexican people are a rebellious people ("Somos muy rebelde, los Mexicanos"). Octavio Paz has summed up Mexican rebelliousness and intransigence in a brilliant passage:

> All of our anxious tensions express themselves in a phrase we use when anger, joy or enthusiasm cause us to exalt our condition as Mexicans: "¡Viva México, hijos de la chingada!" This phrase is a true battle cry, charged with a peculiar electricity; it is a challenge and an affirmation, a shot fired against an imaginary enemy, and an explosion in the air. . . . When we shout this cry on the fifteenth of September, the anniversary of our independence, we affirm ourselves in front of, against and in spite of the "others." Who are the "others"? They are the *hijos de la chingada:* strangers, bad Mexicans, our enemies, our rivals.[2]

Not only does the San Martín episode reflect personalistic and paternalistic tendencies and the capacity for rebellion, it also calls attention to other aspects of the Mexican scene. There is the question of who voices demands. The people who came from San Martín were among the "articulate" in Mexican society. They were not the poor, as described by Oscar Lewis.[3] When they said they had the "absolute" majority, they meant that they had a majority of the articulate group on their side. This would automatically exclude the large number found in nearly any Mexican *municipio* who participate in the "culture of poverty."

The San Martín episode also raises questions relating to modernization. San Martín is on a broad highway reaching into Puebla. How are the articulate ones in more remote *municipios* to acquire the means of

---

[2] Octavio Paz, *The Labyrinth of Solitude,* Lysander Kemp, trans. (New York, 1961), pp. 74–75. Paz points out that the "chingada" is a kind of mother figure which has suffered grave abuse. Though the word has sexual connotations, its more profound meaning centers around notions of failure, violence, deception, cruelty, and the cynical use of power. Those uttering the cry are the defiant victims who derive bitter satisfaction from its utterance. "The magic power of the word is intensified by the fact that . . . no one uses it casually in public. Only an excess of anger or a delirious enthusiasm justifies its use." P. 77.

[3] Oscar Lewis, *The Children of Sánchez* (New York, 1961), p. xxvii. "A critical attitude toward some of the values and institutions of the dominant classes, hatred of the police, mistrust of government and those in high position . . . gives the culture of poverty a counter quality and a potential for being used in political movements aimed against the existing social order."

8 THE BASES OF LEGITIMACY

transportation necessary to visit a party committee in order to reverse an arbitrary and unfair decision? Modernization thus plays a part in terms of the essential nature of transportation in facilitating interaction between those who govern and the governed. Education is also a vital consideration at this point. Had it not been for the superior capacity of the teacher and the doctor from San Martín in the presentation of the case and their knowledge of the party statutes the delegation would probably have failed in its presentation. One then is led to the necessity of pointing out that *municipios* in Mexico frequently do not have access to centers of government, nor do they have educated people to plead a case. The speed with which modernization goes forward thus becomes vital to continued stability.[4]

History and Political Socialization

Certain aspects of Mexican history cluster together to provide the basis of an ideology for the Mexican political system of today.[5] In Mexico an officially recognized, one might say "legitimized," interpretation of Mexican history is widely disseminated. It is inculcated through speeches and actions of community leaders and high officials at all sorts of public events and festivities from the opening of an electric plant in an obscure village to the elaborate celebration of Independence Day in Mexico City. Newspaper editorials, official and semi-official pronouncements, literary figures, and many other persons and groups vital to the communications function make constant reference to heroes and events which are familiar or for which there is a characterization or interpretation that is familiar.

Outstanding events and personalities of Mexican history are central to the maintenance of existing arrangements in the political system of present-day Mexico. The occurrence and direction of change cannot be understood without reference to these matters. Particularly important is the interpretation of the versions and accounts of these events and personalities as presented to most Mexican school children and young people. The general orientation in historical interpretations

[4] Ivo K. Feierabend, Rosalind L. Feierabend, and Betty A. Nesvold, "Correlates of Political Stability." Paper presented before the *American Political Science Association* (September, 1963).

[5] *Ideology* is used loosely in this chapter to refer to a set of norms, goals, and principles for which many Mexicans have developed strong affective ties and which, in this case, have the official blessing of the governing group. It is in terms of these goals and norms that political experience becomes meaningful and the system worth struggling to maintain. Accordingly, the purpose of this chapter is not to provide the most objective statement of Mexican political history. Instead its aim is to inform the student of key events and official interpretations which form the basis of the present myth of legitimacy.

and its ideological stamp are central to the process of political socialization in its more manifest and rational forms.[6]

Mexican history has generated a legacy which raises a number of
problems for political socialization in its most manifest guise, the
formal schooling process. In other words, the problem of what
Mexican children should learn concerning the relationship between
past events and the present system is critical. The Mexican political
culture is a fragmented one in which the violence of internecine
struggle has appeared again and again in the absence of consensus on
fundamentals as to the way government should operate — its relationship to citizens, their relationship to government, and the overall goals
toward which policy should be directed, that is, the basic purposes of
government. All these matters have been much disputed, leaving in
various sectors of society residues of commitment to values regarding
proper uses of governmental power and reasons for existence of
government which are at variance with major characteristics of the present system. These residues of allegiance to values of other periods have
raised more questions of social adjustment because the dominant
groups in the present situation cannot fall back upon some distinct
philosophical system, such as Marxism, which can be treated as

[6] Herbert Hyman has written about "political behavior as *learned* behavior." In connection with this kind of an inquiry into the socialization
process, Hyman points out that norms of participation and goals of action
as well as the democratic-authoritarian directions of those action goals which
are learned by the populace are vital to the characteristics of politics in a
system. It is in relation to this concern with socialization that the official
Mexican ideology of history is treated as a vital aspect conditioning political
behavior in the system. Herbert H. Hyman, *Political Socialization* (Glencoe,
Ill., 1959), pp. 15–17. Particularly we are interested in an explicitly taught
set of norms and goals based upon an historical interpretation which is part
of nearly every primary and secondary school curriculum in the country and
is integral to most interpretive commentary in the media of communication.
The emphasis upon education is important in this connection, as has been
stated by James S. Coleman: "Increased awareness of this functional inter-
dependence between education and polity has stimulated social scientists and
educators to concern themselves with a more comprehensive array of variables. Such broadening is essential if we are fully to understand and interpret the particular facet of the multidimensional development complex
which engages our specialized training. As holists, conscious of this inter-
dependence and interested in the maintenance, integration, and transformation of total societies, political scientists are particularly affected by this new
challenge. It is the holistic imperative that enjoins political scientists to
search for what has been termed 'a more complete and systematic conception
of the political process as a whole.' The same imperative directs our attention to the study of the role of education in the political process and in
political change." James S. Coleman, "Education and the Political Scientist,"
ITEMS, Social Science Research Council, 19. (March, 1965), p. 5.

revealed truth for justification of the present political arrangements.

Fragmentation of political culture is related to many questions over which Mexicans have shed each others' blood in the past. A partial list of these explosive conflicts would include ethnic differences *versus* desire for a unified, national community, absolutism *versus* representative democracy, a political military *versus* a professional one, a political church *versus* an essentially apolitical one, and distribution of opportunity among a few *versus* its distribution among the many.

Any single one of these issues represented a source of conflict; so many sources of ill will in combination made bloodshed inevitable. In the case of ethnic differences involving Spanish and *criollo, mestizo* and Indian, the problem was not only that of physical appearance but also of status differences ascribed in terms of birth which prevented integration of all groups in terms of a national identification common to all. The fact of three centuries of Iberian absolutism and paternalism overlaying an earlier tradition of despotic Indian tribal rule provided little basis for placing in operation some form of representative democracy, a concept which had much theoretical appeal for many Mexicans from the beginning of the nineteenth century. Efforts to establish representative institutions and a liberal approach to human freedoms floundered repeatedly on the shoals of inexperience, a feudalistic class structure, and the determined commitment of the conservative coalition to its particular concept of order and the social status quo. Reaction to unsuccessful liberal political experiments resulted in conservative dictatorship which the liberal group could dislodge only by another resort to violence. Military leaders with their access to arms and men found political activity and internal strife a riper field of endeavor than routine preparation for the defense of national boundaries. A clergy with established privileges interpreted religion for its own ends, holding its position above civil law by exercising its vast influence in education, the economy, and spiritual concerns, and by steering politics toward maintenance of the colonial status quo with regard to clerical secular interests.

Distribution of wealth and opportunity among a few great landholders and leading merchants fitted well with determination of many military leaders and the clergy to maintain privileges above law in the colonial tradition. Privilege was thus the basis of the conservative coalition which kept rising like a phoenix from the ashes of defeat all during the nineteenth century. This Mexican brand of conservatism was repeatedly able to overcome, or at least subvert, as in the years after the Reform, hard-won victories of those who sought wider distribution of opportunity through expansion of popular participation, wider access to learning, protection of individual rights, application of one body of law to all persons, suppression of monopoly privileges, more equitable division of wealth in land, and pride in nationhood and national sovereignty. The above goals and the leaders of the struggles for realization of these aspirations form the core of the nationalist, revolutionary tradition which is not so much a philosophy as an historical experience. It is this tradition which the leaders of modern Mexico attempt to inculcate in the population through education and the communications media.

The Indian

Indianism is one important thread of the nationalist revolutionary tradition. The Indian is regarded as the antithesis of the Spanish heritage, for the Indian is conceptualized as the basis of the truly national tradition and the Spaniard as the epitome of anti-nationalist, colonialist forces working against Mexican self-determination and the progress of Mexicans as a national group. It is for this reason that the Indian leaders who sought to stave off the Spanish conquest have been elevated to the status of national heroes. In the case of the Indian both the glories of pre-Conquest cultures as well as Indian heroes of those times play a part, but the abuses of the Indians under the Spaniards and in later periods are not insignificant.

The cultural achievements of the Maya of Yucatán and of the Aztecs and other tribes of the Central Plateau are taught to school children from first grade on. And just as school children in the United States learn the facts and legends about the fathers of their states and their nation, so Mexican children learn of the Aztec heroes who struggled against the Spanish. Heroes and myths are legion, but one of the outstanding heroes was Cuitlahuac, who organized the rebellion against the Spaniards under Cortez and drove them from Mexico City (Tenochtitlán). Another even more heroic figure, all the more so for the tragedy and futility of his struggle, was the nephew of the Emperor Moctezuma, Cuauhtémoc, who led the last desperate stand of the Aztecs against the Spaniards. There have been other great Indian leaders, as for example, General Tomas Mejía, a leader of conservative forces in the War of the Reform. But there are no statues of Mejía in Mexico today because he regarded Spanish tradition as benevolent and joined with anti-nationalist forces. Death on the Hill of Bells east of the town of Querétaro in company with the Hapsburg prince, Maximilian, pretender to the mythical Mexican throne, left Mejía far outside the accepted group of Mexican Indian heroes.

From the Indian cultural heritage are drawn (whether with justification is not the question) certain contemporary Mexican ideas concerning communal life and collectivism. The extent to which Mexican leaders of today lean toward the patriotic significance of the Indian and the Indian heritage of collectivism — as much or more than dedication to more recent collectivist ideals — marks them as leftist or rightist within the framework of revolutionary experience.

The heroism and tragedy of Indian groups and leaders who rose against the Spaniards or who stood against the efforts of *criollos* and *mestizos* to overrun their lands during the nineteenth century also receive attention from teachers and pupils. Perhaps more important, however, is the instructional emphasis placed upon abuses suffered by the Indians in the colonial period and the first century of independence, and the lesson that these abuses were suffered at the hands of those who were exploiters, alien to the national tradition. However, Indianism is only one of several important themes of the nationalist, revolutionary tradition that serves as the basis for legitimizing today's political system.

The Generation of Independence: Hidalgo, Morelos, and Others

The revolutionary ideas of the latter eighteenth and nineteenth centuries led toward national self-consciousness and pride. The aspirations involved formed the basis for repeated revolutionary efforts against the hardy, exclusive colonial status quo which continued to appeal to various segments of the Mexican population long after independence from Spain was an accomplished fact. Those who supported in one form or another the ideas which led logically to emphasis upon integration of all Mexicans in a coherent national group created the nationalist, revolutionary tradition and provided the stuff of Mexican patriotism as it operates today. The others represented the Mexican style of conservatism which lost out because, above all, its exclusiveness logically worked against integration of a variety of ethnic types and was essentially anti-nationalist.

The revolutionary struggle of the nineteenth century fluctuated both in its intensity and in its success. Historical phases may be distinguished in various ways — according to key personalities, constitutions, battles, or the composition of governments. Because the revolutionary tradition as an ideology relies so heavily upon the ideas and exploits of heroic figures, it may well be that the most fruitful approach is to trace the course of the revolutionary contest with the conservatives in terms of those who played the leading roles.

Our first protagonist is the father of Mexico's Independence Day celebration. Padre Hidalgo issued his cry of rebellion, the *Grito de Dolores,* in September, 1810. Hidalgo, a parish priest, had plotted with others to organize a *criollo* rebellion against the Spanish, but the plot was discovered and instead of appealing to the *criollos* Hidalgo called his Indian and *mestizo* parishioners to arms to protect the

Spanish throne against the Bonapartes and to prevent betrayal of their religion to the French. The most prominent notes sounded by Hidalgo had little to do with the Enlightenment philosophy he had been studying secretly, but they did arouse the feelings of the rural poor who had been the objects of domination by both wealthy Spaniards and *criollos*. The rebellion that had been planned as a *criollo* war for independence from Spanish colonialism became instead a class war of the lower strata against the upper, driving the *criollos* into alliance with the Spaniards. Great success greeted the first efforts of Hidalgo's motley band. Thousands joined his standard, and all resistance was swept away in the initial stages of the rebellion.

The conflict that followed was truly a civil war, since most of those fighting under the Spanish emblem were, in fact, Mexicans, as were Hidalgo's troops. Dissension in Hidalgo's command, coupled with his own vacillation in the face of stiffening Spanish opposition at Mexico City and Guadalajara, brought about the defeat and decimation of his forces as well as the capture and execution of Hidalgo and his lieutenants.

Hidalgo's rebellion was carried on after his death by another parish priest who had once been a pupil of Hidalgo's, José Maria Morelos. While Hidalgo died in a Spanish prison repudiating his rebellious acts in an effort to escape from the onus of excommunication which the church had placed upon him, Morelos, also under the shadow of excommunication, carried on the war. With him were Matamoros, another village priest, and the *mestizo* peasant's son Vicente Guerrero, who like Morelos, has a state of modern Mexico named for him.

Morelos' military leadership was more successful than Hidalgo's, and he was encouraged to set about organizing a government. His ideas for Mexican political organization, first expressed at Chilpancingo in 1813 and formalized as a constitution at Apatzingán in 1814, became an important source of revolutionary thought during the following century. The fundamentals included such revolutionary ideals as racial equality, abolition of clerical and military *fueros* or special privileges, abolition of compulsory tithing, and seizure of church lands. Morelos believed in partition of the great landholdings to provide small farms for peasants. Universal suffrage was endorsed, but was offset by a method of indirect elections. There was to be a plural executive.

Morelos represented a familiar Mexican paradox: he was a devout Catholic who espoused anti-clerical measures. He was also a child of the Spanish tradition of government who sought to formulate a synthesis of that tradition with the Anglo-Saxon and French ideals of democracy. But Morelos was never to have an opportunity to see his ideas tried in practice, for the Spanish forces defeated him in Michoacán and elsewhere. He was eventually betrayed to the Spanish and executed.

Along with Hidalgo the stories of the exploits of Morelos adorn the texts of the early grades in Mexico's elementary schools. It is difficult for Mexicans to have attended school even for a short time and not know that Morelos and Hidalgo stood for equality, the poor, and the *patria*. Their names are immortal in the revolutionary tradition.

Beginning of Independence: Villains and Heroes

It is a paradox of Mexican history that independence was brought about by conservatives reacting against the liberal Spanish rebellion of 1820. The key step involved an agreement between Agustín de Iturbide, a *criollo* officer in Spanish service, and the perennial rebel, Vicente Guerrero. Iturbide's Plan of Iguala provided the basis for independence and at the same time sounded keynotes for conservative programs of the ensuing years. Central to Iturbide's program were Roman Catholic supremacy and the principle of monarchy with a dynasty other than that of Spain to govern a sovereign Mexico where Spaniards and *criollos* were equal. For the moment, liberals and conservatives agreed. For the liberals there was independence; for the conservatives there was a monarch. There was also release from the control of the Spanish government which the conservatives perceived as dangerously liberal under the Constitution of 1820. Iturbide soon tried to make himself emperor and succeeded for almost a year until rebellion drove him from the country.

The leader in the rebellion against Iturbide was a young army officer, Antonio López de Santa Anna, known to historians simply as Santa Anna. Iturbide and Santa Anna had in common a military background and driving ambition. Also common to both is their connection with nineteenth-century conservatism and their place in the gallery of Mexico's villains, fools, and historical mishaps. Iturbide and Santa Anna are two of the "bad guys" of Mexican history. Only the dictator of a later period, Porfirio Díaz, is more universally condemned by the custodians of the revolutionary tradition.

Santa Anna burst into the arena of Mexican politics as a republican and a liberal. Later, in a seemingly effortless about face, he became the leader of the conservatives. With Santa Anna there came to power in the spring of 1823 the old revolutionary element composed of such people as Guerrero, Guadalupe Victoria, and Juan Alvarez, as well as a newer group dedicated to independence and liberal principles. The latter included Miguel Ramos Arizpe, Valentín Gómez Farías, and Manuel Crescencio Rejón. Also on the scene was a former soldier and comrade of Morelos, Nicolás Brava, and a new personage, who was to be aligned with conservative causes in the future, Lucas Alamán. From the deliberations of these men there emerged a method of selecting a president based upon votes of the Mexican states. In such voting under the provisions of the Constitution of 1824, General Guadalupe Victoria became the first President of Mexico.

The discussions and arguments involved in the framing of the Constitution of 1824 raised most of the substantive questions which were to affect the fortunes of liberal reform in Mexico over the next ninety years. Symbols such as rationality, equality, freedom, and progress were to be important. These words, however, had different meanings for different people. For some, the meanings added up to relative regional autonomy; for others, free ports and free enterprise. Some saw expanded educational opportunities as the core of liberal reform. Others felt reform meant principally a clear separation of church and state. The developing revolutionary tradition could not accept the idea of monarchy, nor tolerate the notion of the operation of any arrangement similar to the Spanish Inquisition. Free speech became a major goal. Freemasonry provided a basis for liberal thought and organization. There was emphasis upon rational approaches to natural sciences and to the study of social phenomena.[7]

In the years that followed 1824, the conservative position emerged as one which was pro-clerical in the sense of wishing to help the clergy maintain its dominant position in the society both economically and politically, pro-military in the sense of supporting the privileges and special courts of military officers, and pro-centralization in the sense of supporting the continued control of the core area of Mexico over the peripheral regions. Conservatives were against Freemasonry, which they regarded as anti-clerical, and felt that Freemasonry was connected with other revolutionary, conspiratorial, and undesirable ideas such as political democracy and egalitarianism.

A generation committed to reform dominated the period from 1824 to 1834, but it was an uneasy supremacy with Santa Anna and the conservatives causing more than one government to fall. The leading liberal of the period was Valentín Gómez Farías. Through the efforts of Gómez Farías and his colleagues the thought of the revolutionary liberal tradition became more clearly defined. Basically it was nineteenth century economic and political liberalism molded to the Mexican

---

[7] The reformers saw the Indian as a symbol of freedom. Their model, however, was the idealized Indian of pre-Conquest times. They were ambivalent; there was the glorious Indian, and then there was the Indian who seemed somehow to stand in the path of progress. Liberals did not look to the Indian for their philosophy, but rather to Europe and to the United States.

context. Legal reform, civil controls over the army and the church, as well as progress in education were stressed. More attention was given the concept of nationality. It was pointed out that no truly united nation could have specially distinguishable and privileged bodies above law or with special legal privileges such as existed under the practice of Spanish colonialism.

The clergy, the military, and the aristocracy in general could not tolerate the revolutionary demands for change in Mexico. Issues ran all the way from the general question of the clergy and the church in relation to government to rather narrow ones having to do with plans for improvement of transportation and development of new ports. In the end the reaction to the program for change overwhelmed the Gómez Farías government. Santa Anna came back to assume the presidency and Gómez Farías fled into exile. With the assumption of power Santa Anna completed his change of position from liberal to conservative. The clergy, the military, and the great merchants and landholders became dominant and were able to control the central governing machinery in Mexico City. Liberals fought back from the outer provinces, but Santa Anna succeeded in building an alliance of the interests of Mexico City, Puebla, and Veracruz which was strong enough to hold back and resist liberal efforts from the periphery.[8] Santa Anna and the conservatives dominated the destinies of Mexico for about twenty years after 1834, but were never able to wipe out the ferment of liberalism and the revolutionary tradition.

Liberal ideas drew wider attention as various interests reacted negatively to special privileges given to concessionaires. Those adversely affected by monopoly privileges granted by conservative governments embraced the liberal program of free competition and individual enterprise with the hope of more equal opportunity. Men attempting to begin manufacturing enterprises particularly resented the monopoly privileges of the import-export interests of Veracruz and Mexico City. A new generation came forward to press for change in accord with the core notions of liberalism. For the rising generation of liberals the overriding issue was change and progress. Nationalism, liberty for the individual, popular representation, and the destruction of the old privileged military and clerical cliques were considered by the new revolutionary generation to be the necessary instruments of progress toward a genuinely prosperous nation state.

[8] There was an effort on the part of liberals in Yucatán to wed their cause to the Yucatecan caste war which broke out in 1839. There was unrest in Jalisco and elsewhere. This was also the time of Mexico's great territorial losses to the United States in the Mexican War of 1846–48.

The Reform: Juárez, Lerdo, and Others

Santa Anna was driven from power by the old *mestizo* warrior, Juan Alvarez, who had fought the Spanish and the conservative coalition since the time of Morelos. The names of the men whom Alvarez brought to power in the mid 1850's have become familiar to all Mexican school children. This generation of outstanding leaders included, among others, Benito Juárez, a Oaxaca Indian who had been trained in the law, Melchor Ocampo, and the Lerdo de Tejada brothers. There was also the tragic Ignacio Comonfort who had demonstrated his military talents in support of Alvarez and then, as President, lacked the will necessary to make the Reform a reality in the face of bitter conservative opposition. Comonfort was replaced by the indomitable Juárez, who led the supporters of the Reform to victory first against the conservatives and then against intervention by the French.

Aims of the Reform reached a high point with the laws of Juárez and Lerdo. The Juárez law of 1855 reflected liberal revolutionary concern for unification of the nation under one law by abolishing ecclesiastical and military courts. The Lerdo law of 1856 attacked the material holdings of the church in such a way as to force large amounts of land controlled by the clergy onto the open markets for purchase and use. The Juárez and Lerdo laws were incorporated into the Mexican Constitution of 1857. When that happened, conservative resistance widened into full-scale civil war. This was the War of the Reform or the Three Year War, 1857–1860.

In 1859, as the struggle became ever more difficult, Juárez moved once more against the clergy by decreeing that all their real property belonged to the nation, that tithing was abolished, and that monastic orders were dissolved. Further decrees established civil marriage and freedom of religion. Juárez' policy that church and state were to be separated was clear.

No sooner had the Reform triumphed in January, 1861, than intervention from the outside threatened. Mexico's delinquency in paying foreign debts was the immediate cause. First came Spanish troops, shortly followed by English and French forces. Although the English and Spanish withdrew their soldiers when Juárez promised renewed efforts to make payments on Mexican debts, the French increased their strength and began to move inland from Veracruz. The French purpose was the establishment of a Mexican kingdom with Prince Maximilian of Hapsburg on the throne. Thus the bitter domestic hatred already engendered by the long struggle between conservatives and generations of liberal revolutionaries was compounded by the alignment of the conservatives with the French forces and the establishment of Maximilian as Emperor of the Mexicans. In the face of international developments from 1865 on, Napoleon III of France withdrew his forces, and with them went the conservative cause. By 1867 the liberals were strong enough to surround Maximilian's forces at Querétaro. Maximilian was forced to surrender and died before a firing squad with his Mexican generals, Miguel Miramon and Tomas Mejía.

Thus ended Mexico's second monarchist experiment, a more serious and bloody one than that of Iturbide's. But unlike the situation when Iturbide fell, there was by this time a sense of nationhood. Moreover, the liberal principles and leaders who had fought for them over the years after September 16, 1810, had emerged as a national revolutionary heritage capable of embracing all Mexican ethnic groups and which all Mexicans could perceive as the basis for a new, inclusive patriotism. It is this tradition and these heroes and heroic events that form the basis for the national myth evident not only in textbooks, but in official speeches, in newspaper editorials, and generally in all channels of communication in present-day Mexico. In taking his stand Juárez was able to achieve a clearer synthesis of liberalism and national identity and thus become a "father of the nation" in the Mexican pantheon.

The Reaction: Neo-Conservatism and Porfirio Díaz

In 1871 Juárez announced that he would again run for President, and was elected. Criticism of this fourth term was quite bitter in some sectors. The liberals split into three groups, Juaristas, Porfiristas, and Lerdistas. Porfirio Díaz, military hero of the wars against the conservatives and the French, attempted to bring off a coup directed at the government in the city of Mexico, but was defeated. Then, just as Juárez had demonstrated his mastery, he died in July, 1872. After Lerdo governed five years, Porfirio Díaz rebelled again, and this time succeeded in taking office in the name of "effective suffrage and no re-election."

In order to understand the development of the revolutionary nationalist tradition in the twentieth century it is necessary to touch on selected characteristics of the regime of Porfirio Díaz which began in 1876 and lasted until 1910. The *Porfirato* became the neo-conservative reaction to the Reform of 1857.

The philosophical basis of the Díaz regime became the positivist philosophy of Auguste Comte. Juárez chose a French-trained Mexican, Gabino Barreda, to head the national preparatory school, a school created to give a new focus to Mexican education. The positivist orientation was originally intended by Juárez and his colleagues to weaken ecclesiastical influence through emphasis upon science and scientific method as distinct from teaching theology and metaphysics, and philosophy in general. Positivism itself, however, became a very important philosophical influence. It stressed the capacity to use rational processes to bring about order, to bring about progress, and to bring stability on the basis of which there could be evolution, change, and advancement of the economy.

At first positivism seemed clearly in conflict with the old conservatism, since positivists attacked reliance upon tradition as a basis for making judgments. In the end, however, the new philosophy became an instrument of the conservative reaction in Mexico. In fact, the new education became the property of a select few, much as had been the case with education throughout the entire history of Mexico. Positivism had an inherently elitist character, and its emphasis upon order and progress, particularly in the material realm, substantially altered the outlook of the Reform. Principles of freedom and progress toward democratic institutions were de-emphasized while attention was increasingly focused upon the principle of order and the goal of material prosperity. Gradually, the Reform was pushed aside to make way for a new ideal, that of internal peace and prosperity at any price.

Concern was lost for individual freedom and for the principle of equality before the law. Also lost was the ideal of building a large rural middle class of small proprietors. The whiter Mexicans, the *criollos,* tended to place greater social distance between themselves and the *mestizos. Mestizos* once again began to be faced with the problem of upward social mobility, the same problem that had aroused them in times past. A new generation of officeholders indoctrinated in positivism created their own strange synthesis which formed the justification of the Porfirian regime. The goal value of material progress was harmonized with the old conservative ideals of clerical privilege, distribution of opportunity among the few, and political dictatorship. Progress in an egalitarian sense tended to be written off.

Industrialization and scientific progress became norms to which many people closely connected with government were deeply devoted. The idea that much could be done for Mexico if only foreign capital could be imported was interpreted in practice to provide legislation leading to a great railway boom and to the acquisition of rich oil lands by foreigners at incredibly low prices. The government took the position that foreign capital was enough in itself, that no order need be imposed by the government and no plan. In the case of railroads the result was a series of large and small railway lines without any system or key terminals, except that in Mexico City. Most of the roads were built for short-term gain, sometimes for no other reason than to serve large plantations. There was very little in the way of railroad service east and west in Mexico. The fact that most of the traffic moved north and south considerably limited the benefits the nation might have enjoyed from railway expansion.[9] Mexico under the dictatorship of Porfirio Díaz was a rewarding place only for those few who were able to command great economic resources or who had political favor, or both.

Politically, Porfirianism operated on the principle that politics should be minimized to achieve orderly promotion of economic prosperity. The tools of political stagnation were assassination, imprisonment, and bribery. There was always scrupulous attention to the form of elections, although it became clear before long that there was very little point in participating, since the decisions were made in other ways. As prosperity returned and order was established, Díaz found that the clergy was not the same enemy that as a military leader he had once believed it to be in the generation of the Reform. Anti-clerical moves by the government diminished. The clergy was encouraged to expand its activities once again.

One of the keys to the central arrangement of the *Porfirato* was the elite core of rural police known as the *rurales*. The backbone of this rural police was composed of ex-bandit chieftains who had been reconstituted as a group to hunt down anyone who threatened the rights of property in the countryside.[10] Another was the practice of playing off state governors against each other. Of particular importance (from the standpoint of today's perspective) was the tendency to forget Mexican nationalism in an effort to bring in foreign capital and to import foreign culture. Thus the people who were supposed to be the custodians of the nationalist revolutionary tradition became eminently conservative in the worst sense.

Four major tendencies during the years of the *Porfirato* are worth noting. Poverty of the rural masses increased. There emerged the beginnings of an urban proletariat which was forced to live at a subsistence level. Great landholding companies were formed and frequently kept the land out of production in order to be able to speculate on land values at a later date. There was, finally, the growth of the economy and of political self-consciousness in the north from which eventually came much of the impetus for the rebellion against Díaz.

[9] Harry Bernstein, *Modern and Contemporary Latin America* (New York, 1952), pp. 98–99.

[10] The *rurales* seldom took prisoners, as they employed the *ley fuga,* which was simply the right to shoot anyone in the back who happened to be running from them. The success of the *rurales* made it less necessary to maintain a military establishment. The army under Díaz declined both in numbers and in effectiveness. This condition was regarded by many as a sign of progress.

As the number of those who benefited from the Díaz regime became smaller, and as wealth was concentrated in ever fewer hands, dissension became evident. The protest was both intellectual and political. In the intellectual arena disagreement was reflected most clearly in the writing of Justo Sierra, who maintained that there should be a return to consideration of the political aims which had stimulated the generation of the Reform. Moreover, an increasingly negative reaction to positivism and the regime which it justified was manifest in the occasional writings emphasizing the worth of the Indian as opposed to the positivist position that the Indian was simply a force for inertia and a barrier to progress.[11] There was also the writing of the Flores Magón brothers and others who embraced the doctrines of anarcho-syndicalism as a justification for demands for betterment in the lot of industrial laboring people.[12] In addition, there began to appear more groups or clubs dedicated to discussion of democracy and representative government. Disenchantment was also manifest in the speaking and writing of one of the sons of the wealthy Madero family, Francisco I. Madero. As these evidences of discontent began to emerge, there were at the same time, marks of senility in the Díaz government. The old dictator himself was more and more out of touch, and he even suspected some of his most important colleagues and aids. It was true, also, that it was nearly impossible to get an interview with Díaz. A split developed in Diaz' official family, since there were still some military men of importance such as Bernardo Reyes, governor of Nuevo León, who were disliked and distrusted by the *criollo-cientifico* elite. Perhaps more than any single factor involved in the growing discontent was the ever-dominant situation of the tiny number of *criollo-cientificos* and the seeming occupation in perpetuity of the places at the top, leaving room for no one else — what Howard Cline calls "the full car."[13]

Madero and "No Re-election"

The first major statement of determination to end the *Porfirato* and re-establish the tradition of liberalism and the revolutionary struggle for Mexican nationalism and progress for all Mexicans came

[11] Bernstein, p. 102.

[12] For contrasting views on the philosophical approach of the Flores Magón brothers see: Howard F. Cline, *The United States and Mexico* (Cambridge, Mass., 1953), p. 117, and Daniel James, *Mexico and the Americans* (New York, 1963), p. 125.

[13] Howard F. Cline, *Mexico, Revolution to Evolution, 1940–1960* (London, 1962), p. 22. "The Díaz regime was not only a government of the privileged but also of elderly men who could not resign themselves to giving up power." For a similar statement see Octavio Paz, *The Labyrinth of Solitude* (New York, 1961), p. 137.

from Francisco I. Madero. Madero's emphasis was primarily political. He wanted wider participation and more democratic processes in politics in an effort to end the *continuismo* of the Díaz regime. In 1908, Madero wrote a book, *The Presidential Succession of 1910.* The book was written for some of the newly formed clubs interested in democracy. The bias of the book was squarely in the political tradition leading up to the Reform.[14] Madero's slogan was "Effective Suffrage and No Re-election," and differed only slightly in its emphasis from many aspects of the Plan of Tuxtepec once announced by Porfirio Díaz in the days when Díaz was still a reformer-liberal and not a dictator. The ideals of political liberalism which had survived so many reverses were reflected in the wide popular response to Madero's appeal. There was also a quality of mysticism in his writing which helped to give authenticity to his plea for moral and political reform. It is one of the paradoxes of Mexican history that this man, so small of stature, with his high pitched voice and his essentially moderate views — so unlike the usual political agitator or the stereotype of the Latin American caudillo — became the symbol of the anti-Díaz movement and the spark which touched off the first great social revolution of this century.

A number of key events fanned flames of discontent with the *Porfirato.* A bad harvest in 1909 took the rural population in some parts of the country to the brink of starvation. An interview given by Diaz to the American journalist, James Creelman, turned out to be a disaster because it raised hopes for a free election in 1910. Efforts of Bernardo Reyes, wealthy politician of Nuevo León, to mobilize personal support, and the publication of Molina Enríquez' book which presented a devastating critique of Díaz' agrarian policy all worked to undermine Díaz. Reyes stepped out of the picture in 1909, and more anti-Díaz factions flocked to support Madero. These factions selected Madero to run for President against Díaz with a Reyista as vice-presidential candidate. Madero was imprisoned but released through the influence of his family and crossed the border into Texas. There he issued his celebrated Plan of San Luis Potosí.

Sporadic uprisings followed Madero's *pronunciamiento,* but they were put down easily, as was Madero's own first effort. The rebels then began to have success in Chihuahua under Pancho Villa. Rebel efforts under Emiliano Zapata in the south were also successful. The aged, feeble character of the governing group and Díaz' policy of

[14] In 1909 another important book appeared, Andres Molina Enríquez' *Los grandes problemas nacionales.* Molina Enríquez tied together the liberal-nationalist tradition and the contribution of the heroes of the revolutionary struggle much better than did Madero. See James, pp. 136–143.

weakening the army were good fortune for the rebels. Díaz was forced to resign in May, 1911.[15]

No sooner had Madero gained control with massive popular support than the factions that had for the moment united behind him began to quarrel. With the revolutionary forces divided, the leaders of the reaction were able to carry off a counterrevolutionary coup which resulted in Madero's imprisonment and eventual assassination. At the head of the counterrevolution was General Victoriano Huerta who had himself made President, but who was beaten by the revolutionaries hammering at him from north, west, and south. He resigned July 15, 1914.[16]

And what of the man who died so ignominiously? This man, Francisco I. Madero, was a great symbol, and his political failure could not obscure the fact. He epitomized opposition to the continued tyranny of the neo-conservative regime. As a symbol he did not need an extensive program to become immortal. All he needed was a principle that seemed to fit the times. This he had — "no re-election." The reign of the dictator must end. It is for this conviction and this insight that he is known as the "Apostle of the Revolution." He opened the way for the tides of social change, and for so doing he enjoys an undisputed place among the heroes of Mexico's revolutionary tradition.

Carranza, Villa, and Zapata

Another hero was added to the revolutionary tradition when Venustiano Carranza of the northern state of Coahuila, once a senator under Porfirio Díaz, pronounced the Plan of Guadalupe, thus challenging

[15] "A new generation had risen, a restless generation that desired a change. The quarrel of the generations became a part of the general social discord . . . the Revolution, without any doctrines (whether imported or its own) to guide it, was an explosion of reality and a groping search for the universal doctrine that would justify it and give it a place in the history of America and the world." Paz, pp. 137–140.

[16] The Constitutionalist Army swept the federal troops of Huerta from the north while Zapata closed in on Mexico City from the south. By the end of 1914 victories by the Constitutionalists had opened the way to Mexico City, but there had arisen a split between Villa and Carranza which prolonged the Revolution. The situation was further complicated when the United States Marines, on orders from President Woodrow Wilson, landed in Veracruz to help in the overthrow of Huerta. Nationalist sentiment, already heightened by events, reacted violently to this intervention by the United States. Even the Constitutionalists, who stood to benefit by the Marines' presence, took the position that the United States was violating Mexican sovereignty. The Marine occupation of Veracruz took place at the expense of many Mexican lives; it lasted about seven months and made it very difficult for the United States and anti-Huerta forces to reach any satisfactory relationship after Huerta was defeated.

Huerta's legitimacy in March, 1913. Carranza was a large landholder in Coahuila and had gathered a private army about him even before Huerta completed the coup against Madero. When the news of the Huerta coup reached him, it did not take long for Carranza to assume the role of Madero's avenger under the title of First Chief of the Constitutionalist Army and thus become a part of the revolutionary nationalist tradition.

Two facts assure Carranza a place in the revolutionary tradition. He was, in the first place, an avenger of Madero and a powerful enemy of the counterrevolution. Secondly, he was an adamant nationalist in dealing with the United States and other foreign powers even when his victory in the revolutionary effort seemed very much in doubt. Thus, he symbolized Mexican nationalism when he entered a formal objection to the landing of United States Marines in Veracruz in April, 1914, even though the landing benefited Carrancista forces. Among other nationalist stands were his refusal to allow Argentina, Brazil, and Chile to mediate differences between Mexico and other foreign powers and his determined protests against the Pershing expedition into Mexico in pursuit of Villa after Villa attacked a small town in New Mexico in 1916.[17]

Carranza's revolutionary bent reached no farther than a few vague notions relating to political liberalism and an uncompromising nationalism. His personality, however, did not overshadow those about him as was the case with Villa and Zapata. Consequently, the intellectuals and persons with statesmanlike qualities who for one reason or another attached themselves to Carranza had an opportunity to make their influence felt on Carranza's revolutionary activity. Thus, Carranza's narrow conception of the Revolution did not limit him to policy pronouncements of the same narrow scope. At the urging of Luis Cabrera, Carranza promulgated an agrarian reform decree similar to Zapata's proposals and better thought out. At the same time, on the urging of his best general, Alvaro Obregón, also a gifted politician,

---

[17] Carranza and Villa, allies at first, quarreled. Zapata, whose personality and general view of the revolution as a social movement came closer to Villa's than Carranza's, joined Villa in operations against the First Chief. It was not until the battle of Celaya in the state of Guanajuato in April, 1915, that Carranza's forces clearly were in the ascendant. This defeat of Villa by Carranza's great general, Obregón, was clearly the turning point. Other Carrancista victories followed until Villa's operations were confined to his home state of Chihuahua and Zapata to his stronghold in the southern state of Morelos. By October, 1915, Carranza and his lieutenants were so clearly in command that it was possible to gain recognition from the United States while at the same time rejecting all efforts of the Wilson government to play a part in arranging a new constitutional regime for Mexico.

the fundamental demands of organized labor were granted, and battalions of workers joined the Carrancista armies while labor leaders set up headquarters behind Carrancista lines.

Thus, Carranza, the "limited" revolutionary, became for a time a symbol of leadership to those groups for whom the revolutionary struggle was basically an effort for social change. In a great paradox of history, Carranza, the *hacendado* and former senator under Díaz, became a full-fledged member of the revolutionary tradition, avenging Madero and supporting the principles of the Reform, defending Mexican nationalism, and sponsoring, however unwillingly, the goals of social reform.

Both at the time of the framing of the Constitution of 1917 and later, Carranza attempted to renege upon his social revolutionary commitments. He was opposed in this by most of the able men who had gathered about during the revolutionary fighting. As President he grew continuously more isolated from those whose leadership had made possible the Carrancista triumph over Villa and Zapata. When he attempted to name Ignacio Bonillas as his successor, Obregón, Plutarco E. Calles, Luis N. Morones, and Adolfo de la Huerta rebelled and brought him down.

Another leader who fought against Victoriana Huerta was Pancho Villa. Villa was already a hero of the Madero phase of the Revolution, and his movement represented a popular explosion in the north of Mexico. Villa was a northerner, a man who had made himself a legend as an outlaw before he turned revolutionary. He was an instinctive leader and tactician uninhibited by moral scruples. He was a child of the exploited class, and he found it natural to adopt a style which captured the imagination of the masses of the north. He was a man with whom the small *rancheros,* the range riders, the peons, and the town loafers of the north could identify. He was the man who had laughed at Díaz' police before it came time to defeat Díaz' soldiers.

Villa has a leading place in revolutionary mythology and in the nationalist tradition but not because of his role as a reformer. Intellectuals with him tried to make of him an heroic fighter for social justice, but it was Villa's genius to make Mexicans feel — not think. He was the epitome of the most crude aspects of the cult of virility, *machismo.* He helped pull down a dictator, and he raided into the United States. He inspired songs and legends. He was a warrior, not a statesman, but as a warrior figure he contributes essential zest and color to the nationalist revolutionary tradition.

Emiliano Zapata fought against Díaz, then took up arms against Madero in the south as the revolutionary alliance began to break up shortly after Madero took office. When the counterrevolution displaced

Madero, Zapata grew stronger until he dominated south central Mexico. Zapata's *pronunciamiento* against Madero was the Plan of Ayala. Its demand for "land and liberty" became one of the great pillars of the revolutionary tradition. Almost all the programs advanced by revolutionary leaders referred to the agrarian problem sooner or later, but only Zapata, leading the Revolution of the South, gave top priority to reform in this area of affairs. The program of Zapata was simpler than most. The whole message was summed up in the demands for redistribution of land to Indian villages and expropriation of the great landholdings. Though simple, the message meant a great deal, for it spelled the end of feudal Mexico and opened the door for modernization.

Zapata, and the intellectuals around him who attempted to make explicit his intuitive approach to the Revolution, were essentially traditionalists. Their conception of their role was focused on return of Mexico to its origins along the lines of the pre-conquest communal farming units. There was no place for futuristic dreams in their orientation.

The Zapatista explosion of the south, like Villa's in the north, never succeeded in incorporating its intuitive truths in an organic plan despite the efforts of attendant intellectuals. The Zapatistas were a wind of violence across the land. They did not bring organization in the wake of the chaos they created, but they did raise on high an idea too powerful to be denied because it stemmed from the most fundamental realities of the Mexican situation.

Alvaro Obregón

Nearly devoid of popular support, Carranza still insisted on naming his successor. He passed over Alvaro Obregón for a man with little standing, Ignacio Bonillas. This was the last straw for those leaders of the north who had engineered Carranza's victory. Armies were recruited, and the move on the capital began in April, 1920.[18] The leaders from Sonora entered Mexico City in May. Adolfo de la Huerta was named provisional president by the Carrancista Congress, and the stage was set for Obregón's ascent to the presidency later in the year.

Obregón was a man with great popular appeal, and a systematic, pragmatic turn of mind. He believed in the social ideals of the Revolution, but he recognized the barriers to their rapid achievement. He displayed an unusual capacity to win popular applause while moving forward slowly and methodically toward limited goals. Obregón was the kind of man Mexico needed at the time. He proved to be a clever

[18] Carranza gave up and fled. Supposedly friendly officers betrayed him, and he was assassinated, whether on orders from the top leaders is not clear.

and ruthless politician who was able to play off one group of revolutionaries against another, and he knew how to crush his enemies if the occasion demanded. At the same time his policy was a careful mixture of nationalism with the revolutionary social change for which he had fought so many years. His task was to consolidate and pacify the nation without abandoning the Revolution.

The focal points of Obregón's presidency involved four areas of revolutionary ideals. These were expansion of educational opportunities, concrete recognition of agrarian reform, support of labor and maintenance of a strong nationalist position in international affairs, especially toward the United States and foreign capital. For the task of pushing education, particularly the problem of bringing literacy to the rural areas, Obregón chose José Vasconcelos, whose political views were a strange composite of nineteenth-century conservatism and the Maderista emphasis upon essentially political and legal aspects of liberalism. But there was no doubt about Vasconcelos' commitment to the goal of education for the masses. His measures laid a firm foundation for the expansion of rural schools under succeeding administrations.

In agrarian reform Obregón's course was carefully plotted to avoid the twin dangers of serious disturbance of agricultural production through excessive distribution of land to peasants as well as the wrath of United States landowners in Mexico which might worsen already difficult diplomatic problems. At the same time, land was judiciously distributed in those rural areas of greatest discontent.[19] A good deal of the distributed land went to make peace with militant followers of the deceased Zapata in the state of Morelos — Obregón was active enough on agrarian reform to win support from agrarian leaders in a number of instances. This kept him less dependent upon militant organized labor groups and military chieftains than would otherwise have been the case.

Obregón's determination to support labor was clear enough. Out of the young labor movement there emerged one organization which wielded great power through government support. This was the *Confederación Regional de Obreros Mexicanos* (CROM) which was organized before the end of Carranza's presidency. The size of the organization grew rapidly with Obregón's aid. CROM unions were the only ones that could strike with government support. The CROM was organized along lines of the AFL in the United States, and it was both nationalist and anti-communist in orientation. Labor became a

[19] See Eyler N. Simpson and Frank Tannenbaum for comparative views on Obregón's agricultural policy. Eyler N. Simpson, *The Ejido* (Chapel Hill, N.C., 1937), p. 87. Frank Tannenbaum, *Mexico, The Struggle for Peace and Bread* (New York, 1951), p. 147.

serious force in Mexican politics in these years, and, even though the CROM declined at a later date, organized labor continued to be a vital part of the political system and an important factor in the economy. Through the CROM Obregón provided the urban wage-earning groups with an important place on the Mexican scene.

A major problem area for Obregón involved foreign capital and United States diplomacy as these might affect his position in the nationalist tradition and his hopes of creating a stronger and more stable Mexico. The United States government at this time proposed recognition of Obregón on the basis of an agreement designed to make provisions of Article 27 of the Mexican Constitution of 1917 nonretroactive.[20] The proposal was refused, since Obregón feared such an arrangement would damage his standing as a nationalist and would produce far-flung political repercussions in Mexico that would endanger stability and the possibility of a peaceful presidential succession.

Obregón was able to negotiate a successful agreement with United States bankers concerning funding of debts and handling of railroads. The real difficulty centered around the question of subsoil rights under Article 27, and the uncompromising attitude of many American oil companies. Guarantees were demanded which were politically impossible for Obregón to grant.[21] The situation dragged on with feelings on both sides growing ever more intense until some people in the United States began to urge intervention. Not until 1923 was it possible to develop a satisfactory basis for talks to resolve the conflict. The famous Bucareli agreements followed. Both a General and a Special Claims Convention were signed with United States recognition of Mexico just preceding the event. The United States was temporarily satisfied, but various dissident groups in Mexico used the occasion as a pretext for challenging Obregón's legitimacy as protector of Mexican sovereignty. Obregón in fact gave up nothing of substance in relation to Article 27; nevertheless, the agreement to arbitrate claims worked in favor of anti-Obregón forces and aided them in their plan to oppose Obregón's choice for the presidential succession.

In retrospect, Obregón stands out as a definite contributor to the Revolution and its goals. His was the first in a series of efforts to go

[20] Article 27 of the Constitution of 1917 states in part that "ownership of the lands and waters included within the boundaries of the national territory belongs originally to the nation." The nation at all times has the right "to impose on private property the measures that the public interest dictates." Most important under this article the nation has ownership of all subsoil wealth.

[21] For example, Obregón was asked to promise tax relief and exemption from expropriation. The latter would have been in violation of both the spirit and letter of Article 27.

beyond ideal homage to the Indian of pre-conquest times in order to effect a realistic educational program for integration of the Indian and indeed all rural Mexico as participating members of the Mexican polity. He provided labor with a strong political position as an articulator of interests of the urban masses, and he was so firm in his dealings with the United States that it took him three years to obtain recognition. He was thus an implementer of revolutionary goals and a nationalist in sufficient degree to place him securely as a lineal descendant of the revolutionary heritage. As such he has become an appropriate subject for study by school children, reference for orators, and artistic exercise of painters and sculptors in the revolutionary tradition. Had he lived to serve a second term instead of being assassinated immediately after re-election in 1928, the case might not have been as clear.

Calles: A Controversial Figure

Plutarco E. Calles was clearly a revolutionary and nationalist in orientation, but there is an air of doubt about his place in the tradition of events and heroic actions which constitute the legitimizing heritage of the regime. As a President, many of his policies sought to realize revolutionary goals, but his determination to maintain his supremacy by directing Mexican politics from behind the scenes for several years after the termination of his presidency in 1928 has cast a shadow upon his historical image and has made it more difficult for succeeding generations to award him a place in the revolutionary pantheon. However, his role in developing the modern Mexican economy and political system can never be dismissed, for it was substantial. From the standpoint of the present, Calles remains a formidable figure who made a positive contribution to the existing system.

Plutarco Elías Calles came from Guaymas, Sonora, and his family was well known throughout the state. Calles had a revolutionary turn of mind which demonstrated itself as early as 1900 when he had some trouble with Díaz officials. He was a man who knew a number of occupations and was for a time a school teacher. After the Revolution had gone into its second phase in 1913, Calles joined Obregón and became his most capable military lieutenant. He was one of the Sonoran triumvirate with Obregón and Adolfo de la Huerta who brought about the downfall of Carranza and was a close collaborator of Obregón's during the latter's presidency. As Obregón's term drew to a close, the question of the succession split the Sonora triumvirate, and when Obregón chose Calles, his other friend and colleague, Adolfo de la Huerta, pronounced against the two, gathering strength from Obregón's enemies of right and left in the political spectrum. The rebellion was serious, but the United States elected to help Obregón, whose government it had just recognized, and this help was an important factor in deciding the struggle. De la Huerta had to leave the country, and Calles took over the presidency.

Calles, like Obregón, was faced with several fundamental decisions when he entered the presidency, all of which directly related to the core ideas of the Revolution and the means of achieving revolutionary goals. First, he had to choose between emphasis upon labor support and agrarian support. Obregón had managed to walk a tightrope between them; Calles clearly chose labor. Labor, for all practical purposes, meant the small coterie of leaders grouped around Luis N. Morones called *Grupo Acción,* who ran the CROM, with its million members and the Labor Party. Morones' record as a key member of Calles' cabinet was not as clean as it might have been. On the positive side, the overall wage level of CROM membership continued to rise, and indemnification of injured workers, as well as those dismissed without "adequate" cause, increased. The course begun under Obregón of adapting both ideology and practice to a policy of coexistence with employers was continued. Other items do not read so well. Strikes declined, and labor leaders grew rich on management kick-backs for help in maintaining peaceful labor-management relations. Government-supported attacks on independent unions increased. The privileged position of the CROM and its tolerant attitude toward factory owners fitted well with Calles' encouragement of the growth of a new class of Mexican capitalists centering their activities for the most part in consumption and construction industries, and the acceptance of these business leaders into the governing group.[22] Calles and Morones continued to style themselves "socialists," stressing the compatibility of socialism and capitalism as the money poured in, and all those at the top embarked upon a pattern of conspicuous consumption in fine houses, luxurious cars, clothing, and jewelry which marked them as something totally apart from the rank and file they professed to serve.

Meanwhile, agrarian leaders, concerned as they were with land reform, found their influence and access to the President on the wane in the cabinet and in the Congress. A sense of frustration and neglect developed among the leadership and rank and file of the Agrarista Party, causing a swing away from Calles and ever closer ties with Obregón. Calles' constructive policies in agrarian reform were obscured by his close personal ties with labor and the new business groups among the "revolutionaries."[23]

[22] Henry Bamford Parkes, *A History of Mexico* (Boston, 1938), p. 381.
[23] Procedures to clarify land distribution were written into the law in 1925 and these were followed by sweeping changes in 1927 which gave clearer clarity to the procedures for acquiring land and delineated more

In a second fundamental decision Calles took the position that modernization was vital to realization of all revolutionary goals. A systematic road-building program was launched setting a precedent for Mexico's relatively modern and constantly expanding highway network of the present. He also realized that a sick population can never be an industrious and productive population and provided for programs of sanitation and wholesale vaccinations which set precedents for continued efforts in this area of affairs on the part of succeeding administrations. Calles pursued modernization by expanding the amount of arable land through establishment of an irrigation program. Subsequent improvements in this field have made possible the increasing agricultural production of today's Mexico. Finally, the former school teacher did not overlook the importance of literacy, and carried forward the policy of lifting Mexico's educational level begun by Obregón.

A third problem area confronting Calles was the attitude of the Roman Catholic clergy which had not changed much despite reverses in fortune dating back to the Reform. The old alliance between the higher clergy and the traditionally privileged groups among large landholders and old mercantile families still existed. Calles mounted an all-out attack in this sphere.

In 1926 leaders of the clergy published a political advertisement in a number of leading newspapers denouncing various portions of the Constitution of 1917. Calles reacted by enforcing one of the Constitution's anti-clerical provisions that had previously lain dormant, and a number of alien priests and nuns were deported. The clergy then refused to conduct services anywhere in Mexico. Subsequently, pro-clerical groups raised the standard of rebellion in the western states of Michoacán, Jalisco, and Colima. Violence mounted, and outrages were perpetrated by both sides. The outcome was a definitive victory against political Catholicism.

Mexican nationalism in relation to the United States constituted a fourth area of decision for Calles. Here the crux of the matter was foreign oil holdings just as it had been for Obregón. Toward the end of 1925 the Mexican Congress passed two laws jeopardizing the position of the American oil companies in regard to subsoil rights. President Coolidge attacked the Mexican position in a public address, and a rupture in relations and intervention seemed imminent. With the situation at an impasse and neither side ready to give ground, Coolidge changed ambassadors, and Dwight W. Morrow, an outstanding financier, went to Mexico to see what could be done. Morrow's approach

---

clearly the rights of private landowners. The result was a relatively coherent basis for future reforms and an expansion of land distribution.

was unpretentious and friendly. Calles liked him and so did a good many other Mexican leaders. Thus it is not difficult to understand the subsequent decision of the Mexican Supreme Court to rule out the most controversial provisions of the oil legislation. This decision paved the way for a period of more amicable relations between the two countries, though the issue between the companies and Mexican nationalism remained.

Finally, Calles had to solve the problem of the presidential succession. Involved were such sensitive issues as "no re-election," *continuismo*,[24] and Caesarism. Madero had made "no re-election" an effective symbol of the revolutionary tradition. Calles' actions in this connection did more to confuse his claim to a place in the revolutionary pantheon than did other of his less fortunate policies.

As the time for succession drew near, Calles supported Obregón in the latter's desire to become President once again. Two constitutional amendments were pushed through, permitting Obregón to be re-elected and lengthening the presidential term to six years. Obregón rolled over his opposition, including the formidable CROM, with Calles' support and was declared candidate-elect in July, 1928. Then, just two weeks later at a great victory banquet, the whole political arrangement was thrown into disarray when a young fanatic approached the great *caudillo* on the pretext of sketching him and shot him to death instead.

Obregonistas, especially leaders of the Agrarista Party, who had expected cabinet posts and a generally more favorable political situation once their leader took office, began hunting for a scapegoat. They found him in Luis Morones and the labor leaders around him, the *Grupo Acción*. To the Obregonistas, it was even possible that Calles himself was implicated. An attempt on Calles' part to retain power seemed impossible in the face of these suspicions.

Rather than risk civil war among diverse groups of the revolutionary camp, Calles took himself out of the presidential picture, and at the same time offered an organizational substitute for the personalism that had characterized revolutionary presidents up to that time. In so doing, he demonstrated at that moment in time a high degree of statesmanship. The new concept of machinery for the succession was mentioned in his annual State of the Union message with the Congress, state governors, and high military assembled. Then to satisfy the disappointed Obregonistas, one of their number, a lawyer named Emilio Portes Gil from Tamaulipas, was named provisional president by the Congress. After thus preparing the way Calles set about organizing a Revolution-

[24] *Continuismo* refers to that phenomenon in which one person determines to maintain himself in power by any means on the grounds that he is essential to the welfare of the state.

ary Party which would encompass all factions to which they would swear loyalty and through which procedures for institutionalizing peaceful succession to public office at all governmental levels could be adopted and made workable. Nearly all organized "revolutionaries" swore loyalty to the new party, its program, and procedural rules, and there emerged the *Partido Nacional Revolucionario* (PNR). This was the forerunner of the *Partido Revolucionario Institucional* (PRI) which dominates present-day Mexican politics.

Calles ran the party, the presidency, and the legislature from behind the scenes after 1928. He picked a relatively obscure man, Pascual Ortiz Rubio, as the PNR's candidate to succeed Portes Gil at the end of the provisional presidency, and arranged a lopsided victory over the PNR's popular opponent, José Vasconcelos. Vasconcelos was credited with only 20,000 votes against 1,000,000 for Ortiz Rubio in an election race that clearly was not that uneven.

Ortiz Rubio never finished his term. He had to consult Calles on the slightest question of policy. At the same time he had to work with Portes Gil, president of the PNR. Gil's egalitarian bias did not fit with Ortiz Rubio's political leanings which were to the right of the increasingly conservative Calles. Portes Gil had been able to influence the composition of the Congress, and it was essentially of the left wing faction of the PNR. In a series of moves against agrarian and labor leaders, Ortiz alienated large sections both of his Congress and his party. Confronted with an opposition that ended his usefulness as a political instrument, he resigned, and Calles turned over the presidency to one of his close friends, and business associates, General Abelardo Rodríguez.

Rodríguez, who had become and has continued to be one of the great Mexican capitalists, also had a flair for politics which Ortiz never possessed. He paid attention to Calles' dictates, gave the PNR its due respect as Calles' organ, promoted business, encouraged foreign capital, kept labor prostrate, put the lid on agrarian reformers, tolerated public graft and corruption in which Calles associates were involved, and still managed to keep an air of presidential dignity.

Rodríguez brought a number of younger men into the government, an action which in itself helped allay the resentment against the existing situation. It was some of these younger men who improved on the Calles agrarian legislation and provided the legal framework used in the vast agrarian reforms of the next president, Lázaro Cárdenas. Just at the time that Calles and his conservative friends seemed most powerful, Rodríguez was presiding over a government and working with a political party in which younger men were rekindling the zeal of the revolutionary tradition.

In summary, the contribution of the Calles period to the revolutionary tradition is obscure. His recognition of the needs of his day and attempts to inaugurate relevant programs set useful precedents for subsequent governments. His contribution to the revolutionary fighting is not in dispute. However, his affinity for newly rich labor leaders and business men and his inability to avoid great waste and corruption make his standing ambiguous. Further, his organization of the Revolutionary Party as a mechanism for undergirding the "no re-election" principle is weakened as an achievement by his determination to govern from behind the scenes after saying he would step down. His achievements are clear enough, but his Caesarism removes him from the mainstream of the revolutionary tradition which legitimizes the regime.

Lázaro Cárdenas

The left wing of the Revolutionary Coalition grew more powerful, and its central figure became Lázaro Cárdenas, whose star continued to rise in spite of differences with Calles, the paramount chief.[25] Cárdenas had been one of Calles' successful junior officers in the revolutionary fighting and had held many important posts during Calles' period of dominance, but Cárdenas had never become completely identified in his own mind with his powerful mentor. Nevertheless, Calles preferred Cárdenas to any other leftist from among whom the existing situation compelled him to choose. Cárdenas' intentions were perhaps foretold in his extensive electoral campaign in which he visited even the most remote corners of rural Mexico to let the people know him.

Once in the presidency, Cárdenas began to build the political strength he would need to expand the drive toward revolutionary goals far beyond the limits marked off by Obregón and Calles. He began by moving simultaneously in a number of directions. He created an image of himself as a symbol of honesty and austerity by closing many of the gambling casinos and moving out of the elaborate presidential residence, Chapultepec Castle. At the same time he stepped up the distribution of land to a pace unequaled by any previous administration

[25] "Revolutionary Coalition" is a term which is applied here and will be applied henceforth as descriptive of that cluster of groups and leaders whose political prominence is directly or indirectly connected with the "revolutionary" struggle and the victories that were won in that struggle. These are the men and groups who because of their connection with the Revolution have some influence, or at the very least, hope of gaining influence in decision-making within the Mexican political system. The Revolutionary Coalition is not static. Its membership varies, but there is always the common identifying mark of "revolutionary" ancestry.

and thus assured peasant leaders of the sincerity of his promises. Labor was encouraged to strike with government support, and labor leaders quickly gravitated to the man whose zeal for bettering their power and economic position stood in marked contrast to the policy of the post-1928 Callista presidents.

Calles' intransigent anti-clericalism was turned against him as Cárdenas took a soft line toward the Church, and pro-Cárdenas military elements were quietly moved into key positions while Callistas in the presidential cabinet were neutralized or removed in a complex set of political maneuvers. By June, 1935, Calles felt it necessary to threaten Cárdenas openly, but his move came too late, and the overwhelming strength which Cárdenas had amassed forced Calles, the one-time strong man, to retire from politics and leave Mexico.

Along with his all-out drive toward achievement of revolutionary goals Cárdenas brought about organizational innovations which distinctly altered the Mexican political scene and continued to provide some of the distinguishing marks of Mexican politics. From a mammoth conclave of labor leaders in February, 1936, there emerged the *Confederación de Trabajadores de Mexico* (CTM) which has continued to dominate organized labor to the present. Cárdenas was also determined that *ejidatarios* (peasants to whom land was distributed) should have a unified national leadership. He encouraged the revolutionary agrarian leadership to combine in leagues at the state level and then encouraged the national affiliation of them all in the *Confederación Nacional Campesina* (CNC). The reciprocity of support between government on the one hand and the organized peasants and labor on the other placed Cárdenas in a position to keep on expanding the Revolution to which he had given new life both in agrarian reform and in labor-management relations. In addition, he was able to reorganize the old PNR to include the new militant elements and provide a basis for consolidation of his reforms by later governments. His instrument of unification was the *Partido Revolucionario Mexicano,* which was based upon the concept of four distinct segments of politically articulate persons. These "sectors," as they were called, were considered to include the most vital political forces in Cardenista Mexico. There were peasant and labor sectors as well as the military. A fourth sector was recognized but did not become effective until after Cárdenas' presidency. This was the so-called popular sector which was conceived as a catchall for all those who did not fit in the other categories.

With regard to foreign-held property in Mexico, Cárdenas placed himself fully in the mainstream of the revolutionary heritage by pushing a bill through the Congress in 1936 which made any property defined as having "public utility" subject to expropriation. The constitutional basis of the law was Article 27, and it was designed to fill in gaps in the Agrarian Code of 1934. The President was given nearly unlimited discretion to determine what was susceptible of expropriation. The law was applied to industrial and commercial as well as to agricultural property. Where labor was involved there were strikes for benefits under Article 123 of the Constitution, and if foreign capital was involved, it faced intervention by the government if labor's demands were not granted. Some Mexican owners fell before labor's onslaught, but foreign enterprises were worse hit. In the countryside as well, foreign owners felt the pressure as the government moved to distribute more and more of the available arable land. Foreign-held stock in the National Railways of Mexico was taken over by the government with promise of indemnification. The promise was honored.

There remained the question of oil. This was a major resource dominated by foreign capital, and it was impossible for Cárdenas to overlook it in light of the strong nationalist bias of his government. Cárdenas' solution for the perennial oil question made him a national hero, almost a folk hero before he left office.

A labor dispute set off the series of events leading to Cárdenas' final decision to expropriate all major foreign oil holdings. There were between 13,000 and 19,000 Mexican petroleum workers.[26] Before Cárdenas' time these workers had been organized in a multitude of small, weak unions. Cárdenas brought about their unification under a single leadership which in its turn affiliated with the expanding power of the CTM. The new and powerful petroleum workers union made numerous demands, some realistic and some not, with reference to higher pay and fringe benefits. When the major companies turned down key demands on wage increases and inclusion of Mexican office employees in the union, a strike was threatened. Cárdenas intervened to arrange a six months' period for further talks. Bitterness increased instead of lessening, and the union called a general strike when the "cooling off" period ended late in May, 1937.

To strengthen its position the union petitioned for government intervention under a provision of the Labor Code of 1931 which distinguished between an ordinary strike situation and an "economic conflict" involving an imbalance in the industry detrimental to the national interest. The Federal Board of Conciliation and Arbitration granted the union's request and set up a commission to study the conflict while workers returned to their jobs. The report which ensued was fair or unfair, depending on one's choice of statistics, accounting

[26] Numbers vary according to what types of jobs are included. James gives the higher figure and Cline the lower. James, p. 281, and Cline, *The United States and Mexico,* p. 231.

procedures, and bias. The report, in any case, was not favorable to the companies, since it rejected their position both on wage increases and union jurisdiction over white-collar personnel as well as many lesser questions. The Board accepted the recommendations of its investigating committee and ordered the companies to comply. The companies then made a concrete offer for wage increases which brought a favorable response from the government, but they lost their momentary advantage by demanding that Cárdenas formally swear to support the deal offered by the companies. The demand put them in a position of impugning the honor of Mexico's President and, indeed, of Mexico itself. The demand for a sworn statement was turned down, and the companies then refused outright to comply with the Board's order.

National honor and national sovereignty were clearly at stake from the official Mexican point of view. In this situation Cárdenas switched from what was apparently his earlier position, i.e., to get the most from the companies while avoiding expropriation. The final acts of the major producers, in addition to the blustering attitude maintained by their representatives both in Mexico and the United States throughout the dispute, constituted an unforgivable offense to Mexican pride. Discarding considerations of economic and diplomatic repercussions, Cárdenas went the whole way for nationalism. A presidential decree of March 18, 1938, based on the expropriation legislation of 1936 brought Mexican control of the major British and United States oil properties and shouts of jubilation from the people. Historians seem to agree that the move was supported by nearly all articulate elements in Mexican society; this was unquestionably one of the most widely supported policies ever promulgated by a Mexican President.[27]

Cárdenas' nationalism would have placed him as a direct lineal descendant in the revolutionary tradition of Hidalgo Morelos, Juárez, and the leaders of the conflict of 1910–1917 without much other action on his part. But his other policies formed the essential background for the oil expropriation. Had there not been a new drive toward the goals of agrarian reform and improvements for labor, the organized and

[27] The expropriation decree did not end the matter. Negotiations with the United States government dragged on into the administration of Cárdenas' successor. However, the bitterness which had characterized diplomatic interchange between the two countries in similar crises of earlier times was less intense than before. Neither withdrawal of recognition nor intervention was threatened by the United States. Mexicans for their part maintained a courteous and open attitude, and the moderation of both sides made possible settlement of agrarian claims before Cárdenas left the presidency and paved the way for settlement of the oil claims during the second year of Cárdenas' successor, Ávila Camacho.

militant political force necessary for the oil expropriation might have been lacking. In the agrarian field, Cárdenas not only distributed twice the total amount of land distributed by his predecessors since 1915, he approximately doubled the number of beneficiaries of land distribution.[28] Along with the physical fact of land distribution went a new and expanded conception of agrarian reform which affected for the first time large numbers of rural wage laborers in northern Mexico.

The old concepts of land reform primarily referred to restitution of Indian lands taken from villages under Díaz, and included grants to certain other types of villages with the net result that in many areas of the north and north central region the *hacienda* as a social and economic institution of ancient vintage had continued to dominate the rural land tenure arrangement. Cárdenas changed this situation by pushing distribution of *hacienda* land to groups of landless rural wage earners who could claim no village land rights. Moreover, kinds of agricultural enterprises to be affected by the land distribution program were expanded to include areas involving large-scale cultivation of commercial crops such as cotton, henequen, wheat, and coffee. Expropriation of many rich Laguna region cotton properties in southwestern Coahuila and northeastern Durango in 1936, the organization of formerly landless peasants in cooperatives to run the new *ejidos* and the collectivization of the henequen industry in Yucatán dramatically illustrated Cárdenas' determination to attack the *hacienda* system in all its forms. In addition there was expropriation of coffee properties in Chiapas and American-owned wheat lands in the Yaqui Valley of Sonora. Whether it was a rural *mestizo* group as in La Laguna or Maya Indians as in Yucatán, Cárdenas was set on expanding the agrarian reform for their benefit. By the time he finished his term, half the rural peasantry was organized in an *ejido* of some type.

Hand in hand with the wholesale distribution of lands went a renewed drive to educate the peasantry, and thousands of young people went out into the rural areas inspired by an awakened educational evangelism reminiscent of the days when José Vasconcelos was Secretary of Education in the Obregón cabinet.[29]

Realization of revolutionary goals was also pushed in the urban areas as labor unions affiliated with the CTM struck again and again in all types of industry to push for collective bargaining contracts based on the guarantees of Article 123 of the Constitution. The demands for an

---

[28] Nathan L. Whetten, *Rural Mexico* (Chicago, 1948), p. 127.

[29] Early in the government of President Gustavo Díaz Ordaz (spring, 1965) it appeared that an effort would be made to rekindle enthusiasm for expanding educational opportunity with a view to eliminating illiteracy entirely from the Mexican scene.

eight-hour day, higher wages, and recognition of benefits relating to sickness, unemployment, and recreation facilities were most dramatically illustrated in the great petroleum workers dispute; but other labor-management conflicts followed much the same lines, though with less at stake for the nation.

Mexico's political system, social structure, and economy of the present have been developed through the efforts of many, but Cárdenas more than any other in the revolutionary tradition shaped those political and social structures while at the same time making a substantial contribution to the historical-ideological underpinnings of the existing system. Under Cárdenas, socialist ideals and egalitarian tendencies were brought to the fore, combined with the principle of private property, and developed into a new synthesis. The positive role of private industrial enterprise was linked more than ever to the concept of an active role for public enterprise and public financing; a new approach to co-existence of the economic and political power of managerial groups with the power of extensive and centralized labor organization and leadership was developed. Those holding lands distributed by the government were organized into *ejido* communities with their own national organization institutionalized under the agrarian code, and the old semi-feudal *hacienda* system disappeared forever as the dominant form of land tenure. New large-scale properties which were to spring up in later years could only be justified as socially desirable in terms of higher levels of productivity.

Cárdenas' policies assured the dominant position of the Revolutionary Party on the political scene through incorporation of new groups. The emphasis on inclusiveness and the reputation for social reform gained under Cárdenas contributed greatly to the image of the party as an instrument of the masses. Foreign capital was assigned a new role, no longer controlling the bases of the Mexican economy, but instead collaborating with government and Mexican private enterprise in the vast task of economic development. The way had been opened for expansion of a Mexican capitalist class oriented more toward competition and productivity than toward procurement of monopoly concessions for exploitation of fellow countrymen. There was a new pride in being Mexican. "Mexico for the Mexicans" had become a fact. People had been shown that their country could hold its own with the great neighbor to the north.

Cárdenas accomplished the feat of bringing off a class war, while at the same time subordinating it to the overriding theme of Mexican nationalism. Major surgery was performed upon economic and social institutions of long standing. Social realignments and change in stratification arrangements took place, and national sentiment and unity triumphed in these changes. Modern evolutionary Mexico was ready to emerge based upon the twin assumptions of nationalism and modernization as the overriding values of the future. Change was accomplished without adoption of the totalitarian political styles characteristic of twentieth-century revolutionary reform.

Perhaps most important from the standpoint of political stability as well as the liberal principles for which so many had died in the past was Cárdenas' decision to step down at the end of his term. Thus the tradition in the style of Madero was maintained and strengthened. The "no re-election" principle reigned triumphant.

Government textbooks and other instruments of manifest political socialization do not dwell on the exploits of Cárdenas at great length. Cárdenas is a folk figure whose renown in his own lifetime makes mention of his name in some planned way a matter of only secondary importance. He is a part of the nationalist, revolutionary tradition, the national myth. The actions and goals encouraged in the educational process are either the same or similar to those associated with Cárdenas, and everyone knows it. Barring a series of frightful blunders late in life, Cárdenas will stand out in the teaching of the myth as second to none. He is a "revolutionary" along with Zapata, Villa, and Carranza. The regime is correspondingly strengthened by its close association with Cárdenas' record as President.

Post-Cárdenas Revolutionaries: Ávila Camacho, Alemán, Ruiz Cortines, López Mateos, Díaz Ordaz

Presidents who have succeeded Cárdenas have been milder men with a political style oriented toward evolution rather than revolution, though official interpretation does not recognize "evolutionary" as a prestigious word.[30] All presidents since Carranza have been considered "revolutionary."[31] Cárdenas represents the capstone of that historical line of heroes and events which has legitimized the regime as well as the presidents and their governments since 1940. This is not to say that succeeding presidents and their policies have been unimportant, but their role has been one of consolidation and forward movement along lines marked off by Cárdenas and his predecessors.

[30] The title of Howard Cline's recent book, *Mexico, Revolution to Evolution, 1940–1960,* focuses on this distinction.

[31] Great insight can be gained through reading the free textbooks distributed by the national government through the National Commission for Free Textbooks. See especially Concepción Barrón de Morán, *Mi libro de cuarto año* (México, D.F., Comisión Nacional de los Libros de Texto Gratuitos, 1960), pp. 170–177. The presentation of all presidents since the Revolution of 1910–17 as "revolutionary" is to be clearly observed in this and other similar elementary texts.

Cárdenas' selection as his successor was a mild-mannered general of moderate views named Manuel Ávila Camacho. He was strong enough to steer Mexico on a middle course between the Fascist and Communist extremes which threatened Mexico during the years of World War II, and he was able to ally Mexico with the United States in the great struggle without alienating essential support groups. Moreover Ávila Camacho began policies designed to heal the open wounds in Mexican society left by Cárdenas' revolutionary policies and began to rebuild the agrarian and industrial sectors which had suffered greatly in loss of production under the wholesale land distribution and wave of strikes which Cárdenas had used to effect the second phase of the Revolution of 1910–1917. It was under Ávila Camacho that the expanding Mexican middle class grouped around bureaucrats, professional men, and new Mexican industrialists began to increase its influence through the *Confederación Nacional de Organizaciones Populares* (CNOP) and the national chambers of industry and commerce.

By the time Miguel Alemán Valdes became President in 1946, the stage was set for an unprecedented expansion in business activity based on an influx of foreign capital and growth of Mexican-owned industrial enterprises. Alemán's free-wheeling, pro-business policy was accompanied by a considerable amount of corruption, so that the presidential succession which brought Adolfo Ruiz Cortines to office in 1952 was not as peaceful as the succession of 1946, although there was no real question that the candidates of the Revolutionary Coalition could win the presidency and other elective posts.

Ruiz Cortines was nominated by the Revolutionary Coalition because he was a good administrator, had a reputation for honesty, and had a political style that was moderate, peaceful, and conciliatory. He pushed steadily ahead toward modernization of the country. He emphasized road construction, harbor improvement, literacy, and hard work. Among sectors of the governing party the CNOP (Popular Sector) was clearly in the ascendant although labor and peasant leaders were still influential in the top circles.

Ruiz Cortines' successor was Adolfo López Mateos, who had been Ruiz Cortines' Minister of Labor and had established a reputation for successful handling of labor-management disputes. López Mateos was clearly a product of the Revolutionary Coalition, having begun his political career as private secretary to Carlos Riva Palacio when the latter was a major figure during the Calles period of dominance in 1930. López Mateos had held many prestigious posts, was a forceful orator, and could trace his family lineage back to outstanding members of the generation of the Reform such as Francisco Zarco Mateos — who was Juárez' Minister of Foreign Affairs for a time — and the outstanding writer, Ignacio Ramírez. López Mateos identified himself in his campaign speeches with agrarian reform and generally leftward tendencies within the Revolutionary Coalition. But when it came to the acid tests, his was clearly a pragmatic evolutionary approach emphasizing economic development and peaceful coexistence of Mexican interest groups.

The López Mateos administration took a favorable stance toward the Castro dictatorship in Cuba at first, only to withdraw to an attitude of guarded neutrality as Castro took Cuba rapidly into the Soviet orbit. Wildcat strikes in several industries, notably railroads, met with determined action on the part of the government, and several leaders were imprisoned. Demonstrations that were clearly Communist-inspired were not tolerated, and the famous artist and Communist leader, David A. Siqueiros, was put behind bars for a lengthy stay. At the same time the Mexican government expanded its role in the economy through lending activities, stockholdings in basic industries and purchase of foreign-owned electric utilities. The government continued to stress desirability of foreign investment. López Mateos followed the bias of his long experience in the revolutionary camp as he proceeded steadily toward further land distribution and the creation of new arable lands on a scale unequaled since Cárdenas' time.

As this is written Gustavo Díaz Ordaz has directed the fortunes of Mexico as Chief of State for a few months. It is still by far too early to appraise him. We can say, however, that he was López Mateos' choice. As Minister of Interior (*Gobernación*) he carried out tough policies against the extreme left. His campaign speeches showed the usual preoccupation with such mainstays of modernization as education, agriculture, and industrialization.

In summary, the presidents since 1940 have not been revolutionaries except in the special sense that they are all referred to as "revolutionary."[32] Their focus has been on the means to achieve ever greater material advancement rather than upon ideological precepts and class warfare. They have been essentially conservative within the framework of the revolutionary heritage. However, their attitudes toward change and their policies have remained essentially consonant with the political lineage which they claim as their own basis of legitimacy and the legitimacy of the regime. They have recognized the necessity of maintaining their role within the frame of the revolutionary image. They have maintained the nationalist ideal as the core of the system, and nationalism has been used as the cement for constructing support at the levels of regime and government. So far no President since 1940 has

[32] Jesús Silva Herzog, "La revolución mexicana en crisis," *Inquietud sin tregua* (Mexico, 1965), pp. 23–42.

overlooked the relationship between the revolutionary nationalist aspects of the role and the maintenance of mass support in its various organized and potential forms. Adaptation has gone forward firmly rooted in the national myth.

Summary: Ideology and Political Socialization

History as a kind of ideology is written into government-published textbooks and is disseminated through nearly every media of political communication. The established aim of the regime and its governments is continuous strengthening of support through expansion of facilities for dissemination and assimilation of the revolutionary nationalist myth. The Indian, revolutionary heroes, great events, revolutionary goals, and current policies are woven together to create an orientation in political socialization that supports the legitimizing argument for the system.

Mexico's political culture, as we have seen, is far from homogeneous in relation to values of fundamental importance. In seeking to maintain and broaden consensus through educational orientation, the teacher, the text writer, the popular essayist and historian are all confronted with the fact that there is more than one tradition of values concerning the purpose of government and the authoritative use of governmental power which might be used to legitimize a Mexican regime. The reader has been introduced in the above material to the substance of the historical case which is made under the present regime to provide an ideological basis for "revolutionary " rule. This is the set of values and leaders constituting the legitimate political lineage as opposed to values and leaders which represent the tradition of the usurper.

The concept of "nation" is central to the distinction between the tradition of legitimacy and the illegitimate. Citizens young and old are encouraged to examine which tradition has done the most for the Mexican nation. It is pointed out that the real heroes have been those who have sacrificed personal security and subordinated personal desire for power in order to build a unified, strong, Mexican people. Anyone who has defended Mexican soil with personal integrity and sacrifice, whether he won or lost, is a hero. Anyone who has sacrificed the integrity of Mexican soil on the altar of his own ambitions is cast as a villain. Anyone who has attacked or provoked attack on Mexican soil from without has been an enemy; so are those who have violated the Mexican estate from within. Antonio López de Santa Anna and Porfirio Díaz are the outstanding villains. Santa Anna is notorious because he sold Mexican territory to the United States to maintain himself in power even after his own inefficiency, caprice, and self-interest played a key role in the loss of Texas and of one-third of the original Mexican territory in the War of 1846–1848 between

Mexico and the United States. Díaz is a villain because he delivered great tracts of land and subsoil rights to foreign investors, especially those from the United States. Cuauhtémoc is a hero, even if representative of Aztec despotism, because he sacrificed himself in a struggle to drive out invaders.

The historical facts facilitate the spinning of the national revolutionary myth. Historical circumstance makes it easy to link the conservative coalition which supported Santa Anna with encouragement of French intervention and the effort to establish Maximilian, the foreigner, as monarch of all the Mexicans. Similarly, the propensity to encourage large land and subsoil holdings by foreigners lends itself to interpretation of the Díaz regime as merely a renascence of the old conservative coalition.

In contrast, the revolutionary tradition emerges as centering on the core idea of Mexico for the Mexicans. Cuauhtémoc is, therefore, linked with the *criollo* parish priest, Padre Hidalgo and his pupil, José Maria Morelos, both of whom suffered excommunication and death in the attempt to liberate Mexico from colonial rule. The lawyer from Oaxaca, Benito Juárez, fits into the political lineage of Cuauhtémoc, not so much because Juárez was Indian, but because he sought to forge a nation through establishing political unity of the country under one law devoid of special privileges for military, clergy, and rich merchants — because he stood for national sovereignty against French intervention. Madero's heroic stature is in part a function of his revolt against a pro-foreign dictatorship. Carranza is heroic because, with all his faults, he avenged Madero against the counter-revolution and manifested a determined nationalism in the face of intervention and threats of intervention from the north.

The tradition of revolutionary ideals and revolutionary heroes reaching back beyond Hidalgo and Morelos and their struggle against Spanish colonialism to Cuauhtémoc and the Aztecs has become an historical synthesis fitted to contemporary needs through the policies and pronouncements of Mexicans since the Revolution. In this synthesis being nationalist and anti-colonialist applies to any group or leader with a stance against foreign forces of exploitation whether political, economic, or both. Thus the tradition is broad enough to encompass both Cuauhtémoc and the Aztecs, as well as Lázaro Cárdenas and the workers' and peasants' organizations he used against foreign oil and land holdings. The schisms in Mexican society which were reflected in the wars of Independence, the War of the Reform, the War of French Intervention and the Revolution of 1910–1917 have not ceased to exist, but have become less profound and less capable of producing civil war in the period since the Revolution of 1910–17.

Internal peace and an apolitical military are equated and related to the aspiration for a stronger, more cohesive nation. The value of a unified nation justifies the removal of the clergy as a major political force based upon a legally privileged position. Clerical strength has been confined to spiritual functions as nearly as is possible in a Catholic country. The liberal ideals of individual liberty, popular participation and representative government, as well as the conservative ideal of order, have been forged into a new working combination with the operative norm of "no re-election" as a catalytic agent. The Revolutionary Coalition with its mass, quasi-voluntary organizations and its single, inclusive political party represent an organizational innovation capable of sustaining the principle of no re-election while at the same time practicing a variation of *continuismo*.

In the nationalist revolutionary synthesis progress and modernization occupy high places in the hierarchy of values and are explicitly connected with the goal of a strengthened nation, based upon wider distribution of opportunity and a higher standard of living for the masses. Patriotism is linked with progress through modernization in the appeal for citizens to push the country to greater heights. Patriotism is defined in specifics to include love of homeland and the duty to promote progress for all Mexicans through hard work, punctuality, and sober living. Achievement in the fields of education, irrigation, agriculture and industrial production is praised; so is continued expansion of the distribution of electricity and expanded services in transportation and communication. Social security, medical attention, and sanitation facilities are emphasized repeatedly in conjunction with appeals to the young to become technically proficient, and thus to push Mexico farther along the road of material progress. Evidence of past accomplishments and the educational focus upon continued improvement have been made essential to the political socialization process.[33] Decision-makers are aware that literacy and accompanying indoctrination serve a vital function in nation-building by opening channels through which a relatively common understanding of the significance of historical persons and events can become widespread. There becomes possible a distinct loyalty which is oriented toward the existing political system, particularly in terms of a sense of community and an affection for the regime. Thus, persons in government may be sus-

---

[33] See the references to these matters in such seemingly diverse sources of official thought as the presidential inaugural address of Gustavo Díaz Ordaz and the *Libros de Texto Gratuitos*. In fact, such sources are not so diverse as they seem for there is an ideology which is called upon for all occasions and in all circumstances whether in school orientation or political ceremonial address.

pected of participation in all kinds of self-aggrandizement at the expense of the multitude, but the populace at the same time (1) can identify as a community, and (2) remain loyal to the general framework of fundamental rules. This has happened in Mexico.[34]

We have been speaking of an interpretation of history as a unifier of Mexican society and a builder of support for the political system at the levels of community and regime. The historical orientation of which we are speaking, then, functions as an ideology without partaking of the nature of a closed philosophical system such as Marxism. The revolutionary ideology is a clustering of facts, myths and legends around certain core feelings and philosophical conceptions. This ideology of history is not static; it changes in its secondary aspects all the time. The primary or basic elements, however, remain the same from one generation to the next and will do so unless new forces destroy the system and install a new set of norms and roles. There has tended to develop a common language concerning the political antecedents of the present regime which makes possible a more meaningful dialogue between various strata of urban society, as well as between urban and rural people. The interpretation of history thus provides a pragmatic ideological bias which gives direction and meaning to political style so that leaders increasingly are able to act and speak in an understandable fashion to urban and rural dwellers alike. More Mexicans than ever before have a sense of membership in a tradition.

> Villa still gallops through the north, in songs and ballads; Zapata dies at every popular fair; Madero appears on the balconies, waving the flag; Carranza and Obregón still travel back and forth across the country in those trains of the revolutionary period, causing the women to flutter with alarm and the young men to leave home. Everybody follows them . . . It is the Revolution, the magical word, the word that is going to change everything . . . By means of the Revolution the Mexican people found itself . . . [Its superiority] compared with our nineteenth century movements . . . resulted from the profound manner in which its heroes, bandits, and myths stamped themselves forever on the sensibility and imagination of every Mexican.[35]

[34] This refers to that portion of the Mexican people who have been exposed to some education and have learned a little about the functioning of the existing political arrangement. There is another Mexico for which the outlook is not so promising, as will be pointed out later.

[35] Paz, p. 148.

2

Parties and Elections

The Revolutionary Party

Mexico's political system is frequently referred to as a one-party system, but there are in fact several parties. The one which wins, however, in the country's electoral contests is the Revolutionary Party, which has been called PNR and PRM — and most recently, PRI. The organization of the PRI sets an example for organizational efforts of the other parties.[1]

The role of the PRI is the subject of controversy among observers. Robert E. Scott, for example, sees the PRI as a dominant, non-authoritarian party, which functions as an aggregator of the various interests of its sweepingly inclusive rank and file.[2] Frank Brandenburg, on the other hand, regards the PRI as nothing more than an appendage of government, especially the executive branch of government. He views the existing arrangement as a benevolent despotism with the President of the Republic and a small coterie of trusted associates making the only significant decisions. In this latter view the constitutional limitation of no re-election provides the only deviation from an essentially authoritarian pattern of rule.[3]

While the writer does not regard the PRI as an aggregator of interests

[1] The party has changed names three times and has undergone six changes in organizational rules since 1929. When first organized at Querétaro in 1929 its title was *Partido Nacional Revolucionario* (PNR). In 1938 it was *Partido de la Revolución Mexicana* (PRM). Finally, in 1946 the party became the *Partido Revolucionario Institucional* (PRI). Changes in the party rules or "Statutes" occurred in 1933, 1938, 1946, 1950, and 1953 with further alterations in March, 1960

[2] Robert E. Scott, *Mexican Government in Transition* (Urbana, Ill., 1959), p. 146.

[3] Frank Brandenburg, *The Making of Modern Mexico* (Englewood Cliffs, N.J., 1964), pp. 3–7.

after the fashion of a major party in a two-party system or a more stable multi-party system, he does see the party as facilitating the final aggregative decisions emanating from the President's circle. The party is thus considered a significant element in the process culminating in aggregation. As such, the party is discussed both in terms of evolution and structure to clarify the manner in which it contributes to interest aggregation in the political process.

The party came into being as a result of a felt need for stabilization of relationships among competing groups. The varying orientations within the normative framework espoused by the victors of the 1910–17 Revolution produced thirteen years of post-revolutionary strife often marked by violence among divergent groups and their leaders. These difficulties culminated in the assassination of General Alvaro Obregón, Mexico's president-elect, in 1928. The assassination disrupted the presidential succession and raised the threat of an all-out civil war among the "revolutionaries" who had established the constitutional norms and progressive goals that were designed to lead the country out of a situation of economic stagnation and backwardness.

The intense hostility between the Agrarista Party, principal supporters of Obregón, and the groups supporting the outgoing President, Plutarco E. Calles, made it necessary to find some new solution to avert bitter civil strife. It was at this point that Calles introduced the idea of an inclusive single party which would incorporate all wings of the revolutionary tradition and provide established procedures by which all factions could work together to make decisions involving the succession to office at all levels.

Historians interpret in different ways Calles' motives in calling for the formation of a Revolutionary Party during his State of the Union message in September of 1928. One interpretation sees it as a clever, calculated move to achieve control of the presidency and all revolutionary politics without violating the norm of no re-election.[4] Without entirely rejecting this view one can at least suggest that the innovation of Calles was more than a mere political maneuver. Calles made a choice which helped establish the basis for peaceful change in a country where violence was endemic and rule by military parasites might have been easily perpetuated. If the Revolution has not terminated in another

[4] "Calles emerged the full-fledged caudillo he had said Mexico would be well rid of. The chief difference between himself and Obregón was that he had the backing of a highly organized and united political party, which he ruled with an iron hand. He became, in short, the modern political machine boss so familiar in American politics. . . ." Daniel James, *Mexico and the Americans* (New York, 1963), p. 246.

Porfirato as did the Reform, it is in part because of the decisions made by Calles in 1928–1929.[5]

The party which Calles brought into being was at first a loose coalition of regional parties and functional or economically based groups. With the exception of the tiny Communist following and the labor leaders affiliated with Luis N. Morones, all other groups identified in some way with revolutionary ideals sent delegates to Querétaro in March, 1929, to participate in the founding of the National Revolutionary Party (PNR). Not only was the new structure loosely knit in organizational terms but its very inclusiveness presupposed an extensive range of views on agrarian reform, workers' benefits and treatment of the oil problem. Somehow these differences had to be resolved in terms of broad policy decisions. Calles was able to orient most of the choices in a generally conservative direction until after Lázaro Cárdenas became President in 1934. From that time on the views of the left wing of the party dominated Mexican government policy until Cárdenas left office in 1940.

The party was organized to unite the divergent revolutionary groups and reconcile personality differences among leaders. It was a political device created to provide the far-flung, leader-centered groups of the revolutionary tradition with a symbol of common interest, and the *Pact of Union and Solidarity* which they signed at Querétaro provided a degree of moral pressure for conformity with established procedures in decisions concerning candidates.[6] The burden of proof morally — after March, 1929 — rested upon any civilian or military leader who considered rebellion as a viable alternative against party decisions. Thus an institution surmounting exclusively personal ties came into operation. Within the framework of this institution views could be expressed without immediately reflecting personal animosity, and divergent groups could compete for advantage. The result was a situation in which no man could maintain himself as boss of the machine indefinitely. Two events have pointed up this condition. One

[5] "He . . . use[d] this moment of tension and strife to attempt a bridge between the tradition of the *caudillo* and political democracy. The moment was tense with implicit tragedy, for the logic of political tradition required either a tyranny or a convulsion. That neither came to pass is to the credit of Calles, and it must be recognized as the beginning of that change in the political atmosphere which has since brought relative peace to the country." Frank Tannenbaum, *Mexico, The Struggle for Peace and Bread* (New York, 1951), p. 67. The term *Porfirato* is used by Mexicans to describe the distinguishing characteristics of the regime of Porfirio Díaz.

[6] L. Vincent Padgett, *Popular Participation in the Mexican "One-Party" System* (unpublished dissertation, Northwestern University, 1955), p. 45.

was Calles' acceptance of Lázaro Cárdenas, the candidate of the left wing of the party in 1934, followed by Cárdenas' action to force Calles to leave the country in June, 1935. A second was the Ruiz Cortines compromise accepted by President Miguel Alemán in 1951.

That the party has remained subordinate to the presidency in most cases has been demonstrated again and again; yet it cannot be denied that the party has also provided a way of legitimizing the choice of new presidents in a manner distinct from choice based solely on the will of the presidential incumbent. As an institution the party has durability beyond the personal popularity of individuals, and it is this fact which has contributed greatly to a change from personal continuism to the pattern of party continuism. The difference has been significant for political stability in presidential successions and thus has aided Mexico's continued economic and social advancement in recent years.

The organs of the party at the national level have always been three in number. Formally speaking, the highest in rank is the National Assembly. The National Assembly generally has had the major function of naming the candidate of the party for President of the Republic and rearranging various aspects of the party rules or statutes, the party statement of principles and the program. The National Assembly under the Statutes of 1929 and 1933 was called the National Convention and was composed of delegates elected indirectly through a series of conventions arranged in hierarchical order from the municipal level to the level of the electoral district, the state level and finally the national meeting. When the PRM was formed in 1938, a new arrangement for selecting delegates to the National Assembly emerged. The bases of delegate choice were the sectors which were titled agrarian, labor, popular, and military. Each sector included one or more groups for interest articulation, and each sector was to have a number of delegates assigned by another party organ, the National Council.

In 1946 when the party became the PRI the idea of a party primary based upon electoral districts as defined by federal law was introduced for selecting National Assembly delegates, but this was abandoned under the rules of 1950 and 1953. Under the rules of 1960 three sectors — agrarian, labor, and popular — formed the basis for selection of delegates.[7] The delegates are chosen directly by sectors as well as

[7] Under the rules of 1960 a distinction is made between assemblies and conventions at all levels. The assemblies are concerned with proposed revisions of rules and program, the selection of highest ranking party executive committee officers — national, state and local — and reports of retiring executive committees. The term "convention" is applied to distinguish meetings called for the purpose of nominating party candidates and stating the

by state assemblies or conventions. The rules of convocation set the basis for apportionment of delegates.

A second of the three major organs at the national level has appeared under all the statutory arrangements from the beginning of the party in 1929. It has been variously referred to as the National Directive Committee, the National Council, the Grand Commission, and finally, in 1960, was called once again the National Council. The National Council has sometimes been able to select its own officers, but the most recent arrangement is one corresponding to some earlier periods in which the president or secretary general of the party's National Executive Committee presides over the National Council.[8]

Under the rules of 1960 for the first time the presidents or chairmen of the party's state committees are given membership automatically in the National Council. In addition, there are fifteen representatives for each sector — agrarian, labor, and popular — chosen on a national basis. The president and the general secretary of the National Executive Committee are members and presiding officers for the National Council. The National Executive Committee determines which organization in each of the three sectors will select leaders as representatives on the National Council. The number of persons affiliated with an organization is stressed explicitly. In formal terms, the larger the rank and file of an organization or *central* the more likely it is to have one or more sector representatives.

The National Executive Committee (CEN) summons the National Council to meetings. The vote of the president of the National Executive Committee is the deciding vote in case of a tie in its deliberations. These are the overriding considerations. The only conceivable way in which the National Council could really affect decisions at the highest level in the party would be in the case of a drastic rupture of relations among persons who constitute the top leadership of the Revolutionary Coalition and of the party. Under such circumstances authority to approve orders of convocation issued for national assemblies by the CEN, powers of review with regard to sanctions and reestablishment of party members in their rights and the power to name a CEN president or general secretary on an interim basis might become important.

Probably the most significant fact about the National Council under

---

party's proposed governmental program or platform. *Statutes of the PRI* [Approved by the III Regular National Assembly] (Mexico, 1960), pp. 19–20.

[8] The size of the National Council has varied considerably from one set of statutes to the other. The size has apparently been greater and its author-

the rules of 1960 is the representation of state party committees. Their presidents, as mentioned above, sit on the National Council. In 1953 an effort began to bring the state committee presidents together at least once every year.[9] The purpose was to strengthen the party as a structure among other political structures in the Mexican political system and by so doing give life to various types of party programs at all levels. Under the rules of 1960 it is no longer necessary to call a special annual council of regional committee presidents. Instead, these presidents meet together with leading representatives of the various *centrales* of the three sectors and the two highest ranking officials of the National Executive Committee to talk over problems thus facilitating a broader interaction in perpetual effort to maximize consensus on major policy questions. Gearing state party presidents into an existing national party organ instead of calling for a special meeting is also a way of giving greater status to the state committee leaders and thus providing more effective communication with the CEN.[10]

The National Executive Committee (CEN) has more power than either the National Assembly or the National Council. Under the rules of 1960 the CEN is empowered to convoke national assemblies and specify the criteria for choice of delegates. It also convokes the National Council and specifies criteria for choice of the National Council's sector representatives. It oversees the discipline of the party as a whole in accord with official acts of assemblies as well as party principles, program and statutes. It checks on members in discharge of their obligations as citizens and their missions as members of the party. It sets up commissions for independent reporting on regional political situations and appoints "zone supervisors" and "delegates" to observe party functions at all levels. It convenes state party assemblies and authorizes state party committees to convene municipal and district assemblies, and it settles controversies or difficulties that arise between organs or members of the party. It has power to make interim appointments of presidents and secretaries of state committees when these fail to complete their terms, and it can remove members of state, district, municipal and sectional committees for specified causes relating to failure to abide by party rules. It is able to determine political style by specifying norms of organization and methods of political action. It can arrange its own internal procedures and those of district, municipal

---

ity less during periods when the statutes have been drawn at the beginning of presidential terms and the size less and the formal authority greater when the statutes have been drawn toward the end of presidential terms.

[9] Padgett, p. 148.

[10] Padgett, p. 149.

and sectional committees as well. It passes on the validity of results of nominating conventions for positions as federal legislators, governors, state legislators, and municipal presidents. It issues convening orders for all nominating conventions and rules on the legality of proceedings including the necessity of another convention in the event of "irregularities." It supervises state committees in their conduct of training centers for teaching basic educational and technical skills and dissemination of party propaganda. It has ultimate responsibility for expansion of party membership through supervision of recruitment drives.

The president of the CEN stands above the committee itself and like the general secretary is chosen by the National Assembly of the party. However, the decision as to which person will be president of the CEN and which person will be general secretary under normal conditions is made by the President of the Republic. The reasons for this are clear enough in terms of the Mexican tradition of politics and political decision-making which centers around the presidency of the nation. Mexico's presidency is in fact a decision-making organ without peer among Mexican political structures. If the president's decisions are to be fully supported, other political structures in the system such as the Revolutionary Party must be headed by a man who is considered trustworthy by the leading decision-maker.

Insofar as the party structure is concerned, the CEN president is clearly the apex. He has the authority to call the CEN meetings, and he presides over its sessions as well as those of the National Council; he also carries into effect the agreements reached in the sessions of the CEN and the National Council. Since his approval is necessary for all expenditures of the CEN, he controls the budget, and he exercises the powers of the CEN in urgent cases. He acts as the representative of the party before all authorities and institutions in the country, or he can delegate this representative role to others.

The general secretary, like the president, is named by the National Assembly and selected by the incoming CEN president. The general secretary keeps a record of all meetings of the CEN, reports to the president of the CEN on all activities within the jurisdiction of the secretariat including all of the various bureaus of the CEN, and reports discussions of the CEN and the National Council to leading persons in other political structures, for example, the President of the Republic.

The CEN is composed of six officers in addition to the president and the general secretary. The officers are the secretary of agrarian action, the secretary of labor action, the secretary of popular action, the secretary of political action (senator), the secretary of political action (federal deputy), the secretary of organization, the secretary of press and propaganda, and the secretary of finance. The two oldest offices among these are the secretariats of agrarian action and labor action. Both offices were formed in 1933.[11]

In recent years the person acting as secretary of agrarian action of the party has usually been the general secretary of the National Peasants Confederation (CNC). The secretary of agrarian action operates as a liaison officer between the party and the peasant organizations, particularly, of course, the agrarian leagues in the states and the national confederation which brings them together. In his role he proposes concrete action programs for improvement of life in the peasant sector, operates as an investigating officer in various types of conflicts affecting the rural person affiliated with the party, encourages party loyalty of the rural dweller and seeks to bring more persons in the countryside into affiliation with the party. The primary emphasis has been upon persons who live on *ejidos*.[12] Rural day laborers and small property-holders have also been included.[13]

The secretary of labor action forms a link between the party and the affiliated organizations of the labor sector. He is supposed to work for achievement of the party's announced social goals and programs for the benefit of all workers affiliated with the party. Specifically, he is to hear and investigate complaints of workers and workers' organizations. In practice, however, the perennial occupation of this post by a leading figure in the large *Confederación de Trabajadores de Mexico* (CTM) has isolated other union groups from any services provided.[14]

A secretary of popular action was first incorporated in the CEN under the statutory changes of 1938. By 1950 it had become established that this member of the CEN should also be general secretary of the increasingly powerful popular sector organization, the CNOP. Like the secretaries of agrarian and labor action, the popular action secretary is supposed to represent the interests of his sector members in deliberations of the CEN, to promote the party program within the popular sector, to strive to increase the membership of the party, and to encourage militant support of the party within the popular sector.

The rules of 1960 make it clear that the secretaries of agrarian, labor, and popular action are regarded as direct links between the party and their sectors.[15] It emphasized that this role involves responsibility for

[11] Padgett, p. 30.

[12] The plots of land set aside under the land distribution program.

[13] See Padgett, p. 130, for the history of the development of the statutes on the agrarian secretariat.

[14] Scott, p. 163.

[15] The word "sector" refers to one or more confederations of peasants, workers or professional people grouped together according to function and given representation in the party as a "sector."

proposing concrete "educational and action" programs, for stimulating "militancy" of party members, for promoting loyalty to the "principles of the Mexican Revolution," and for establishing "close coordination" among the sectors in the interest of party unity and strength.

In 1960 a totally new idea appeared with regard to relations between the CEN and the sectors. It is related to the perennial problem of political communication in the Mexican-style inclusive, dominant party arrangement. Each sector — agrarian, labor, and popular — is supposed to have a consultative council with members chosen by the CEN "taking into account the importance of the distinctively different organizations active in each sector and the numbers of persons affiliated with each organization."[16] These councils are convened and presided over by the president and general secretary of the party CEN.

The importance attached to the creation and maintenance of communication channels linking the leadership of the primary political structures is reflected once again in the provision under the party rules for a secretary of political action (federal deputy) and a secretary of political action (senator). These persons have been assigned a liaison or communications function to promote unification within the Revolutionary Coalition. Their special concern is the coordination of party pronouncements with executive aims and legislative action. This has always been the mission assigned these posts by the party statutes since the positions were first made part of the CEN in 1946.

The 1960 party rules created the new CEN posts of organization, of press and propaganda, and of finance. The provisions concerning the secretary of organization and the secretary of finance deserve mention because they refer explicitly to an aspect of political organization formerly missing from the party rules. These provisions set up new guidelines with regard to recruitment of members. The party secretary of organization, for example, is to maintain an up-to-date record of party membership, to oversee state and municipal committees so that they maintain adequate membership records, to see that the lower level committees are prepared to submit reports on the past and current records of party members, and to ascertain whether party members register to vote and act in accord with existing electoral laws. The secretary of finance has been charged with responsibility for collection of regular dues and special contributions. He has charge of all accounting procedures.

With the addition of these two roles the party has for the first time a structure providing for operation in the style of a democratic party in Western Europe. The rules of 1960 have provided the organizational

[16] *Statutes of 1960.* Art. 36, pp. 36–37.

basis for a clearly definable rank and file and for less dependence upon government officialdom and leaders of interest groups for financial support of party activities.[17]

A meeting of party functionaries in February, 1965, along with the selection of the veteran and dynamic Carlos A. Madrazo as president of the party, seemed to mark the beginnings of some important changes in party practices. Specifically, the party's popular image and the necessity of a loyal membership stood out as major concerns. With regard to the former, Madrazo led the party forward on several fronts, particularly in the emphasis upon democratization of the choice of party municipal committees and party nominees for local government posts. The idea was to lessen the pre-assembly decisions made among sector organizations and reduce the influence of higher party levels which often resulted in unanimous votes in the municipal assemblies. Madrazo pointed out that the growing image of the party as the instrument of a few must be changed through actual expansion of popular participation at the grass-roots level of party organization. This was the meaning of the focus upon party nominations for municipal committees in most states during the first six months of 1965.

Moreover, attention was turned repeatedly to the problem of corruption within the Revolutionary Coalition. Madrazo, who had distinguished himself by mid-1965 as one of the most dynamic and controversial presidents the PRI central committee had ever had, supported the formation of a Commission of Honor and Justice to work with the Attorney General (*Procurador de la República*) in order to clean up some of the racketeering among politicians. Pedro Vivanco, a leader of the Petroleum workers and Norberto Gómez Solis of the agrarian department (DAAC) were among the first singled out. Some enthusiastic younger politicians suggested that the great labor figures, Fidel Velázquez and Jesús Yurén, ought not to be overlooked.[18]

In still another move to provide more substance for the party struc-

[17] The party in the early 1950's operated through a series of executive committees at the national, state, and municipal levels. The mission of these committees was to provide communications centers between sector leadership and rank and file on the one hand and the group holding formal governmental positions on the other. In addition, the committees were to organize demonstrations and rallies for party candidates at election time, and participate in the selection process relating to choice of party candidates. The party depended for its rank-and-file supporters almost entirely upon organized groups within the sectors. The chain of command was not very clearly spelled out with regard to relations between the national committee and the state and municipal committees. See L. Vincent Padgett, "Mexico's One-Party System: A Re-evaluation," *American Political Science Review,* 51 (December, 1957), p. 994.

[18] *Excelsior,* June–August, 1965. *El Día,* June–August, 1965.

ture and alter the party's character Madrazo ordered the PRI and all its affiliated organizations to set up a record of all persons in their membership. The importance of providing independent financing for the party from the grass roots was recognized in the first systematic effort to record the "pledge" of each member for financial support. This effort along with the other changes in policy represented the conviction of Madrazo and the powerful circle to which he belonged within the Revolutionary Coalition that the party must become more vital and have greater autonomy in order to function with a higher degree of effectiveness in organizing mass support for the regime.

With regard to membership recruitment and a dues-paying rank and file, it is worth pointing out that the CEN has been expanding its services, setting the pattern for party committees at all levels. The CEN now has offices for the organization of sports activities known as "Revolutionary competitive events," for the organization of women, for the organization of youth up to twenty-five years and encouragement of militant party spirit among them,[19] for organization of discussion meetings at the national level and promotion of political, economic and social writing favorable to the party's position on the part of professional people.[20]

Party state committees, called "directive committees" (CDE), have a table of organization nearly identical with the CEN. Municipal committees and sectional committees (deputy electoral districts) are very similar in organization to those higher up. Committees at each level have two principal officers, president and secretary, who bear primary responsibility for finance, staff appointments, major projects (such as the training centers already mentioned), and records of

[19] Madrazo said publicly that the party was in danger of losing the university students and that more must be done to recruit the able, politically articulate student. However, Madrazo's many efforts at reform in this and other areas came to an abrupt close when he was removed from the presidency of the PRI in the fall of 1965.

[20] Three offices important to CEN operation are not mentioned in the textual material above. Civic Action is responsible for assisting and supervising the executive committees at the state level to promote the training centers already mentioned. It also organizes celebrations for all patriotic days, e.g., birthdays of heroes and dates of great battles in the revolutionary tradition, "in order to propagate the doctrine of the party." Social Action organizes social services for women and children affiliated with the party who could not otherwise afford such expensive items as medical aid. It also is supposed to intercede with government authorities concerned and tries to arrange housing for needy persons. The long-standing Legal Affairs (*Asuntos Jurídicos*) whips into proper legal form the party initiatives sent to the federal congress and composes the *convocatorias* for party assemblies issued by the CEN as well as reviewing those issued by the state committees.

membership and dues as well as committee resolutions and files.[21] These officers are the party's key men at its respective levels of organization for carrying out functions such as communication and consensus formation. Door-to-door distribution of campaign literature and other similar electoral activities are principally carried on by municipal and sectional committees.

The procedure for eliminating aspirants prior to the nominating conventions was never made explicit in party rules prior to those of 1960.[22] Convening orders for nominating conventions recognize the circulation of petitions as the legally approved way of becoming a party candidate. Aspirants have a stipulated period of time to circulate petitions to be signed by a given number of party members in the territorial division pertaining to the office, e.g., an electoral district drawn for the office of federal deputy. A petition must contain information on the candidate, including civic, professional, and political activities as well as his previous experience in public service so that

[21] Committee presidents and secretaries are chosen in assemblies which are convened by authorization of the CEN and decisions ultimately depend on the CEN for approval. Roughly the same procedure of CEN authorization and approval takes place in the case of nominating conventions. Both assemblies and nominating conventions have some delegates from sectors and some "at large" from gatherings at lower levels.

[22] The writer learned of the procedure as early as 1953 from a frustrated pre-candidate for federal deputy. Not until seven years later was it written into the rules. The procedure does not apply to the office of the President. Procedural requirements are particularly important with regard to such public offices as municipal president and state legislator as well as places in the party organization on the sectional, municipal and municipal subcommittee levels since it is at these points that dubious political antecedents might most easily escape close scrutiny under cover from some established politician who lends support for reasons of family connections or business advantage. No person is supposed to be selected as party candidate for public office if he has had a record of previous political activity as functionary or prominent member of an opposition group — or any kind of systematic opposition to the party. (A notable exception is Ezequiel Padilla, losing presidential candidate in 1946, who became a senator in 1964.) Other requisites on the more positive side include full position of citizen's rights under the *Federal Electoral Law,* a minimum of one year's formal affiliation with the party, and a record of "militancy." "Militancy," which has become a key word in the vocabulary of party leaders, means unequivocal support of agrarian reform, rights of labor, and benefits for the poor as well as fulfillment of party work assignments and obedience to orders from higher echelons. The same requisites hold for persons aspiring to become members of party executive committees at any level. As a further measure to maintain control and discipline all candidates go through a solemn ceremony in which they swear an oath of loyalty to the party. Newly selected party functionaries also are sworn in by the executive officers they are replacing.

potential signers and higher party officials can have a look at his attested political career record. Petitions are evaluated by the CEN and in some instances by state and municipal committees. The committees that check the petition also send a delegate to the electoral entity in question to gather information as the basis for a more objective evaluation of the candidate's political career and community standing. Thus, in the case of candidates for municipal president three party committees and three delegate reports are involved — municipal, state, and national committees and their representatives. The extent to which the procedure works in practice is difficult to determine because the committees keep scanty records.

Centralization of decision-making as well as multiple channels of information characterize the process described. There are Mexican as well as foreign observers, however, who think of the nominating process as entirely a result of an arbitrary decision by the President of the Republic and his closest associates. The writer does not deny the arbitrary factor, but it is his opinion that the scale of direct presidential intervention is less than is often imagined and that the process described in the rules is usually followed even if this does not eliminate situations in which decisions are made for candidates with credentials inferior to their rivals. Clearly, not only numbers of petition signatures count but also qualitative considerations, such as the status of the signatories and their ties with persons at top levels of the Revolutionary Coalition. However, the explicit statement of the process in terms of petitions can be assessed as reflecting an interest of the elite in rationalizing the process, i.e., an interest in providing a more objective basis of choice designed to produce candidates with a better record and better chance of securing popular approval in the electoral area.

The rules of 1960 differ in three important ways from the earlier organizational formulations: (1) they treat duties of party committees at all levels in greater detail with regard to records of membership and payment of dues; (2) they are more explicit in formalizing the control of the CEN over selection of party candidates, the selection of party committees, and the work of the committees themselves at all levels; and (3) they specify more types of organizational activity for party committees at all levels than ever before and do so in considerable detail.

In the first case it is reasonable to interpret the formalized concern for maintenance of up-to-date records in membership and funds as reflecting renewed interest in creating a political mechanism more capable of facilitating interest aggregation, i.e., effective combination of interests into major policy. Conversely, the goal is less dependence upon related functional groups and government in such matters as rank-and-file support and financial assistance since such dependence tends to foreclose the possibility of interest aggregation through the party. On the second point, the expanded control of the CEN over internal nominating conventions, selection of committee chiefs, and work of party committees seems a clear indication of intent to increase the party's potential for playing a part in decision-making through strengthened, centralized instruments of discipline and control. Finally, the detailed obligations of the committees with regard to organization of women, of young people and of training centers for the under-privileged clearly are compatible with the emphasis upon an expanded dues-paying membership affiliated directly with the party and under party discipline.[23] The tendency is toward recruiting greater popular support from a wider political base.

It can, of course, be argued that changes in the rules are unlikely to eliminate the intermittent structural characteristics of functional performance most clearly observable in the dependence of the party upon President, government, and quasi-official interest articulation groups.[24] On the other hand, the party has a broader and more explicit set of instructions regarding membership, finance, central control, and coverage of non-functional groups than ever before. The formal basis has been provided for sharing the interest aggregation function with the presidency and the associated inner circle of the Revolutionary Coalition as distinct from merely facilitating aggregative decisions. The new formal emphasis upon centralization and financial support may reflect agreement in the higher echelons of the Revolutionary Coalition that the party be given greater strength apart from government circles and other outside centers of power, i.e., more voice in nominations for electoral posts and more capacity to aggregate demands effectively. The writer is not crossing off the possibility that the PRI will some day have relative autonomy in the matter of nominations and win elections independently of highest government circles.[25]

The party has performed certain observable functions in the political system for some time and probably will continue to perform these functions regardless of other considerations, such as changes in rules and the related issues of the degree of party autonomy and its capacity to combine interests effectively for purposes of policy formation. It is

[23] Padgett, "Mexico's One-Party System: A Re-evaluation," pp. 995–996.

[24] Cline, *Mexico, Revolution to Evolution,* p. 156; Scott, p. 117; Manuel Ramírez Reyes, "El desarrollo histórico de los partidos políticos mexicanos," La Sociedad Mexicana de Geografía y Estadística, Sesión Académica Ordinaria (October 8, 1963), unpublished.

[25] For a reverse opinion see Brandenburg on "The Liberal Machiavellian." Brandenburg, pp. 141–165.

important to remember what the PRI is and is not. It is not at present an institutionalized autonomous structure for the aggregation of demands articulated by the various interests of the Mexican political system. It is, however, an agency with its own personnel, its own procedures, and its own internal hierarchy of command. As such it performs functions vital to the existing mode of operation.

The party is an important mechanism for facilitating political communication. Key decisions aggregating interest and producing policy are made by the President, but the party provides an important sounding board and listening device by which trial balloons can be released among the rank and file of power-seekers in the lower echelons of the Revolutionary Coalition, and reactions at these levels can be reported for an assessment of support and/or ease of producing consensus. The party itself, the officials and other political acquaintances and friends, can be useful in propounding arguments in favor of projected policies among the politically active while at the same time functioning as an organ for the distribution of propaganda to the masses.

The party also has an important function as mediator of disputes and promoter of consensus. Choice of "revolutionary" leaders is characterized by a kind of co-optative action on the part of top decision-makers which is accompanied in a seemingly paradoxical way by preoccupation with achievement of consensus among lesser influentials and power aspirants. Moreover, the goal of maximizing consensus is pursued without resort to standard methods of totalitarianism in the treatment of opposition and mobilization of support. Thus devices are at premium for bringing about consensus by means as nearly voluntary as possible. The party in fulfilling its role helps to avoid the totalitarian solution on one hand, and on the other, works to prevent the chaos that would follow an outbreak of internecine strife among members of the Revolutionary Coalition. It is a role the functions of which involve more careful consideration than would be the case if the party were viewed as a mere appendage of government — say another bureau of the Secretariat of the Presidency. Particularly important in this connection is the apparently simple fact that party offices serve as useful meeting places for members of diverse groups within the Revolutionary Coalition. In addition, a part of mediation and promotion of consensus is involved in the liaison work through party offices and officials in which messages are carried back and forth, and "diplomatic" representations made by the party as a neutral body among sometimes competing factions.[26]

Another set of party functions is related to the special conditions of

[26] The party in the context of this statement refers to the officials of the various committees at the different levels of party organization. Although

Mexican elections. Under Mexican circumstances, firm decisions concerning the candidates of the Revolutionary Coalition are basic to the whole succession process. This is because the party serves as a symbol of unity for the coalition during the period of elections. In part it is able to serve this purpose because it is the only organization in a position to act as a legitimizing symbol of candidate selection. The presence of the party makes the many high-level decisions concerning presidential succession and succession to lesser offices seem less arbitrary because there is a set of procedures for resolving disputes among organized groups of the party's three sectors and between these organized groups and government.

Finally, the party is an electoral instrument which serves the Revolutionary Coalition as a device for meeting the norm of electoral participation. In fact, the party symbolizes the electoral norm for leader selection. Not only in this symbolic way, however, is the party important as an electoral device, for the party also contributes substantially to the mobilization of popular support through activation at election time of essentially dormant loyalties.

In summary, the party should be perceived as a legitimizing symbol for the selection of candidates and a repository of procedural devices for minimizing arbitrary choice in the nominations of candidates at various levels. It should also be viewed as a vital communications center through which messages are flashed to keep all segments of the Revolutionary Coalition informed and a mediating and liaison device facilitating congruent policy stands among interest-group leaders and officials of government.

As one political structure among several, it is quasi-independent of the executive branch, but it is still more a creature of the executive organizational network than the executive branch is a creature of the party. In practical order of importance the President and his colleagues in government and their top echelons of organization make decisions which control party decisions. Nevertheless, the party has an independent administrative life of its own with corresponding loyalties, and its personnel have dreams of expanding the power of the party as a structure vis-à-vis other structures. This tendency is reflected in the evolution of the statutes and in recent statutory change.

Other Parties

Opposition groups in the Mexican political system may be regarded as parties, or simply publics. Brandenburg has separated all the dif-

---

members of these committees may be parties to an intra-Revolutionary Coalition dispute, the committees as such frequently function as neutral and conciliatory bodies.

fering clusters in relation to the Center, Left and Right of the political spectrum. Without specific organizational identification of these clusters, he terms them "publics."[27] He assumes that policy orientation is critical because organized parties are supported by government with the intention of creating and maintaining an impression of considerable variety as ideological arguments and policy positions.[28] In contrast, the writer feels it more useful to treat most of the duly registered political parties of Mexico as independent, voluntary organizations which may on occasion receive financial aid or some other kind of support from government but only as the exception — not the rule.[29]

The Transient Political Party

One type of opposition group that has appeared in the past, and conceivably might appear again, could be referred to as the transient political group, since it arises and disappears on the occasion of the approach and passing of the presidential election. Apart from its lack of permanence, the transient group has as its salient characteristic a pattern of personalism with all the attention and loyalty focusing on the leader. In the second place, that leader is himself a person who was once a part of the Revolutionary Coalition and who has withdrawn from the revolutionary circle because his aspirations for the presidential nomination were frustrated. Characteristically, the transient leader and his group have had no intention of becoming a permanent, loyal opposition. Their objective has been the division of the Revolutionary Coalition in such a way as to challenge the presidential decision which has deprived the leader of his expected "revolutionary" candidacy. An underlying assumption of such groups has often been the necessity for use of force, and this is not surprising in the light of the fact that the leader more often than not has been a military man. The pattern of the transient group began as early as Obregón's rebellion against Carranza. It was manifest in de la Huerta's rebellion against Obregón in 1923 and in the election efforts of Vasconcelos in 1930. It was clearly represented in the elections of 1940, 1946, and 1952.

[27] Brandenburg, pp. 119–140.

[28] Brandenburg, pp. 144–165.

[29] Many officials and strong partisans of the various parties staunchly maintain that their organizations exist on the basis of private donations — some very small from the rank and file and a few large amounts from wealthy supporters. The rumor persists that most of the money comes from government, but no one will say whether this is literally true in terms of payments of money or whether it is figuratively true in terms of advantages through letting of public contracts and other business dealings in which government plays a part. Mexicans do not talk freely of these matters when they are in a position to know what is really going on.

In 1940 a very popular man in the Revolutionary Coalition was frustrated in his presidential ambitions and went outside the coalition, divorced himself from the "revolutionary" circle, and formed his own Revolutionary National Unification Party (PRUN). General Juan Andreu Almazán represented a real threat to the supremacy of the inner group dominating the Revolutionary Coalition and to the carefully erected procedural framework of the party for validating decisions of the inner circle of influential persons; but in spite of his connections with peasants, some labor groups and other factions of the Revolutionary Coalition, Almazán was unable to muster enough support to reverse the decision against him and gain the presidency. The Almazán-Ávila Camacho contest of 1940 was a bitter one and sometimes bloody, but it was fought in the area of civilian organizations.[30] Military rebellion never materialized. When the moment of supreme trial had passed, the Almazanistas never were able to re-group, and a few months later both the group and the leader had disappeared as major factors in Mexican politics. Some of the details of the Almazán affair are worth noting as typical of such cases in the past and likely patterns for the future in the event of a split in the Revolutionary Coalition.

The organization of vast sectors of Mexican society into functional groups with strong commitments to support the existing control structure was an accomplished fact by the time General Juan Andréu Almazán campaigned for the presidency against General Manuel Ávila Camacho. Almazán had had a considerable amount of contact with both peasant and labor organizations through his position in the military. As Zone Commander in the state of Nuevo León he frequently had occasion to befriend peasants of the *ejidos* against the local *hacendados*. Although in doing so he merely carried out the policy of President Lázaro Cárdenas, Almazán saw to it that the peasants remembered his part in aiding their cause. Similarly, with labor, the general did his best to secure the most political advantage for benefits rendered.

When it became clear that he could not obtain enough support among the groups in the effective power pattern, the so-called "revolutionary" groupings, Almazán moved outside controlling political circles and tried to lure their elements of support to his cause. He asked for endorsements from peasant and labor leaders whom he had aided, then had these printed and circulated among the workers and peasants everywhere. A pledge of support from the officers of the *ejido,* Granja

---

[30] Civilian organizations in this context means that bodies of the organized military did not struggle against each other — rather it was organized peasants and labor who played key roles.

Sanitaria, El Alto, in the *municipio* of Montemorelos, Nuevo León, will illustrate this approach and point up the impression which Almazán sought to create among the peasants while he was Zone Commander in the north.

Señor General of Division
Juan Almazán, Monterrey, Nuevo León.

The undersigned [belonged] to the *ejido* of La Granja Sanitaria at the moment of the taking possession of the *hacienda* of El Alto which it pleased you to cede to us. [We are] thankful to your excellency for [the] great favor that we have received from you in . . . the grand extension of land that amounts to 854 hectares, or twenty times that which had been conceded by donation to us in Monterrey. [We are also grateful for] the draft animals, plows and other instruments of cultivation that you have given us in addition to the allowance of seed corn that is benefiting us and the water that guarantees our crops. [We] wish to offer you at this time a vote of confidence with our gratitude and that of our families for the ever-so-generous way in which you helped us to resolve our problem.

Attentively,
"Land and Liberty"
El Alto, Nuevo León
14 July 1939

Comisariado Ejidal —
Julio Flores
Consejo de Vigilancia — Vincente Bocanegra, Luciano Sánchez.
Antonio Rodrigues, David Castillo, Nicolas Rodrigues, Isabel Contreras, Juan Hernández, Jesús Martínez, Manuel Gonzales [and so on down the list of *ejidatarios*].[31]

Almazán especially tried to woo the labor organizations that had been identified with the "revolutionary" group but had remained outside the CTM. In Puebla he had notable success and won the Revolutionary Federations of Workers and Peasants (FROC) to his side. The Federation had significant strength in Puebla. However, the storm troops of the CTM attacked the FROC headquarters and broke its organization in the process. Thus, Almazán's base for a raid on the labor fold was cut out from under him.[32]

---

[31] *Excelsior*, September 27, 1939. Almazán was already campaigning in this fashion against Ávila Camacho and his own former colleagues before the election assembly of the PRM. The assembly began on November 1, 1939. By September 23 General Heriberto Jara, president of the CEC of the PRM, had already announced to the Chamber of Deputies that Almazán would not be considered as a PRM candidate.

[32] *Excelsior*, September 12, 1939. It took the FROC a number of years to recover from the loss of this trial of strength.

In 1946 Ezequiel Padilla made an effort to break the Revolutionary Coalition by forming the Mexican Democratic Party (PDM) to lead interest group leaders in a secessionist movement. As in 1940, however, the effort failed, and the threat to the dominant position of the Revolutionary Coalition and its inner circle of decision-makers was less real. In 1952 the frustrated office-seeker who deserted the Revolutionary Coalition to challenge its choice of leadership for the presidency was General Miguel Henríquez Guzmán. This effort to split the Revolutionary Coalition was better planned, better financed and more intensely emotional than that of Padilla. In these respects it was more like the Almazán episode. Both Almazán and Henríquez were "revolutionary" generals who had had important commands as well as important political jobs and high political standing in the Revolutionary Coalition. Both men had had extensive relationships with the grass roots leaders as well as close personal connections with the inner circle of the Revolutionary Coalition. Henríquez' party, the Federation of Mexican Peoples' Parties (F de PPM) made it seem like a real contest in 1952, just as the PRUN of Almazán had done in 1940.

Permanent Opposition Parties

Since 1952 no political groups have appeared corresponding to the transient groups led by Almazán, Padilla, or Henríquez. Other political groups which have manifested opposition to the dominance of the Revolutionary Coalition have had a different style and have, in some cases at least, shown genuine staying power. Staying power, or permanence, on the Mexican scene, so far as political groups are concerned, must be evaluated in terms other than participation in presidential elections alone. The real test as to whether a group can be considered a permanent opposition group hinges on whether it shows an inclination to involve itself in the contests that arise between the presidential elections every six years. The posts involved might be those in the federal Chamber of Deputies, in state legislatures, or municipal councils.

The two parties which have lasted and have shown a disposition to compete in off-year elections have been the National Action Party (PAN) and the Popular Socialist Party (PPS). The PAN and PPS have in common the fact that they are both younger than the PRI. They have customarily entered elections for some local and state as well as federal offices, but they have won very few of the elections in which they have taken part. The PAN and the PPS also have in common the role they have played as political gadflies, that is, they have helped to educate the public by emphasizing alternatives other than those presented by the government. They have also performed a public service by helping to prick the public conscience and thus encourage an airing of some policy questions. The organizational features of both parties closely resemble those of the PRI.

These two parties are different in spite of their similarities. The PAN, for example, is identified with the Right of the Mexican ideological spectrum; the PPS is identified with the Left. The PAN is older than the PPS, having been constituted by an assembly held in September, 1939, whereas the PPS did not emerge until nine years later, in June, 1948. Also different are the backgrounds of the leaders. The founders of the PAN, Manuel Gómez Morín and Efraín González Luna, never had any position in the Revolutionary Coalition. Their background has always been a combination of harmony with church-oriented conservatism in matters such as education and a traditional liberal position regarding property and the relationship of government to business. In contrast to the leaders of the PAN the leader of the PPS, Vincente Lombardo Toledano, was once a militant member of the PRI, and was pushed out because his views were too far to the left to fit with the orientation of the party as it evolved after 1940.

The extreme wings of the PAN and the PPS shade off respectively into the militancy of the Sinarquista and the Communist groups.[33] With the exception of the years 1937–1942, when the Sinarquistas raised their membership to an estimated 1,000,000 persons, neither the Sinarquistas nor the Communists have shown consistent tendencies of growth necessary to make them a threat to the established order.

The Sinarquistas and the Communists stand against the going system, both in terms of the existing pattern of influence and power relationships dominated by the Revolutionary Coalition and its leading members as well as the formal or constitutional aspects of the existing arrangement. In contrast, the PAN and the PPS both appear more willing to function within the framework of rules and pattern of power. Their aim seems to be simply a series of modifications to permit more

[33] The Sinarquistas, later known as the *Partido Fuerza Popular,* derived the name of their movement from two words, *sin anarquia,* meaning literally "without anarchy." Indeed, the principal theme of the Sinarquistas has been *orden,* or order. They were strong immediately preceding and during the first part of World War II. Their orientation was that of the Spanish Falangist movement, and they were outspokenly pro-Axis. Since the war they have suffered from repeated schisms among their leaders, and their militant tactics have caused them trouble with the government — always to their detriment. A definitive discussion of the Mexican Communist Party is to be found in Robert J. Alexander, *Communism in Latin America* (New Brunswick, N.J., 1957), pp. 319–349.

effective pressure from their sectors upon the process of political choice and decision-making. Both the PAN and the PPS would make changes in the formal political structure, the Constitution and its correlates, to fit the emphasis of their respective doctrines, but they would not abolish totally constitutional rules of the game.

The PAN. Paradoxically the PAN emerged at a time when Mexico had been carried far to the left by the policies of President Cárdenas. Originally it was formed by a small but highly influential group of intellectuals and professional men and was led by Manuel Gómez Morín. Gómez Morín helped to form the new group because of his opposition to the leftward orientation of the Cárdenas government. The group had economic and human resources far beyond what its small number would indicate.

It is important to remember that the PAN never has represented all sides of the conservative opposition in Mexico. It began with the definite elitist orientation thinking only in terms of a small number and refusing to compete for mass support. This meant that the PAN to be effective at election time had to support some group that was appealing for endorsement of the masses. Thus the PAN in 1940 supported Almazán and in 1946 Padilla. However, in 1952 the PAN began to think in terms of larger-scale involvement in electoral activity on its own and nominated Efraín González Luna as its presidential candidate. This set the new pattern, and the PAN again put forward a candidate for the elections in 1958 with Luis H. Alvarez as standard bearer. In 1964 the PAN presidential candidate was José Gonzáles Torres.

Table 1

The Record of the PAN as a Mass Party: Presidential Vote

	PRI and Related Parties PPS PRI PARM	PAN	Transient
1946 Alemán	1,787,425	67,762	443,416
1952 Ruiz Cortines	2,713,419*	285,555	579,745†
1958 López Mateos	6,769,754	705,303	
1964 Díaz Ordaz	8,368,446	1,034,337	

* PPS ran its own presidential candidate in this election. He received 72,482 votes.

† The 1952 election was the last one to have a voting record for a transient party.

Becoming active in presidential politics placed considerable stress upon the cohesion of the innermost circle within the PAN. Clearly, in order to make any headway as a contender for votes it was necessary for the PAN to expand its membership and in so doing to broaden its appeal. Essentially, it was a small group with an elitist focus representing church-oriented political views, the views of some of the older and more prosperous businessmen and drawing to it a number of upper- and middle-class professional people.[34] To develop a mass following, however, it was necessary for the PAN to create new associations or find some group that already had something approximating wide popular support. To some extent the PAN did this in 1952 and followed much the same course in 1958, working with the Sinarquista group, which had wide support in some rural areas, particularly in North Central Mexico and Northwest Mexico. A few labor unions also joined the PAN, as did many lower-middle-class white-collar workers. Support was particularly widespread in the states of the North, where many felt that Mexico City under the PRI had forgotten the interests of their area. In 1952, however, the PAN could only run a poor third against the overwhelming strength of the PRI and the very strong challenger, the Henriquistas (F de PPM). With the defeat came disillusionment on the part of those organized groups that had joined the PAN. Some of them disbanded, and others found their way into the ranks of the PRI as part of the Revolutionary Coalition.

One group of leaders under González Luna argued that PAN should forget its attempt to muster mass support and return to the original idea of an elitist opposition with an orientation against accommodation within the existing legal and political framework. Another group, however, argued that the more the PAN attempted to recruit broad support and function as a more-or-less loyal opposition, the more the party could influence decisions made within the Revolutionary Coalition and that this latter course was clearly the most beneficial. The modified conception of a "loyal opposition" won as the election of 1958 approached. For the most part the Sinarquistas dropped away, but many votes were gained through the outspoken and hard-driving campaign launched by the PAN candidate, Luis H. Alvarez. Alvarez did not demand abolition of a revolutionary program. Instead, he demanded reforms to provide more popular benefits. He particularly emphasized social welfare benefits and better administration of existing

---

[34] Professor Kenneth F. Johnson of Colorado State University has done extensive field observation in the political attitudes of PAN adherents. See his "Ideological Correlates of Right Wing Political Alienation in Mexico" (a paper delivered at the annual convention of the Western Political Science Association, March, 1965).

programs. He denounced corruption and argued for doing away with the existing rulers because of their ineptitude and failure of devotion to the public service.

As in 1952 the PAN was successful in attracting many supporters in the North. But in general throughout the country the showing was poor, and the PAN claimed that it had been defrauded in the electoral count. Six members of the PAN were declared elected to the Chamber of Deputies, but the PAN subsequently ordered that the persons elected not take their seats as a protest of the way votes were handled in other districts. The PAN deputies-elect were threatened with expulsion from the party if they took their seats in the chamber. By December, however, four of the six elected PAN deputies had risked expulsion and had become members of the Chamber of Deputies where they spoke out clearly against many policies of the government.

The struggle within the party on the question of whether or not to seek mass support continued, and in 1959 a split occurred. The moderates, led by Gómez Morín, were defeated by the more militant elitist group led by González Luna and a young firebrand, Felipe Gómez Mont. The victorious group was in favor of an intransigent policy toward the Revolutionary Coalition, a policy to which they referred as "direct action." The results were riots in the states of Chihuahua and Baja California during the state and local elections of 1959.

By 1964 the pendulum had once again swung back to the more moderate position. The PAN nominated as its candidate José Gonzáles Torres, who had already served as the party's president and its secretary general. He had also been president of several Catholic lay organizations. Under González Torres the party debated and wavered but eventually adopted the more moderate position and a style more in keeping with that of the concept of loyal opposition. During the election campaign candidate González Torres essentially argued for improvement within the existing framework of power relationships and legal provisions.

Although the approach of the PAN in 1964 can be characterized as moderate, it nonetheless launched numerous barbed attacks against sensitive aspects of the system. For example, it clearly challenged the justice of the electoral arrangement. The PAN charged that there was lack of equitable treatment in the distribution of political information and urged that there be more concern for impartiality and truth. It was also argued that there was too much pressure on the voters. Of particular importance among the PAN arguments was the demand that government should cease supporting a political party, and that the colors of that party cease to be the same as those in the Mexican flag.

With regard to the vote itself, spokesmen of the PAN demanded a truly impartial body to count and judge the vote so that "the real vote" of the people would be taken into consideration. In explaining the reason for its participation in the election, the PAN leadership recognized its disadvantageous position in relation to the government party, but pointed out that the PAN was fulfilling a civic need in struggling for political liberties and electoral reforms, and that it felt any small opportunity to participate in the system through holding, for example, seats in the Chamber of Deputies represented a useful way to contribute to "democracy" in Mexico.

Leaders of the PAN hammered home the notion that a Communist conspiracy well planned and administered was being carried out in Mexico, and that to defeat this conspiracy there was a need to strengthen organizations in an intermediate position between the people and their government. Labor unions were mentioned as an example of such organizations. The PAN complained that labor unions were unable to fulfill their rightful function because of their tendency to exploit workers for political purposes. To make unions more vital and socially useful organizations it was urged that balloting in the unions should be secret in order to avoid pressure by leaders, that leaders should be forced to account fully for their handling of funds, and particularly that union funds should not be used to advance the personal political goals of the leaders.

Unexpectedly, for a right-wing group, the PAN argued that a system of cooperatives would be a useful way of reducing the inequitable distribution of wealth in Mexico. The PAN further recognized that cooperatives were very much in existence on the Mexican scene but charged that they had been deformed and obstructed by government — that cooperativism had been "surrounded by a series of bureaucratic obstacles."

The problem of the local political boss, the *cacique,* was raised by the PAN, and it was argued that *caciquismo* and the problem of municipal autonomy both presented great difficulties, but could be resolved. The real difficulty, said the PAN, is that authorities are "imposed" and are for that reason "arbitrary" and "illegitimate." As the presidential candidate, José González Torres, put it: *"Caciques* have continued even though it would be easy to get rid of them because the government is illegitimate in its origin and in its exercise and finds in the *caciques* the point of support for organization of mass demonstrations. The government is most interested in keeping the public ignorant, poor, and fearful."[35]

[35] *Excelsior,* April 3, 1964.

Not only is the *cacique* a problem of municipal government — there is the problem of federal interference itself. At one point in his campaign, González Torres used the Frontier Improvement Program (PRONAF) to illustrate the fallacy of federal government interference in the *municipios*. The federal government, he said, has taken away legitimate income, imposed authorities, usurped powers, and converted municipal government into something like a police force for "collecting fines from drunks." Rather than to authorize greater participation in the use of public money by the town councils, new organizations have been imposed from the federal level, and in the case of PRONAF, said González Torres, the effort has been "useless and sterile." In relation to municipal elections and federal interference, he said it was not the people who elected their officials, and he elaborated by saying that in more than 3,000 *municipios* of Mexico only eight had legitimately elected officials.

The PAN also attacked one of the major pillars of the "revolutionary" regime, the agrarian program. PAN speakers maintained that one of the most grave problems was a land tenure arrangement in which the government demands political submission of the peasant in exchange for the loan of some land. The PAN position called for all Mexicans to be owners of a small portion of land. In any case, said the PAN, neither small property owners nor *ejidatarios* can be successful where there is lacking accessible and inexpensive credit. Such an arrangement has been missing in Mexico, and credit ought to be reorganized so that it would come to the peasant without the customary bureaucratic red tape and high interest rates.

Another difficulty plaguing the life of the farmer, argued the PAN, has been governmental interference as a middleman in the marketing process. It was charged that the National Popular Subsistence Corporation (CONASUPO), the government marketing corporation, was fixing the value of products at a rate below the market and forcing farmers to sell at that rate while other products remained free under the laws of supply and demand. It was also said that livestock raisers had been suffering undue hardship because the government cancelled certificates of inaffectability. A government which does not take into account the popular will, as in the case of imposing price levels on agricultural production without consulting the producer, has adopted a totalitarian attitude and this attitude must be changed. Further, in censoring agrarian policy the PAN pointed to difficulties in the region of La Laguna. The destruction of small private property holdings in this area and the creation of the *ejido,* according to the PAN, were errors which have led to misery in which some men lose their land altogether, and others have only insufficient land given as a loan in return for which they "must surrender their dignity and liberty."

In an attack on still another pillar of the revolutionary system the PAN hinted at widespread corruption in the petrochemical industry, collaboration between a corrupt union and inept management, and failure to develop adequate distribution nets as a basis for industry and jobs in much of Mexico.

The foregoing would seem to indicate that the PAN pulled few punches in the campaign of 1964. In addition to these charges and demands, there were many others just as strongly advocated. However, an interesting insight into Mexican attitudes is provided by the insistence in some quarters that the PAN was clearly in a "deal" with the government throughout the campaign. The only evidence which the writer can find to support this is the consistent position taken by the PAN candidate in urging a rejection of the use of force. After an outbreak of rioting during a public appearance of the PRI candidate in Chihuahua, González Torres told his audience, "By that road we reach chaos and National Action wants to achieve social order." Over and over again the theme of the importance of a legal and orderly political opposition was emphasized. Perhaps it is this concept of the loyal opposition so alien to the Mexican scene that has encouraged both domestic comment as well as statements by foreign observers to the effect that the campaign represented a sellout. Is it impossible that in Mexico someone might support in good faith the concept of the loyal opposition?

The PPS. Vicente Lombardo Toledano was the founder and has been the guiding spirit of the Popular Socialist Party (PPS). The party was formed in the latter 1940's when it became clear to Lombardo that he no longer had any chance of regaining his once high place in the inner circle of the Revolutionary Coalition. Using all of the contacts which he had developed over the years in the left wing of the PRI and all the organizational tricks in his repertoire, Lombardo set about building a party which at the outset he hoped would challenge the PRI. Later his purpose was more limited — to make a good enough showing that his party could be considered an interest important to a degree that it must be recognized and conciliated. There was also the hope that such a party might have a significant ideological impact upon a large section of the Mexican people.

It is important to note that, in spite of Lombardo's pre-eminent role in the PPS, the party has encompassed other strong personalities. A number of outstanding leftists gathered around Lombardo. In the group who joined Lombardo were independent Mexican leftists and also some Communists. The Communists had as their goal the unification of the small Communist party with the non-Communist Left in Mexico so that there might be a large single mass party which the Communists themselves could dominate. As sympathetic as Lombardo had been to the Soviet Union throughout most of his career, he was not so far committed to Communism that he would permit this latter kind of development at the expense of his own predominant position in the party. For example, when the Communists wanted Lombardo to give up his proposed presidential candidacy to join with them and other leftist groups behind General Henríquez in 1952, Lombardo could not see the desirability of this move.

In addition to the Communists, of course, it was necessary to have other groups, and Lombardo set about forging a confederation of labor unions. This effort resulted in the General Union of Mexican Workers and Peasants (UGOCM). He also succeeded in obtaining the support of a confederation known as the Unified Labor Confederation (CUT) which may have numbered for a short time at the beginning of the 1950's as many as 350,000 persons in the rank and file. Lombardo was also able to attract an organization which had been clearly Communist-dominated for some time, known as the Mexican Farmer Labor Party (POCM). In addition, fronts and groups of various kinds were formed to help Lombardo, with leftist painters such as Diego Rivera and David Alfaro Siqueiros participating, along with leftist writers and professionals with a leftist bias.

The Left was far from unified in Mexico, and the many diverse groups began to drop away, pointing up the instability of the coalition which Lombardo had built. During the weeks and months following the election of 1952 Lombardo lost the CUT and then the POCM. His UGOCM was unable to obtain the necessary government recognition as a bargaining agent for workers and factories across the country and became defunct. The situation became so bad that in 1954 Lombardo attempted to bring his group back into the Revolutionary Coalition. The maneuver did not work for Lombardo as it had for some others in the past. Various organized groups, particularly among labor, dropped away or lost their utility for the PPS, and the association with the Communists also provided many difficulties. Since the Communist Party as such had been unable to gain registration from the Ministry of Interior (*Gobernación*), many Communists hoped to make the PPS their own electoral instrument, but in this they failed. Lombardo himself saw greater political utility for his own purposes in keeping the PPS as a more general leftist opposition party. The struggle, however, did the party no good, and its weakness was shown by the fact that it achieved only one of the 162 seats in the Chamber of Deputies at the time of the elections in 1955.

Matters did not seem to improve much for the PPS over the next few years. A large group of sugar workers left the party as the 1958 elections approached and swung in line behind López Mateos in an effort to see what fruits participation in the Revolutionary Coalition might bring. Meanwhile, the Communists associated with the PPS began a fresh attack upon Lombardo, blaming him for establishing a personality cult and for the losses of support which the party had been suffering. The struggle finally became so bitter that Lombardo was forced to bring about the expulsion of a number of Communists from the party in order to maintain his own position of leadership.

By December of 1957 Lombardo had consolidated his position in what remained of the PPS and had effected a temporary reconciliation with the Communists. The critical decision concerning the party's electoral role in the elections of 1958 was made. The decision was to place the PPS in the position of supporting the presidential candidate of the Revolutionary Coalition while at the same time presenting its own candidates for a number of senatorial seats and federal deputy posts. Weakened as the party was from internal bickering, it was unable to command strength for more than one victory in the contests for seats in the Chamber of Deputies. In order to express discontent with the electoral count in other districts, Lombardo, like the PAN leaders, refused to permit his deputy-elect to be seated. As in the case of several PAN deputies the PPS deputy, Macrina Rabadán, refused to follow party dictates and took her seat in the chamber. The result was another period of unrest in the PPS. The deputy who had taken her seat and a number of Communists as well were stricken from the party rolls.

The outlook for the PPS following the election of 1958 was not bright. The problem of how to deal with the Communists or whether to deal with them at all continued to plague Lombardo. There were scars left by the fight over the seating of Macrina Rabadán, and there was the problem of organizing new labor groups and professional groups to give the sagging rank and file the boost it badly needed.

The complexion of Lombardo's problems and the general status of alignments on the Left of the Mexican ideological spectrum were greatly affected by the victory of Fidel Castro in the Cuban Revolution. The more militant groups of Mexico's Left turned on Lombardo for his gradualism and announced their determination to organize their own brand of militancy. Under the auspices of the World Peace Council there was held in March, 1961, a Latin American Conference for National Sovereignty, Economic Emancipation, and Peace. The Mexican representatives at the council were able to agree on tactics and came out with a plan to unite in a so-called Movement of National Liberation (MLN).[36]

From the start the leadership of the MLN characterized its orientation as "democratic" and non-Communist, but despite this manner of presenting themselves it seemed that Communists whose names were well known took an active part in the movement. Another meeting was held in August, 1961. It was entitled the First National Assembly for National Sovereignty, Economic Emancipation, and Peace. There were members from the Mexican Communist Party (PCM), the Mexican Farmers and Workers Party (POCM) and the Popular Socialist Party (PPS). The meeting was held to outline a program and provide an organizational basis for the new MLN which had been agreed upon at the March inter-American meeting. The major theme of the conclave was that the Revolution had been betrayed by the Right but that it could be revitalized through the MLN program based upon revolutionary measures.

The program decided upon included provisions calling for complete application of the Constitution, completion of agrarian reform and control of all Mexican national resources by Mexicans. Further nationalization of industry was called for along with a more equitable division of the national wealth. A plea was entered for release of political prisoners (an obvious reference to the men who were incarcerated following the wildcat strikes of 1959). The program also demanded solidarity with Cuba and revitalized commerce with the Soviet bloc countries. United States "imperialism" was denounced.

The MLN leaders maintained that they were trying to organize all people of good will — whether Catholic, Protestant, or of any other belief or creed. By 1962 they claimed as many as 500,000 members. But also by 1962 there was trouble with Lombardo and the PPS. Lombardo, who was the major reason for the continued existence of the PPS, somehow managed to go on commanding popular support in and around the Federal District and in a few states. For this reason the dissent by the PPS from the general line offered by the MLN represented a serious blow to the overall effort on the part of Mexico's Left to organize and take a more militant stand.

---

[36] A very useful interpretation of the Left and its changing alignments is provided by David T. Garza, "Factionalism in the Mexican Left: The Frustration of the MLN," *Western Political Quarterly* (September, 1964), pp. 447–460. Another helpful work is Ann Wyckoff de Carlos, *Mexico's National Liberation Movement — The MLN* (Institute of Hispanic American and Luso-Brazilian Studies, Stanford University, 1963), unpublished.

In June, 1962, less than a year after the MLN had held its conference on program and rules, Lombardo in a public statement took his PPS out of the MLN, claiming no further association with the movement. There were several reasons why he did this. For one thing, he himself had always desired to be the head of a unified Mexican movement of the Left, but other leaders in the MLN had taken control of the delegation which the Mexican Left was sending to the World Conference on Disarmament and Peace scheduled to meet in Moscow in July, 1962. The Mexican Peace Committee in Moscow was managing the Mexican delegation and was dominated by MLN leaders other than Lombardo; as a result he took his PPS out of both the Peace Committee and the MLN.

Lombardo's ideological position, all questions of personal advantage aside, was different from the other leaders in the MLN, because he claimed that the existing government of Mexico could achieve progress in some areas and that it should receive selective support. He also claimed that the road taken by the Cubans could not be readily copied by the Mexicans. Apart from differences in policy orientation, Lombardo was not happy that the MLN had fallen into the hands of the Mexican Communists, nor was he happy about the prominence of Lázaro Cárdenas in the whole MLN effort. He realized, moreover, that he was being pushed into the background as the Cubans were brought forward by international Communism to head the organization of a new inter-American labor movement to replace his own Latin American Labor Confederation (CTAL). The situation was made more confusing because two of Lombardo's aides in the PPS, Jacinto López and Jorge Carrión, were serving on the national committee of the MLN and participating in its sessions while Lombardo claimed that these men were not really on the National Committee of MLN at all — or, if they were, it was against their will. Finally, López, heading the PPS front organization, the General Union of Mexican Workers and Farmers (UGOCM), split with the MLN. Meanwhile Carrión continued to write for *Política,* a periodical closely associated with the MLN, and even attacked the approach of Lombardo as being too gradualistic.[37]

The MLN developed its own peasant arm, the Independent Farmers Confederation (CCI), and from the movement emerged also a small political party. The Peoples' Electoral Front (FEP) was created in April, 1963. For the most part the Mexican Communist Party (PCM) went along with the MLN and the CCI in support of the FEP and yet there was a division within the MLN concerning the FEP. The

[37] *Política* provides many valuable insights into the maneuvers of groups and leaders on the Mexican Left.

Mexican Farmers and Workers Party (POCM) did not follow the PCM as it was expected to do. Thus, the POCM announced that it would not go along with the FEP but instead would fuse with the PPS. The leader of the POCM referred to some of the leaders of the MLN and FEP as being "irresponsible leftists." Lombardo, always on the lookout for political advantage, then turned from the POCM to urge the PCM itself to join with him. This invitation, however, was refused.

The FEP did not gain sufficient support to permit registration for the 1964 election. This failure was forecast in the opposition to the FEP among leftists outside the MLN and the division within the MLN as to the proper role of the FEP. Lombardo took a stand against the FEP and was joined by Sánchez Cárdenas at the head of the POCM. Lázaro Cárdenas himself maintained complete silence with regard to the FEP, demonstrating what could reasonably be interpreted as a growing dislike for the dogmatic, militant views of some of the leaders of the MLN. In the end it appeared that the MLN might very well be faced with a dilemma. Either it could follow a more gradual approach and suffer drop-outs in its rank and file and internal quarrels among its leadership, or it could make an effort to bolster the will and sense of purpose both among members and leaders by closing ranks in direct militant activity against the government and thus risk quick suppression by authorities.

Meanwhile, Lombardo and the PPS survived. Not only did they survive, but they did rather well under the new electoral law. In spite of the increasingly personalist nature of the party and the scarcity of its support both in the Federal District and in the states, it was decreed that the PPS had in fact a sufficient percentage of the vote cast in the elections for federal deputies to permit the seating of ten PPS candidates in the Chamber of Deputies under the new electoral arrangements.[38] Lombardo took one of the ten seats with his usual aplomb and bland self-assurance while comment in the press and elsewhere acidly underscored the "personalist" character of his party and its lack of mass support.[39] There were broad hints that an unsavory "deal" with the government electoral agencies raised the number of votes attributed to the PPS and thus provided for its seats in the lower house of the legislature.

As the new presidential term of Díaz Ordaz got under way the outlook for unity on the Left appeared less bright than it had at the

[38] See the section on elections, below.

[39] For a devastating commentary on Lombardo and the PPS in relation to the election see Julio Manuel Ramírez, "Desayuno," *Excelsior*, July 12, 1964.

opening of the decade. The PPS had come to exist largely in terms of Lombardo, and that wily old leftist was not going to submit to the leadership of others if it could be helped. Among other leaders also there were jealousies, and in some quarters there were signs that financial support had worn very thin. Unless new forms appeared, the Left would not constitute a major threat to the regime for some time to come.

Elections

Luis Cabrera, one of the prominent figures of the "revolutionary" regime in times past, once remarked that "so long as . . . the electoral college judges the elections of its own members it will not be possible to have true elections."[40] Cabrera was referring to the Chamber of Deputies as the electoral college. Members of the chamber are elected at the time of the presidential balloting and are then approved by the outgoing members. It is the Chamber of Deputies which finally decides the outcome of presidential elections. The judgment of the outgoing chamber with regard to the seating of newly elected members and their judgment in turn on the election of the President has always been overwhelmingly in favor of the Revolutionary Coalition and its candidates under the banner of the party. Practice in the past has been such as to warrant little supposition that some outside group is likely to achieve a majority position in the Chamber of Deputies and thus outweigh the Revolutionary Coalition representatives in review of the presidential ballots. Cabrera made his statement in the conviction that only given the seeming impossibility of an opposition gaining a majority in the Chamber of Deputies could some candidate from outside the Revolutionary Coalition become President of the Republic.

Statements of Mexican observers and commentators repeatedly contain the notion, which seems to be generally held among Mexicans, that no majority group dominating the election machinery is likely to give a fair hearing to other potential majorities. This is a point of view which has remained predominant in spite of the increasing sophistication of the electoral machinery in Mexico, beginning with the electoral reforms of 1945.[41] Events have supported the general assumption that the Federal Electoral Commission will not fall out of

[40] Luis Cabrera, "Sufragio efectivo y no re-elección," *Una encuesta sobre la cuestión democrática de México,* ed. Alberto J. Pani (Mexico, 1948), p. 98.

[41] PRI, *Ley para la Elección de Diputados y Senadores del Congreso de la Unión y Presidente de la República* [a pamphlet containing the electoral law of 1945 and subsequent changes through 1949], (Mexico, 1949). Secretaría de Gobernación, *Ley Electoral Federal* (Mexico, 1951). [Amendments through 1964.]

step with the majority of the Revolutionary Coalition and the Chamber of Deputies. Certainly the interior ministry (*Gobernación*), which is also concerned with elections, has never been out of harmony with the Federal Electoral Commission and the Chamber of Deputies. All electoral units have functioned smoothly as part of a single machine which has continued to legitimize the majority control of the Revolutionary Coalition. Such has been the case in spite of continued reforms and refinements written into the electoral law.[42]

A recent change in the electoral law is directed towards broadening the opposition in the Chamber of Deputies — or as the cynics might put it, giving an appearance of greater opposition within the Chamber of Deputies.[43] Under this change small political parties which are able to capture only a fraction of the votes throughout the country nevertheless can be assigned a certain number of seats in the Chamber of Deputies on the basis of that small vote.

In order to be a legally registered party it is necessary to have 75,000 members on the rolls throughout the republic and have these 75,000 spread throughout two-thirds of the federal entities with no less than 2,500 registrants in each of the entities thus distinguished.[44] Under Article 54 of the Constitution as amended there are two ways of gaining seats in the Chamber of Deputies. Seats may be filled through direct popular election; they also may be taken on the basis of a small percentage of the total vote for deputies acquired by a party throughout the country. Thus a national party that has met the registration requirements and gains 2.5 per cent of the total vote for the Chamber of Deputies will receive five additional seats in the chamber. For each additional .5 per cent of the vote a party will receive an additional seat up to a maximum of twenty seats for the total vote obtained. Under the new provisions it is conceivable that a party might fail to win any seats in the Chamber of Deputies through direct popular election and yet have as many as twenty seats in that house on the basis of votes totaled throughout the entire country. The outcome, given this new provision in the elections of 1964, is indicated in Table 2 with a comparison to 1958.

The famous Mexican jurist, Ignacio Burgoa, in evaluating the amendment to Article 54 of the Constitution, has pointed out that the

[42] Great skepticism concerning the validity of Mexican elections is shown by Philip B. Taylor, Jr., in "The Mexican Elections of 1958: Affirmation of Authoritarianism?", *Western Political Quarterly,* 13 (September, 1960), p. 742.

[43] This is the amendment to Article 54 of the Constitution of 1917 with a supporting provision in the Federal Electoral Law, 1954, Article 127 as amended.

[44] *Ley Electoral Federal,* Arts. 29, 33, and 127.

Table 2

Seats in the Chamber of Deputies

| | 1958 | | 1964 | |
	Seats	Per cent	Seats	Per cent
PRI	153	94.5	175	83.3
PAN	6*	3.7	20	9.5
PPS	1	0.6	10	4.8
Other†	2	1.2	5	2.4
Total	162	100.0	210	100.0

* Only four took their seats.
† Includes the PNM and the PARM, both parties declining in importance.

idea of deputies for a party (*diputados de partido*) in addition to deputies on the basis of direct popular election (*diputados populares*) will probably become applicable to state legislatures in the near future. He also gave his considered opinion that the new way of assigning deputies constituted a very noteworthy "advance toward democratization of our country." Burgoa pointed out that he assessed the reform in this fashion because it seemed to him to give more different types of groups an opportunity for representation than had been the case in the past — that groups which could not win a majority in given districts could obtain seats in the legislature on the basis of their total vote.[45]

Mexicans explain the continued supremacy of the Revolutionary Coalition in one of two ways. The first explanation is simply the denial of the possibility of a just count. In this first case the concept of an opposition as reflected in the presence of the PAN and the PPS is accepted, but the acceptance of the reality of opposition is coupled with a denial that the system will deal fairly with the opposition even if it could command a majority. The second explanation goes beyond denial of a just count and denies further that the opposition parties themselves can be considered a true opposition. It is held that the PAN, the PPS, the PARM and any other parties that obtain legal registration are really mere instruments of the Revolutionary Coalition, paid and used by the leaders of the coalition to provide the appearance of a contest and thus make a gesture towards the required norms.[46] Either way there is a considerable difference from the ordinary post-

[45] *Política*, July 1, 1963, pp. 1–6.
[46] Brandenburg, pp. 156 and 165.

election explanations of defeated parties and candidates in the United States. In the United States losers tend to explain election losses by referring to large government payrolls, the coddling of some special interest with a large rank and file, such as labor, or "giveaway" programs for interests such as the aged or farmers. These are all explanations which accept the reality of opposition and focus on the reasons for the triumph of one side.

The two differing Mexican explanations do not necessarily support each other. To deny a just count is not the same as denying the existence of opposition. In either case it would be very difficult to put together an adequate empirical case substantiating the judgment. No one has yet indicated from what ministry or from what account the funds must come to pay off the bogus opposition parties if in truth they are simply a façade. Nor is it easy to point out at what juncture in the voting process fraud is consummated. Incidents in which soldiers turn would-be voters away are infrequent. Ballots in federal elections are not separate and distinguishable by party, in contrast to the former practice which enabled observers to know how a man voted by the stack of ballots from which his was selected. Charges of fraud are seldom carefully documented. However, the belief continues widespread among Mexicans that somehow the elections are a farce.

Perhaps the best prima-facie evidence for the belief that elections are meaningless one way or another is the continued success of the Revolutionary Coalition. However, more than the continued success of the Revolutionary Coalition is involved. There are deeply rooted historical facts which have made it very difficult to accept the ballot as an institution central to the operation of political choice. Experience with representative institutions, of course, was extremely limited during the time of the Spanish colonial rule. After independence the country was racked by military rebellions, civil war, and foreign intervention. It finally settled down under an old-style dictatorship only to suffer seven years of revolution at the beginning of this century. In this span of time there was no point at which electoral procedures had an opportunity to become rooted. The social structure itself has worked against institutionalization of just elections. In earlier times the Indian and *mestizo* masses were kept in tutelage by small minorities having all the wealth and learning. This was not conducive to respect for the ballot. Lack of national unity, stemming in part at least from the geography of the country, also worked against peaceful change through the ballot box.

People frequently judge their national institutions by first-hand experiences. In the case of Mexico, persons in rural areas frequently have had to contend with the institution of the *cacique,* the local small-scale political boss.[47] The local political boss (*cacique*) is a man who has been able to form a small group of henchmen willing to stop at nothing so that the *cacique's* will is law in the area. The rule of this political entrepreneur is always despotic and often approaches a genuine tyranny. Usually his power is buttressed by relations with persons of influence in government at higher levels. In another day the support of the largest landowner of the immediate vicinity was required. One thing is certain: a *cacique* does not lose office because a reform party managed to hold elections and vote him out. The *cacique* either dies a natural death, is shot from ambush, or occasionally is routed by a mob. If he is routed by a mob, however, powerful connections might bring him back with the only result being punishment for the dissenters.

The institution of the *cacique* came into being during colonial rule and has endured until the present. The more remote the rural area and the farther it is from ready accessibility to a large city, the easier it is for the *cacique* to establish and maintain himself in power. The stronger the village culture, the stronger the *cacique* can become because the suspicion and fear which villagers often feel for those outside their community circle keep them from seeking outside help against the local ruler. A norm stressing unanimity, along with suspicion of the outsider, tends to make people draw together and protect the local boss, even though there may be a well-intentioned person

[47] *Cacique* in Mexican political usage originally meant simply *chief,* and its first major political connotation stemmed from the fact that the Spanish conquerors found it easier to keep a people subjugated as long as the chiefs were cooperative. Chiefs were thus given special favors in return for keeping the people pacified. Later the term *cacique* came to be applied to any person who could build a following sufficient in his local community to provide the influence necessary to keep the people there from demanding rights from higher governing authorities. The *cacique* not only keeps order in the local area but is the one person who has contact in any meaningful way with the officials at higher levels. He becomes known as the spokesman for his area and frequently receives money from his own constituents as a reward for bringing certain problems to the attention of higher authorities. There are thousands of these persons throughout the country, and, as Mexican commentators point out, there are *"caciques* of *caciques,"* i.e., bigger chiefs over smaller ones. These are the intermediaries by which rural people and some urban people contact their government. The farther from the effects of modernization including education and transportation the more dependent the people are upon their *caciques.* Thus, although we cannot say how many *caciques* there are in Mexico today, we can however speak of the modification of the worst aspects of the institution the more Mexicans find their lives touched by modern influences. One of the strengths as well as one of the problems of the governing party has been its reliance upon the *cacique* as intermediary between party officials and government on one side and the people — especially rural people — on the other.

from a higher level of government seeking to rectify inequitable situations.

The emphasis upon unanimity in village culture is pointed up in anthropological studies.[48] The village norm of unanimity is reflected even in the more modern political groups of Mexico — including the urban areas. One tends to find the close in-group feeling which, when members of the group achieve official position, becomes almost a proprietary attitude towards government. This is very similar to the way the local *cacique* and his group hold tightly to their position of preeminence and pass around local government positions and the fruits of power among themselves.

The norm of unanimity and the institution of the *cacique* combine in Mexican experience. First of all, no one imagines that the *cacique*, once in power, will allow some upstart among his own followers, or some other group for that matter, to take away the hard-won prize of control. Moreover, unanimity as a norm works against the principle of the majority as a method of making decisions to oust the *cacique*.[49] With unanimity valued so highly, holding government office and acquiring political control tend to become functions of superior strength through military superiority or through political style in a context where legal rules do not effectively set operating limitations. Under

---

[48] See Elsie Clews Parsons, *Mitla — Town of Souls* (Chicago, 1936), p. 167, and Victor Goldkind, "Another View of Social Stratification in Chan Kom: Conflict and Cacique" (San Diego State College, 1965), unpublished manuscript.

[49] "In what way are consensus-based decisions arrived at? In a great many non-Western societies, particularly at the village level, this process — though well institutionalized — is often more subtle and difficult to observe than is the case in the West. Here the Western-trained researcher is likely to encounter consensus-based decisions which resemble more closely the Quaker 'consensus' of the meeting idea than the simple numerical majority decision usual in the Western environment. In fact, to many non-Western groups accustomed to decision-making based upon unanimous accord, it is difficult to understand how majority decisions are compatible with the minimum degree of inner harmony required by the group or community." Professors Kahin, Pauker, and Pye, "Comparative Politics of Non-Western Countries," *American Political Science Review,* 49 (December, 1955), p. 1040. Rupert Emerson points out the "assumption of Sukarno and many others that the kind of democracy traditionally characteristic of Asian and African countries is a confrontation of all opinions in free discussion which ultimately achieves an agreed version of the community's will . . . The formal promise of full freedom to oppose the leader and to challenge the desires of the party hierarchy is all too likely in reality to lead to political retaliation against the dissident faction." Rupert Emerson, *Political Modernization: The Single-Party System,* in The Social Science Foundation and Department of International Relations Monograph Series in World Affairs, University of Denver (Denver, 1963), p. 27.

such circumstances elections tend to be made through the *pronuncia-miento* and *cuartelazo* (barracks rebellion) at the national level or by assassination or riots at the local level.

Since 1945, as pointed out above, leaders of the Revolutionary Coalition have shown a disposition from time to time to formulate an institutional framework which might permit peaceful succession to government on the part of groups outside the revolutionary circle through adequate electoral machinery. The prospect of change by peaceful means is connected with the growing urban character of the country, the diminishing number of old-style *caciques,* and the expanding communications and transportation nets as they link up more and more out-of-the-way rural places with modern centers of urban development. There is the observable rise of the middle class and of other gradations which make the stratification arrangement more complex and lend more substance to the growth of divergent political views. However, it is not easy to depart from ancient practices and ancient attitudes. The belief in the impossibility of fair elections, the high value placed upon the appearance of unanimity, the long-standing experience with the institution of the local *cacique* all will continue to work against the emergence of the hard-fought, crucial election so familiar in modern democracies.

Summary

The official party, the opposition parties, and the electoral process all have distinct functions in the Mexican political system. This is not to say that such functions are unique, but only that they are among the most essential characteristics of the Mexican system as presently constituted.

The standard functions of the official party do not differ greatly from what they have been and what they probably will be in the future. The party symbolizes unity of the Revolutionary Coalition, and it provides the coalition's vehicle for participation in an electoral act which is itself more symbolic than substantive. Basic to the maintenance of the coalition are the liaison and communications functions the party performs as well as its machinery for legitimizing candidate selection at all levels and for resolving disputes in case of otherwise irreconcilable interpersonal conflict among the top leaders of the coalition.

The opposition parties are organized very much along the lines of the official party. Their weakness clearly does not lie in their method of organization. Instead, the opposition parties are attempting to play roles that have no traditionally defined place in Mexican politics. There are no patterns of emotional responses and established values which permit the existence of a thriving "loyal opposition." Quite the contrary, the initial reaction is to suspect the opposition of disloyalty to the regime with a strong tendency towards armed revolt. Under these circumstances it is surprising: first, that opposition parties exist; second, that they have the degree of autonomy which they manifest in terms of public pronouncement and electioneering; and finally, that they are able to recruit overtly so many supporters. The parties are articulators of alternatives which otherwise might not be heard in the dominant party situation.

Elections have their special place in a system such as this. Perhaps most important, they mark off periods at the end of which the Revolutionary Coalition and the dominant party change the personnel in public office. Thus, they modify the *continuismo* of the coalition and give substance to the expectations of many potential office-seekers. Moreover, elections symbolize at least the goal value of democracy which is expressed many ways in the Constitution and laws of the country. Finally, elections provide a remarkably useful device for mustering large audiences, propagating the "gospel" of the regime and stirring a sense of participation in the masses. Thus, elections, while not fulfilling exactly the same function as expected in classic democratic theory, are not without their utility for the stability of the system, and in the context of Mexican political culture they contribute to the freedom and sense of individual worth for a people confined by party *continuismo*.

3

Labor Organizations

The simple threefold division of the official party's organizational scheme tends to obscure the complexity of the Revolutionary Coalition and the many groups and alignments involved in the support network for the existing system. The labor sector itself has a long historical background and many well-organized groupings with extensive memberships. The major confederation which brings together federations of state and local union chapters, as well as the leadership of the major national unions, has been the Mexican Workers' Confederation (CTM).

Labor confederations have been organized according to a vertical-horizontal pattern which in some respects resembles the arrangement of the party executive committees. The confederations are really central group governments with a set of formalized rules of procedure. These central governing groups preside in turn over an association of groupings that have some functionally oriented interest in common or some other attributes which make it possible to bring them together in an associational form. Federations are the state-level counterparts of the national confederations, and it is these federations and their formalized leadership which direct the activities of organized groups at the state, regional, and local levels.

The formalized structure of operation within each confederation from the national level to the level of the *municipio* or subdivision of the *municipio* as well as the style of politics which has developed over the years among leadership at all levels in these organizational frameworks tends to bring them into contact at their respective levels with the committees or groups operating the PRI mechanism as well as those who are holding public office. Not infrequently men may hold public office, party office, and office in the executive committee of their functional organization at any given level, national, state, or local.

Historical Antecedents of Organized Labor

Historical antecedents of labor organizations reach far back in Mexican history, but it serves present purposes to begin with the years of the Díaz era when gradually there grew among the more aware artisans and small businessmen a determination to organize in some way in order to reduce the hazards of misery and ruin which made life precarious in those times. Mutual aid groups were formed to provide some minimal insurance against natural disasters such as death and accidents, as well as a pool of funds for small loans to constitute a cushion against bad business years and the ever-present threat of failure.

Eventually, some artisans and elements among the industrial workers began to talk among themselves about the "right to strike." Cooperative societies with a more militant orientation than the mutual aid associations began to appear. Agitational papers sprang up in which the concept of the right to strike was frequently mentioned. Anarchism, syndicalism, and Marxism all contributed to the beginning of a new ferment. From the most militant cooperative efforts there emerged in the last decades of the nineteenth century the First Congress of Workers, Mexico's first labor confederation, and the Grand Circle of Workers. As has often been the case, rural workers remained generally unaware of the new ideas.

The growing awareness of Mexican workers as well as miserable working conditions brought demonstrations at Cananea in Sonora and at Rio Blanco-Orizaba in Veracruz during the 1890's, and these occurred in greater intensity during the period 1900–1910. Especially violent were the strikes at Cananea and at Rio Blanco-Orizaba. Troops were habitually used to crush the demonstrations and prevent the strikes from spreading. In Cananea not only Mexican soldiers but also armed men from the United States side of the border took part in breaking the strike.

The aspirations and determination of Mexican workers in the more prosperous and more established industries were strengthened by the behavior of the foreigners beside whom many Mexicans worked. The living conditions of these imported workers, not to speak of conditions for higher level technicians and managers, were of such a quality that Mexicans began to ask why higher wages, better housing, medical care, and other benefits should go only to foreigners. When the foreigners themselves struck for even better conditions, as the railroad workers did, the message that poverty and misery were not necessarily inevitable facts of life became clear for the first time to many Mexican laborers.

Mexicans applied the concept of American railroad brotherhoods in organizing themselves as early as 1888. By the latter 1890's Mexican railroad workers were pushing hard for better hours and an increase in wages. Finally, in 1904 there emerged ties with the leadership of railroad workers in the United States.

When revolution on a large scale finally resulted in the fall of Díaz and the inauguration of Francisco I. Madero as President of the Republic, the new strength of organized labor was reflected in the organization of a labor office in the Mexican government. There were repeated strikes to convince the government of Madero that better hours and higher wages should be awarded the workers. The new labor office formulated projects for the benefit of labor, and at the same time a large labor organization known as the *Casa del Obrero Mundial* was formed. However, the Madero government fell before most of labor's goals could be written into the law.

One of the most important things to remember about the *Casa* aside from the fact that most of organized labor was affiliated is the extent to which labor leaders of the future were recruited from the men who formed this organization. The *Casa* was not dispersed during the period of Victoriano Huerta's dominance. When Huerta fell, the *Casa* was still very much a force. In recognition of its importance, General Alvaro Obregón, chief lieutenant of Venustiano Carranza in the three-sided revolutionary conflict, succeeded in building a close working relationship with leaders of the *Casa*. Obregón gained six battalions of workers in return for a decree from Carranza in support of unionization and government recognition of the right to strike in labor disputes. Carranza signed a pact with the leaders of the *Casa* in February, 1915.[1]

Labor leadership and Carranza clashed again and again throughout the year 1916, although Carranza was not willing to go all out to suppress such an important organized force. The labor battalions, after all, had helped defeat Villa and Zapata. However, Carranza did act under the old laws drawn up by the generation of the Reform as early as July, 1916, on the occasion of a strike in the Federal District. Several leaders were imprisoned. Later Carranza ordered the doors of the *Casa* in Mexico City closed after a major clash between workers and various anti-labor groups in Avenida Madero. Finally, he reconsidered and allowed the *Casa* to operate in Mexico City while

[1] The first labor leaders, those that were to be very important in the 20's and 30's and even later, came from the *Casa*. The doctrine of these people was at first anarcho-syndicalist. Later, some of them became Communists. Most of them were anti-clerical. Many participated in the organization of the red battalions which aided Obregón and Carranza.

leadership of the organization was suppressed with his blessing in the states.[2]

When the constitutional convention which Carranza had arranged met in November of 1916, there were not many delegates who supported the labor position. However, Alvaro Obregón had not forgotten the contribution of labor battalions to his own and others' victories. Also, the energetic and dedicated General Mújica pressed hard to make sure that the demands of labor were not overlooked in framing the new constitution. It was a bitter fight in which Mújica stood numerically almost alone among those who had assembled to frame the Constitution. What saved Mújica's position was support from Obregón and a few lesser generals. Quality of leadership, and the presence of organized mass strength of the labor battalions who had served under Obregón carried the day for the labor partisans.

Earlier Groups and Group Alignments

The new Constitution in February of 1917 encouraged various labor leaders to call a meeting of all concerned. In Tampico in October, 1917, it was decided to set up a central committee in Torreón, Coahuila. The governor of Coahuila at that time was somewhat more favorable to labor leaders than most other governors, and it was felt that a central committee could safely count on the state as a base from which to work for expansion of labor influence. Then, in Saltillo, Coahuila, in the early part of 1918, a great congress of labor leaders was held and from this congress there emerged the first great Mexican labor confederation of the post-revolutionary period. The *Confederación Regional de Obreros Mexicanos* (CROM) was founded March 22, 1918. The CROM began by claiming a membership of 7,000; by 1920 it claimed membership of 50,000; by 1922, membership of 400,000, and by 1926 the CROM claimed a membership of 2,000,000 or more.[3] It was from the circle of CROM leaders that the impetus arose for the subsequent organization of the Mexican Labor Party with the aim either of taking complete power, or at least of exercising great power within the existing post-revolutionary political framework. The latter indeed happened during the governing period of Obregón and even more so in the years of Calles.

In addition to the CROM, there emerged another confederation, the General Labor Confederation (CGT), whose leaders for the most part went Communist and turned against the administration of Obregón on the grounds that it was essentially bourgeois. Although the CGT

[2] Roberto de la Cerda Silva, *El movimiento obrero en méxico* (Mexico, 1961), pp. 121–122.
[3] de la Cerda, p. 140.

never obtained a membership much greater than 80,000 it did at least raise an important issue — whether the labor movement should affiliate with the Communist movement. Some leaders of the CGT attended an international red convention (*Convención Radical Roja*) in Moscow in July, 1921, and they brought back with them an eminently revolutionary approach.

The CGT, because of its radical position, stimulated the organization of Catholic labor groups, basing their doctrine on the *rerum novarum*. Catholic labor groups were more like the old-time labor organizations in Mexico with a strong mutual aid orientation and some emphasis on the eight-hour day and limitations upon child labor.[4] They published several newspapers and several regional confederations were organized in connection with this movement. By 1925 the national grouping called the National Catholic Workers' Confederation had about 22,000 members and close to 400 unions, but most organized workers, though considering themselves Catholic, were affiliated with the CROM and the CGT rather than with the Catholic organization.

Emilio Portes Gil became interim President after the assassination of Obregón in 1928. His major emphasis was upon agrarian reform, but he did not entirely overlook the power of organized labor. It was in part through his efforts that the first statutory labor code of national standing was enacted in 1931.[5] By the time General Lázaro Cárdenas became President in 1934, there were many splinter groups throughout the country with no major unifying organizational cover. Altogether there were 13 confederations, 51 federations, and 2,781 unions registered.[6] A major reason for the chaotic condition of the labor movement had to do with the decline of the CROM. In the years following the assassination of Obregón in 1928, leaders of the CROM were credited by many with an effort to stimulate that assassination, and the unpopularity of the group stemmed at least in part from this as well as from abuses of the leadership. Another union, the CGT, was unable to fill the gap in terms of providing a nationwide organization because it could not get governmental support from the presidents who succeeded Calles, and it had become clear that no existing labor confederation was in a position to obtain sufficient support from the

[4] Marjorie R. Clark, *Organized Labor in Mexico* (Chapel Hill, N.C., 1934), pp. 86–96.

[5] This seems to be the case although Ortiz Rubio had become President by this time. Neither Ortiz Rubio, who left office without finishing his term, nor General Abelardo Rodríguez did much for the labor movement during their presidencies. By the end of 1933 labor was weakened and divided. The once proud CROM was but a shadow of its former self, reflecting the loss of presidential patronage since 1928. See Clark, pp. 135–144.

[6] de la Cerda, p. 141.

government to permit the kind of expansion that would be necessary to the formation of a really large nationwide confederation. The proliferation of splinter groups continued at a rapid pace as different leaders split away from the CROM and the CGT. A new group known as the General Confederations of Workers and Peasants (CGOC) was formed, as well as the Unitary Confederation of Mexico, the National Chamber of Labor, the Union of Railroad Workers, the Union of the Electricians, and the Miners' Alliance.

President Cárdenas was determined that the many labor groups should have some kind of overall organization. Thus, with Cárdenas' manifest encouragement, most of the outstanding labor leaders of the country, with the exception of those in the CGT and the CROM, gathered early in 1936 to produce a new organization known as the Mexican Workers' Confederation (CTM). The CTM was a product of the Workers' Coalition and the Committee for Proletarian Defense, both of which were organized through the encouragement of Cárdenas. It was certainly through the backing of the government that the CTM was able to claim 500,000 members shortly after its organization early in 1936. Leaders of the CTM immediately began to reach out for international contacts. Representatives were sent to the World Labor Congress held in London in 1936. Later, CTM leaders promoted establishment of an organization designed to provide leadership for the Latin American labor movement. This organization was known as the Confederation of Latin American Workers (CTAL). The CTAL came into being in 1938 with Vicente Lombardo Toledano, the general secretary of the CTM, also acting as leader of the new international group. The orientation of the group was essentially anti-United States and pro-Communist. The CTAL, like the CTM, had a class struggle orientation.[7] This class struggle bias tended to create a different situation with regard to relations between the Mexican and United States labor movements from that during the superiority of the CROM in the 1920's.[8]

Following Cárdenas' departure from office, the presidential term of Manuel Ávila Camacho saw a number of labor disputes. The dispute between the CTM and the Confederation of Workers and Peasants of Mexico (COCM) was one of the most bitter labor struggles of the period. There was also conflict between the CTM and the National Proletarian Confederation (CNP). Although President Ávila Camacho

[7] The original motto of the CTM was "For a society without classes."

[8] Although Cárdenas supported the CTM unequivocally, conditions never ripened to the point that it was convenient to crush the CROM and the CGT as well as some other unions and state federations which remained outside the CTM.

was able to bring about a settlement of these outstanding quarrels, he, like Cárdenas, fell short of the goal of bringing all of labor under one organization. Thus, in the case of the CTM as in the case of the CROM at an earlier date, the ideal of a single confederation acting as spokesman for all labor was not realized in spite of overt government support.[9]

Although the CTM never succeeded in stamping out the CGT, the CROM and many autonomous state-level labor organizations, it is true that the story of labor in the late 1930's was essentially the story of the expansion of the CTM and its general organizational success based in part on government support throughout the country. However, when Cárdenas left office, the CTM lost not only much of its stimulus from the presidency but also much of its ideological militancy. The new orientation could best be summed up as abandonment of the Marxist class struggle position and determination to function within the framework of the nationalist orientation of Mexico's social revolution collaborating with the government and with industry for the economic development of the country. Its motto reflected the change in outlook. The motto became "For the economic independence of Mexico." The change helped to bring about a split in the CTM, the formation of new rival confederations, and a drop in the number of its members.

During the presidencies of Miguel Alemán (1946–52), Adolfo Ruiz Cortines (1952–58), and Adolfo López Mateos (1958–64), the tendency to support the CTM above other labor groups continued. Labor organizations meanwhile went on seeking new alliances, always working without success toward the goal of unification of the labor movement. In 1949 Vicente Lombardo Toledano, who had been pushed out of his leading position in the CTM some years before, attempted to create a new confederation which he called the General Union of Workers and Peasants of Mexico (UGOCM). The UGOCM had a Marxist ideology in line with the position usually taken by Lombardo, but seemed to operate more in terms of an effort to exploit discontent for pragmatic goals rather than ideological purposes. After the organization participated or conspired to participate in several large strikes, the government of Miguel Alemán finally ran out of patience.

[9] It is commonly recognized that leaders of the great worker confederations such as Luis N. Morones, Lombardo Toledano, and others have always been dependent upon government to help them carry out their organizational feats. In spite of the splintering tendency of labor, it seemed evident by the mid-1940's, if not earlier, that the labor movement had definitely arrived as a permanent fixture on the Mexican scene with more than two thousand unions in the rolls of the Ministry of Labor.

The registry of the UGOCM was refused approval in the Ministry of Labor in 1950, only to spring up again several years later.[10]

In the 1940's mining and electrical workers' unions ignored presidential efforts to stimulate labor unity. A national labor congress was held to try to bring these divergent interests together along with still others, such as the CROM and the CGT, but this effort met with only limited success in reconciling labor-management interests. Moreover, the pact the CTM and the National Chamber of Manufacturing Industries (CNIT) signed in 1945, the Industrial Labor Pact, did not change the fact that many labor leaders and rank and file were unwilling to accept the CTM's conciliatory policy toward management. In spite of the pact of 1945 — perhaps because of it — there emerged subsequently the Single Workers Confederation (CUT) with leaders who felt that too close a relationship was growing between the CTM and government and that there was too much repetition in leadership. Luis Gómez separated from Fernando Amilpa and took a group of railroad workers with him to form the CUT with some other small unions and their leader, Valentín Campo. The confederation used a very aggressive statement of principles reminiscent of the earliest railroad workers' associations and stressing particularly the defense of labor against foreign interests.

At least one authority has spoken of the "decadence of the CTM which began in 1947 . . . once again a group of confederations and independent unions were criticizing the situation created by too close a relationship between the CTM and the government. . . ."[11] In addition to the CUT and other confederations organized from discontented workers splitting off from more established unions in the years after 1945, there was the effort by Vidal Diaz Muñoz, who organized the Workers' and Peasants' Alliance of Mexico (AOCM). This confederation had as its purpose the achievement of unity of principle among industrial unions, but was not successful.

In the early 1950's, when there was uneasiness in some Mexican political circles with regard to the presidential succession, another labor confederation emerged, the CROC; for a short time it enjoyed high favor in government, though it never was able to challenge the CTM. Meanwhile, in an effort to maintain its supremacy and move forward toward the goal of a more inclusive, if not all-inclusive confederation, the CTM banded together in the later 1950's with a number of other confederations and large national industrial unions to form a front known as the Workers' Unity Block (BUO) in which were included

[16] Guadalupe Rivera Marín, "El movimiento obrero," in *México: cincuenta años de revolución* (Mexico, 1961), II, p. 264.

[11] Rivera Marín, p. 264.

the CROM, the CGT, the Railroad Workers' Union, the Telephone Workers' Union, and the Motion Picture Workers' Union, along with a number of lesser unions.

Those who were unwilling to band together with the CTM began working toward their own national labor front. This series of groups first called itself the Revolutionary Workers' Coalition and later went through some reorganization, emerging as the National Confederation of Mexican Workers (CNTM). This anti-BUO coalition included the Mexican Electrical Workers' Union (SME), the Union of Electricians of the Republic of Mexico (STERM), the Revolutionary Confederation of Workers and Peasants (CROC), the Revolutionary Confederation of Workers (CRP), the Federation of Revolutionary Textile Workers (FROT), the Workers' Revolutionary Federation (FOR), and the National Federation of Sugarcane Workers (FNC). The organization was born on the fourth of December of 1960 under the motto "unity and class struggle."[12]

The CNTM, now generally known as the CNT in Mexico, had its first regular national assembly June 21–24, 1963, in Mexico City. It was important enough that the President of the Republic saw fit to attend, along with the president of the PRI, Alfonso Corona del Rosal, and the head of the labor ministry, Salomón Gonzales Blanco. The new organization had the following message for its competitors:

> We have sent a cordial greeting to all labor organizations and even though it is true that we have differences with some confederations, and in certain cases very deep ones, it is also true, fortunately, that all of us are agreed on the importance of working for the country within the postulates of the great revolution. Therefore we proclaim ... that we are determined to put forth our best effort in any activity involved in the battle for the well-being of the proletariat and the progress of the Mexican nation.[13]

One Confederation v. Several

The preceding record of maneuvering for position among Mexican labor confederations represents an aspect of the problem which centers around the question of one versus many unions. Another aspect of this problem is the question of which arrangement — one or several — is best suited to the maintenance of support for the system. Briefly, a good statement of the most prevalent view which favors unification is

[12] Old hands in the anti-BUO coalition were much in evidence in the CNTM as Rafael Galván of the electricians was named president while Manuel Rivera of the FROC of Puebla, Enrique Rangel and Rafael Ortega were named to the central committee.

[13] *Excelsior,* May 24, 1964.

that "the atomization of the labor movement represented by the federations and confederations is a fact contrary to labor unity; there ought to exist only one great *central* to seek the achievement of the goals of the proletariat."[14] The pluralist case, on the other hand, stresses that unification of all union leadership, given the conditions of the Mexican political system, might well exaggerate some of the most important existing difficulties. One should consider at this point the position of labor organization and the pattern of leadership within the framework of the Revolutionary Coalition. Abuses under the unification scheme could result in stepped-up frustration in the rank and file and among aspirants for leadership which would result in a greater threat to political stability than is the case with the frustrations accompanying conflicts stemming from the plurality of confederations.

The case for several confederations can also be argued in terms of the "possible." Even when the government has provided great support for a single *central,* as it did for the CROM in the 1920's and for the CTM in the 1930's, it has not been possible for these leading confederations to dominate all worker organizations throughout the country. The CROM was never able to wipe out the CGT, and the CTM was unable to do away with either the CROM or the CGT. President Calles in the 1920's and President Cárdenas in the 1930's saw themselves as catalytic agents in the formation of a giant labor confederation that would encompass all of Mexico's organized workers. Neither man realized the goal. All the efforts — first of Calles and later of Cárdenas — to resolve the internal conflict of organized labor and to unify the labor movement as a single instrument under a single directorate, placing it unconditionally at the command of the group in government for use as political exigencies might dictate were not sufficient.

The monolithic ideal was never hammered into the operating institutional form of a single great all-encompassing confederation because men like Calles and Cárdenas were unwilling to suppress fully dissident groups. The absolute goals of the preferred doctrine of unification were thus tempered by pragmatic considerations in which it was deemed necessary to take into account the personal ambition of leaders, the discontent and the highly volatile temperament of Mexican workers, and the diverse and conflicting convictions concerning labor's role and tactics held both among the members and in the competitive leaderships of the labor movement. Viewing these latter considerations, the leaders decided it was a lesser good to crush all obstacles if this meant

[14] de la Cerda, p. 150. The Spanish word *central* may be used as a substitute for "confederation."

total intervention on the part of the government. In their wisdom, policy-makers decided it was necessary to take into account the special characteristics of the Mexican political environment which militated against the single all-powerful confederation of unions.[15]

Lack of a single great union is regarded in one view as an invitation to chaos and in fact a manifestation or a reflection of the existing chaos in the labor movement. On the other hand, the multi-confederation picture can be interpreted as the mark of a freer, more liberal society. It becomes the basis for more effective choice on the part of workers. The liberal approach is reflected in the federal labor law itself. Here it is provided that "both workers and owners [have the right] to form a union . . . without there being necessity of previous authorization. . . . [Moreover, the law has provided that] no one can be compelled to form part of a union or not to form part of a union."[16]

Several other provisions from the Mexican labor law provide us with a framework for understanding the legal basis of pluralism in the Mexican labor movement. First of all, the public character of unions is recognized in the provision that unions must be registered with the particular council of conciliation and arbitration having jurisdiction in the union area. If the union is within the scope of federal control, it must also be registered with the Ministry of Labor. Secondly, the authorities with whom the unions are registered may rule acts of union officials null and void when such acts seem to conflict with labor law provisions. Particularly important for the range of choice open to the Mexican worker is the provision of Mexican law which recognizes the existence of a "coalition." A "coalition" is essentially an agreement among a group of workers that they are going to band together to defend their common interests. The "coalition" is related to the right to strike in the sense that the right to strike is defined in at least one provision as the "legal and temporary suspension of work as the result of a coalition of workers." In support of the concept of "coalition" the law also says that "any affiliated union shall be able to retire from a federation or confederation at any time — even though a pact to the contrary may exist."[17]

[15] L. Vincent Padgett, *Popular Participation in the Mexican "One-Party" System* (unpublished dissertation, Northwestern University, 1955), pp. 224–225.

[16] *Ley Federal del Trabajo* (Mexico, 1951 as amended), Art. 236.

[17] *Ley Federal del Trabajo*, Arts. 242, 245, 256, 258, 269. The federal Constitution of 1917, Art. 123, XX, is the basis for the system of councils of conciliation and arbitration that have come into being in accord with provisions of the *Ley Federal del Trabajo*. There are councils having only local jurisdiction and there are those having federal jurisdiction. In either case they are composed of an equal number of representatives from labor and

In the study of worker alternatives from the standpoint of labor legislation many other provisions would have to be discussed. The important point for purposes of this study is that the *Ley Federal del Trabajo* has left the workers freedom to choose whether or not they will continue their affiliation with a given union. Individual unions in a similar way, have been afforded the opportunity to decide whether or not they should maintain connections with some larger group, i.e., a federation or confederation.

The provisions of the federal labor law guaranteeing certain rights of choice in labor organization and affiliation no doubt have been abused from time to time by those with authority to administer and execute the law. We do not need to discuss the CROM in this connection because its period of great strength took place before the development of a full-scale labor code. But in the case of the CTM, unquestionably there were times during its period of great expansion in the 1930's when it received government preference over other confederations in the struggle to achieve power through the organization of Mexican workers. It became very difficult for unions to shift away from the CTM to some smaller confederation even if they wanted to. However, the outstanding fact is that, even when workers' unions and smaller confederations refused to affiliate with a government-supported confederation such as the CTM, and were sometimes crushed on that account, there nevertheless were others among the weaker groups which successfully resisted all efforts at incorporation.

As we have indicated, the restraint which groups in government have shown in pursuing the realization of one giant confederation to replace the pluralistic pattern is related to some extent to the norms of the labor code and, of course, Article 123 of the Constitution itself which is the basis of that code. Perhaps it is even more important that there has been a healthy respect among Mexican politicians for the character and attitudes of their countrymen. Politicians, in other words,

---

capital and are presided over by a representative of the executive branch. Federal councils at the state level may be either permanent or temporary. An inspector from the Secretariat of Labor and Social Protection presides over their sessions. In the Federal District the Federal Council of Conciliation and Arbitration functions on a permanent basis. The councils — local or federal — make judgments in labor disputes, although the role of the council may be merely that of arranging a compromise. The judgments are considered binding unless, as in various cases, they are susceptible of appeal to the Mexican courts. The councils help greatly in speeding solution of disputes and in reducing the burden on the Mexican judiciary. Rafael de Pina, professor of law at the *Universidad Nacional Autónoma de México,* discusses the role of these councils in a study of Mexican labor law. See Rafael de Pina, *Curso de derecho procesal del trabajo* (Mexico, 1952), pp. 56, 209–237.

seem to understand that the workers' attitudes and aspirations relative to efficient administration of union funds and democratic procedure center for the most part on the individual union, i.e., the basic unit of labor organization. In the overall picture workers have tolerated the fact that promises of better living standards have often surpassed actual benefits. Certainly over the years there have been many glowing promises, and workers have learned not to expect very much in the way of sudden improvements, although they do expect some gradual indication of change for the better. Great promises followed only by very gradual improvement have been accepted as a part of the game and therefore legitimate. What has never been accepted as legitimate is tyranny and mismanagement on the part of union committees. These things may often be facts of life, but they are always just cause for rebellion in the workers' eyes. It is at the point of the local union that the rank and file have demanded a degree of participation, and their loyalty to the going system rests to a great extent on the grant of this demand.

These considerations are related to the old question of the one great confederation versus rival groups and rival confederations. As Mexican confederations are organized, the confederation committees and below them at the state level, the federation committees, have had a tendency to dictate the selection of leaders in affiliated unions. Workers would not object so much to the practice of selection of their leadership from above if the leadership so selected would do a good job of running the union. Sometimes it does. The crisis situation develops only when the top echelons have persisted in supporting a union committee named by themselves which has abused authority and power to the detriment of the workers under its jurisdiction. Two situations have frequently occurred. First of all, there is the alliance of union officials with management for the purpose of speeding up the worker and quelling protests when guarantees and security provisions of the union collective bargaining contract have been ignored. Secondly, union leadership may abuse workers through the establishment of unwarranted quotas or membership dues in order to benefit the leaders personally. Usually these abuses have to go on for a considerable length of time before the workers undertake the difficult task of making the case that they are in effect being exploited by their own leaders.

The important point is that when federation or confederation committees have persisted in supporting a delinquent union committee, workers have had some opportunity under labor law to mobilize and demand a genuine voice in the selection of their leadership. Although it may be necessary on occasion to defy the usual hazards of *pistoleros* and hired bullies, there exists the very real possibility that an assembly of workers can be held and a new committee elected. Such a committee has the opportunity to seek recognition and be duly registered with appropriate government authorities. This can be done through affiliation with some other confederation. The most substantial aspect of what is sometimes called union democracy, *la democracia sindical,* in Mexico has to do with this opportunity under the law for the worker to separate himself from one set of leaders and join with another which promises something better.

Labor Pluralism: A Case Example

There seems to be ample reason that one of the principal criteria by which workers evaluate the existing political system and those who govern is their own personal experience with leadership in their local factory. Since poor leadership is often closely tied to higher echelons at the federation, state federation, or national confederation levels of the organization, it is sometimes very difficult to get rid of the poor leaders within the framework of the confederation. It is, therefore, of great importance that potential leaders who head the wave of discontent in the local union have some opportunity to affiliate with another confederation and seek a new registry for the union within the framework of another organization. The moves and countermoves involved in this sort of effort to achieve a new and more satisfactory leadership for a local union were observed by the author.

In the textile factory of La Covadonga members of a long established union, including most of the workers, found themselves involved with a corrupt leadership named by the federation officials and approved by the confederation leaders of the CROM. The union had been affiliated with the CROM in the days of CROM supremacy during the 1920's and had stayed on with that confederation during the years of CTM supremacy. Due to the loyalty of groups like that at La Covadonga, the CROM was able to maintain considerable strength in the Puebla-Tlaxcala region. The CROM and its affiliated state federation apparently overestimated the affective ties felt by the rank and file at La Covadonga. Neither the CROM central committee nor the federation committee respected the expectations of workers with regard to the conduct of union officers. Corrupt practices became characteristic of the leadership. Pressure was brought to bear upon union assemblies in order that the persons selected by the federation and central committees might be elected union officers. Sometimes these officers were outsiders who had never held jobs at La Covadonga. The union leaders failed to insist that management respect the wage scales assigned to different classes of workers in the collective bargaining contract. Labor leaders surrounded themselves with spies whose jobs were to search out any malcontents in the membership and punish them. When the tension did not diminish, some workers lost their jobs because their attitudes made them unacceptable to union leaders. Discontent with existing abuses heightened when the leadership ordered a seemingly unreasonable increase in the rate of union dues. A number of workers were beaten up as unrest increased.

Finally, opposition to the leadership coalesced, and the dissenters held their own union meeting as permitted under labor law and selected a new leadership. The records of the meeting were sent to the Department of Associations in Mexico City, which registers unions and union leadership and presides over judgments on union election in conjunction with regional and national labor arbitration and conciliation councils.

Of course the regular leadership also sent its report of the events at La Covadonga. In this report the existing leadership said it would be willing to cooperate with the rebels if the latter made "reasonable" demands. Leaders of the revolt, however, realized they either had to leave La Covadonga or stand in jeopardy of life and limb should the old group stay on in power. Thus, the leaders' offer of a compromise, while it won over some people in the factory, did not resolve enough problems to quiet the unrest. In this opening round of battle the Ministry of Labor refused to recognize the dissident group as having legal standing. The group then appealed to the leadership of the CTM in Puebla, realizing some "friend in court" was needed if the federal authorities were to accept a proposed change in leadership and registration. The CTM, however, refused to take in the new group under a different name to be registered as an affiliate of the CTM.

Meanwhile the old CROM committee held a meeting to provide for election of new leadership. Some members of the the committee were replaced, and a number of promises were made. Particularly revealing was the pledge that leaders would no longer be selected from persons who had not worked in La Covadonga. It was also promised that many of the workers which the old committee had voted to exclude from work in the factory would be reinstated. However, a list of persons who could not be reinstated was also submitted. These were the leaders of the intransigent group. The old committee promised that it would procure jobs in other plants in Puebla and Tlaxcala for the expelled persons. A quorum of workers was present for the meeting, so also was a representative of the governor of the state, and several other high officials. Some of the labor disputants who were to be ousted refused to accept the decision of the assembly, but in general the union group seemed favorable to the compromise arrangement and voted accordingly. The Ministry of Labor promptly recognized the new compromise committee. The settlement was only superficially satisfactory, however, and peace did not last at La Covadonga. The discontented group again gathered more and more support, and another move was made to enlist the help of the CTM in order to achieve a change of registry and recognition of the dissident group in the Ministry of Labor. This plea was again turned down.

In desperation the rebels turned to the state organization of the CROC in Puebla.[18] At CROC headquarters there was a warm reception. The CROC made available its meeting hall in the city of Puebla, and the workers met there to vote unanimously to separate from the CROM and affiliate with the CROC. Interestingly enough, the charges were the same as had been made against the original CROM committee. Signatures of all those attending the meeting were collected and organized in the form of a petition. This documentation, along with a letter stating the case, was sent to the Ministry of Labor. The ministry then sent out two inspectors to review the situation and conduct a formal count of the preferences of all workers. The formal voting was conducted with both the CROC group and the CROM group having equal representation as observers to make sure that the count was valid. When the tally indicated the group favoring the CROC had the most votes, the way was open for the Ministry of

---

[18] There have already been mentioned various manifestations of discontent in the 1940's during which new confederations from time to time were formed. Another organizational effort was that of the Revolutionary Confederation of Workers and Peasants (CROC) in the early 1950's. Its original declaration of principles made a very clear-cut distinction between two classes of people in a society, the exploited and the exploiters, thus giving a kind of class-war orientation to its organizational program. See CROC, *Declaración de principios, program de acción y estatutos* (Mexico, 1952), p. 11. Adolfo Ruiz Cortines, upon taking over the presidency from Miguel Alemán, seemed to find it expedient to offer various opportunities for growth to the CROC. This, of course, did not help the strength of the CTM. As Professor Scott has pointed out: "During his administration, President Ruiz Cortines seemed to be playing the CROC off against the CTM, permitting the former to organize in direct competition with already existing CTM unions and even allowing its leaders to make public attacks charging the CTM hierarchy with having betrayed labor's interests and with having lined their own pockets at the expense of the working man." See Robert E. Scott, *Mexican Government in Transition* (Urbana, Ill., 1959), p. 164. Professor Scott's interpretation is supported by Guadalupe Rivera Marín, who has emphasized the growth of the CROC relative to other confederations in the period of 1950–1960 in terms of total numbers of affiliated union organizations. See Rivera Marín, p. 276.

Labor to change the registration of the union at La Covadonga and recognize as legitimate the changes in leadership at that factory.[19]

The case points up the relationship of labor pluralism to the problem of support maintenance for the system. The pattern of multiple confederations makes possible change from one confederation to another and through such change provides opportunity for altering leadership and policy in accord with demands of local unions. Degree of choice has varied with local circumstances, the general labor situation and the composition of government. However, pluralism has never disappeared in the sense that the one great confederation has replaced all others. The existence of alternatives for union committees to choose from has made it possible for workers to hold a special assembly in order to vote out a venal committee and elect a new one even though opposed by the upper echelons of the confederation. The presence of more than one confederation has made it possible for a committee elected by aroused workers to secure aid and a promise of the privilege of affiliation from an alternative association.

Recent Labor Alignments

When the dissatisfaction with the old leadership reaches a high point and few opportunities are forthcoming for changing leadership, forming new unions, or joining new confederations, there exist ample reasons for discontent and even violence. Another important consideration is the spiraling cost of living which has usually stayed ahead of wage increases. It was a combination of such factors which created the outbreak of unrest among organized workers, other wage and salary groups, and students in 1958–59.[20] There were too many old faces in

---

[19] The case became so well known that a final victory celebration was held in one of the largest theaters in Puebla attended by the military commander, the governor of the state, and the Minister of Labor of the federal government. In addition, the entire central committee of the CROC came in from Mexico City.

[20] One frequently cited source on Mexican politics explains the labor difficulties of this period in terms of the jealousy and troublemaking of the "leftist anti-BUO faction in the Mexican labor movement" whose "ambitious leftist leaders . . . sought to take advantage of the change-over of administrations to enhance their power." Scott, pp. 65–67. No explanation of the term "leftist" is offered, and this is unfortunate since we need to know what the author means when he applies the term to the Mexican context, especially in the context of this particular situation. In addition there is too simple an explanation of cause in heaping the blame upon the anti-BUO group. One could not argue that anti-BUO leaders did not, from time to time, involve themselves or give at least moral aid and comfort to many of these strikes. However, it seems that more than the sympathy of anti-BUO people was needed to create the degree of unrest which swept across Mexico in this fifteen-month period.

high positions, and these faces had not produced enough results; as a matter of fact, in many cases they had produced nothing but suppression and corruption as reflected in appointments from the highest officials to the local union chapters. Of course it was clear that Soviet money and influence were involved in support of the rail strike led by Demetri Vallejo, but the widespread mass following which Vallejo got from railroad workers to support his demands would indicate that prevailing conditions had resulted in a high degree of resentment.[21]

Once the labor disturbances of 1958–59 quieted down, the forces in the Mexican labor movement included the collection of confederations joined together in the workers' unity bloc (the BUO) as well as a large number of autonomous unions and some federations not affiliated with any confederation. Finally, there were a series of federations and confederations joined together in a bloc generally opposing the BUO, and this opposition was formalized in 1960 with the organization of the CNTM, the National Workers' Confederation of Mexico mentioned above. By 1960, then, anticipating the tendency of subsequent years, there was established a pattern of alliances of confederations each encompassing a number of formerly powerful or still powerful *centrales*.

In the BUO block the strongest numerical element is the CTM, followed in importance by the railroad workers' union, the mining and metal workers' union, the petroleum workers' union, the CROM, the CGT, the telephone workers, the motion picture workers, and several smaller and lesser known unions. Most important in the CNT (CNTM) is the CROC with the organization of greatest numerical potential being the newly organized National Federation of Sugar Cane Workers (FNC). Both the Union of Mexican Electrical Workers (SME) and the Union of Electrical Workers of the Mexican Republic (STERM) have great importance, not so much because of their numbers, but because of their tactical position in the Mexican economy. Other organizations, such as the CRT and the FOR, encompass workers in less strategic industries and are not outstanding quantitatively.

Perhaps the greatest possibility for CNT to rise to supremacy in labor lies in the future of the FNC and its capacity to organize sugar cane workers, of which there are some two million throughout the Republic. Some of these have already been organized by the CTM, but opportunities for organization are still open and the FNC may be able to capitalize upon them, thus becoming a major force not only within the CNT but throughout the entire labor movement. The diffi-

[21] Soviet diplomats were expelled from Mexico because of their part in this event.

culty in organizing rural workers perhaps militates against this possibility, and only the future can tell what this organizational effort will
bring. One can speculate upon various consequences of this division
into two great alliances of confederations which appears to have taken
place in terms of the BUO and the CNT. One prognosis would be a
great waste of energy involving a fight between the two great alignments. This, essentially, is Scott's prediction:

> So far, the struggle between the right and left wings of Mexican
> labor has tended to weaken the Labor sector's relative position in the
> national structure of power, but because of the preponderant strength
> of the CTM behind the BUO, coupled with the government's crack-
> down on leftist unions after the 1959 strikes, the battle has been too
> onesided to threaten disintegration of the sector itself. If, however,
> the revolutionary government continues allowing the CROC and
> its allies to build their relative power, a crisis could occur. . . . If
> these organizing attempts should prove successful, the anti-BUO
> labor group could surpass the BUO in total membership. Even
> though the farm laborers may not be so politically effective as their
> numbers seem to indicate, because of their less sophisticated back-
> ground and rural location, the Labor sector of the PRI might split
> wide open. At any rate, more labor energy and influence may be
> wasted on internecine battles than applied to the broader function
> of influencing the national policy-making process.[22]

Another interpretation based on the preceding analysis is that the
presence of two rather loose associations of confederations are better
than one single all-encompassing confederation. Still another possible
interpretation is that unity, regardless of desirability, is now closer than
it ever has been in the sense that many unions have been combined into
the two great alliances, thus reducing the number of independent
smaller federations, confederations, and unions. But this last point
is qualified by the fact that neither great alignment is completely unified
internally.[23]

[22] Scott, p. 168.

[23] The pluralistic pattern was under attack again as the Díaz Ordaz presidency got underway. All labor organizations were persuaded by the new
President to agree to the idea of unity in principle. A national assembly of
labor organizations was planned, but the talks preceding it indicated differences among principal leaders that would be hard to overcome. The major
question as might be expected was how to divide up the spoils. In a unified
labor movement what would be the role of such leaders as Fidel Velázquez
and Jesús Yurén of the CTM or Enrique Rangel and Rafael Ortega of the
CROC — not to mention numerous other important but less prominent
figures? Because of their stronger political position the leaders of the BUO
took the position that the most desirable step would be immediate creation of
a single national labor confederation fusing all pre-existing labor groups.

Schism in the great alignments was seen in the 1958–59 period when the railroad workers and petroleum workers pulled away from the BUO, although nominally remaining within it. At the same time the electrical workers' unions tended to divorce themselves from the anti-BUO faction which was lending some cooperation to Vallejo and other pro-strike leaders among the railroad workers' committees. Weakness in the BUO camp has also been shown in the ambiguous stance sometimes assumed by the CGT. Another confusing aspect of the BUO stems from the fact that much of its support has come from a group that is not even regarded as a portion of it; namely, the Federation of Unions of Workers in the Service of the State (FSTSE) or federal bureaucrats' union which normally belongs in the so-called "popular sector" of the PRI. In the same way, it is not at all clear, as indicated above, that the CROC, which generally tends to be the most important single group in the CNT, can always get along with the electrical workers. Moreover support for the CNT by the CRT, the FOR, and the sugar cane workers has not been fully tested. Thus, the appearance of two great alignments of confederations may be somewhat misleading.

Relative Strength of Labor Groups

One of the most difficult tasks in analyzing the condition of the Mexican labor movement and the factions within it involves the effort to assess the numerical proportions assigned to the types of unions, federations and confederations. The first thing to note is that leaders have a tendency to inflate estimates of the numbers of members in their unions. It is a natural inclination, since the man who speaks for several million as opposed to several hundred thousand may expect to receive somewhat more attention when he makes a pronouncement. Thus, in arguing for better treatment of workers on the part of employers in a major speech in 1958, the perennial general secretary of the CTM, Fidel Velásquez, was reported to have called on all labor leaders affiliated with his group to put forth greater efforts in order to achieve the economic improvement of "more than three million workers [*Cetemistas*] in the country."[24] For the same approximate period Scott

---

The CNT, including the CROC and many relatively independent unions had a counterproposal. They wanted to set up a coordinating body, a National Labor Council with representation from all major labor groups, which would leave existing organizations intact. Major questions on which there were divisions of opinion aside from the assignment of positions to the leaders included such matters as labor housing, minimum wage legislation, setting salary levels for various industries, the problem of company unions, intra-labor organizational conflicts and corruption among labor leaders.

[24] *Excelsior,* February 26, 1958.

estimated 1,500,000 in the CTM and a total of 1,873,000 for all federations and unions affiliated with the BUO.[25]

Another example of the difficulty involved in setting numerical strengths for the various union and confederation memberships may be illustrated by the following contrast in estimates. Scott limits the labor sector of the PRI to 2,113,000 organized workers in both BUO and anti-BUO or CNT groups. On the other hand, the total number of workers organized in Mexico is estimated by Guadalupe Rivera Marín on the basis of official releases from the General Statistics Office (DGE) as including only 1,202,917 persons.[26] Still another line of estimates indicates the doubtfulness of any firm statement about numerical strength. A recent commentary on Mexican labor placed the membership of the CTM in 1936 at the time of its founding at about 500,000.[27] Another source credited CTM membership with a one hundred per cent increase and membership of approximately 1,000,000 in 1940.[28] A report published in 1954 emphasized the difference between estimates of CTM leaders during the course of interviews in which different spokesmen quoted 1,300,000 and 1,400,000 respectively while the investigator in that case estimated less than 700,000 in the CTM rank and file.[29] The writer was told by a member of the national committee of the CTM in 1953 that there were 1,200,000 in the rank and file. An amazing contrast to all these estimates comes from a report for 1948 showing the CTM membership as low as 91,436 while the short-lived CUT was credited with 98,218, and the total for all unions throughout the country was set at 771,646.[30] With regard to other organizations besides the CTM in the BUO, Scott's estimate of the latter 1950's set the membership of the CROM at 35,000 while Davis gave as a maximum figure, 71,244.[31] López Aparicio placed the number of the CROM membership at 50,000.[32] On the anti-BUO side Davis placed the maximum figure for CROC membership at 436,015; Scott placed it at 150,000.[33]

Even given some leeway for the different impressions upon which

[25] Scott, pp. 166–167.

[26] Scott, p. 166 and Rivera Marín, p. 277.

[27] de la Cerda, p. 149.

[28] Alfonso López Aparicio, *El movimiento obrero en México* (Mexico, 1952), p. 219.

[29] Horace B. Davis, "Numerical Strength of Mexican Unions," *The Southwestern Social Science Quarterly,* Vol. 35 (June, 1954), p. 48.

[30] José E. Iturriaga, *La estructura social y cultural de México,* Vol. II (México, 1951), pp. 43–57.

[31] Scott, p. 166, and Davis, p. 49.

[32] Aparacio, p. 181.

[33] Davis, p. 49, and Scott, p. 166.

these estimates were founded, as well as differences in years, the wide variations in estimates are hard to reconcile. The picture is one of considerable confusion and does not provide grounds for a reliable statement. Use of such statistics should be accompanied by elaborate caveats.[34]

A major factor in making the estimate of membership strength so difficult has to do with changes in types of union affiliation. Information of this type also points up the changing character of labor organization in general. In 1939 there were about 5,886 unions registered in the country with the General Statistical Office; 7,564 in 1950, and 8,607 or a little over by 1960. A little over 54 per cent of these were craft unions in 1939, and close to 60 per cent were craft unions in 1960. About 15 per cent of the unions were organized on the basis of a particular enterprise in 1939 and about 17 per cent in 1960. Industry-wide unions were a little over 17 per cent in 1939, and close to 18 per cent in 1960, while the unions based on various types of activity difficult to classify were nearly 14 per cent of the total in 1939 and only about 6½ per cent of the total in 1960.[35] In the last years of the 50's the number of unions based upon individual enterprises, such as a textile mill, or upon an industry-wide organization, seemed to be increasing after relative declines in the early 50's.[36] For the two major confederations, it can be noted that the CTM suffered a decline in the number of unions affiliated with it during the 50's, going from 58.5 per cent of all registered unions in 1950 to 44.3 per cent at the end of the decade. In contrast, the CROC began with 25.7 per cent of all registered unions in the early 1950's and reached 35.5 per cent.[37]

Viewed from a distance the labor movement in Mexico represents a remarkable kaleidoscope of organizational types and doctrinal views with relatively deep historical roots. It is a pluralistic picture set in the frame of an official orientation toward the monolithic. Great diversity

[34] Howard F. Cline, *Mexico, Revolution to Evolution, 1940–1960* (London, 1962), pp. 345–346. In Appendix Table 12, Cline uses Scott's estimates of the labor membership as a basis for his own analysis of a changing stratification arrangement in Mexico.

[35] The small increase in industrial unions and the larger increase in craft unions would seem unexpected in light of Mexico's gains in industrial development.

[36] Rivera Marín, p. 272.

[37] The changing pattern of Mexican economy and accompanying changes in types of union alignments and types of activity in which unionized men are to be found, is clearly visible in terms of the increases of union workers in certain kinds of activities, and decreases in others. Thus, unionized workers in manufacturing increased nearly 90 per cent during the decade of the 50's, while those in commerce increased well over 100 per cent. Rivera Marín, pp. 276–277.

and a remarkable amount of official tolerance are present considering the dependent position of unions upon government. Nearly all the unions, federations, and confederations have in common their adherence to the Revolutionary Coalition despite the differences in orientation internal to the movement. The great weakness of the labor movement is the *continuismo* of labor leadership which is mitigated to some extent by the legal capacity of rank and file to change leaders at the local level. Labor continues to be a positive factor in support of the regime, but the leadership problem does not make this a foregone conclusion for the future.

4

Peasant Organizations

Development of Peasant Organization

Attempts to organize the peasantry were integral elements of the Revolution and continued in evidence as the fighting ended and men worked to establish a post-revolutionary equilibrium. There were, of course, the militant armed followers of Emiliano Zapata. Later there were labor organizers who expanded their activity to the countryside and attempted to organize the peasantry. By 1920 an agrarian group, the National Agrarian Party (PNA), led by Zapatistas had been founded.

Local peasant movements in the early 1920's were particularly in evidence in Yucatán, Tamaulipas, and Michoacán. Of importance in these grass-roots organizations which took the form of peasant leagues were Ursulo Galván and Graciano Sánchez. These men and other leaders finally brought together the peasant leagues of fifteen different states and the Federal District in an organization known as the National Peasant League (LNC) in 1926. Later, many members of the LNC banded together to oppose conservative tendencies in Calles' government and some even joined the Communists. Some of these refused to give up Communist membership to join the National Revolutionary Party (PNR) when it was formed. However, in 1930, a majority of the LNC leaders voted to join the new PNR.

Graciano Sánchez was one of the National Peasant League leaders who joined the PNR and it was his leadership, along with the efforts of Emilio Portes Gil, which made it possible to hold a peasant convention in the spring of 1933 from which emerged a strong agrarian reform plank that was written into the program of the PNR at the time of the presidential nomination of Lázaro Cárdenas. In place of the National Peasant League the peasant meeting of 1933 formed a new group known as the Mexican Peasant Confederation (CCM). The fact is, however, the CCM did not succeed in uniting even a majority of the potentially organizable peasants in the country. Some labor unions had peasant groups affiliated with them; other peasant groups refused to join any national organization. Labor groups, particularly the CROM and the CGT, struggled to expand influence into the countryside by organizing the peasantry. Moreover, in addition to the new Mexican Peasant Confederation, remnants of the National Peasant League continued to function.

Cárdenas and the CNC

Lázaro Cárdenas decided to build an agrarian group which would have the members of the *ejido* communities created under the agrarian reform program as the basis of the membership. Cárdenas' ideal involved a national association organized as a single confederation which would bring together all of the rural people related in some way to the agrarian reform program. In a decree in July, 1935, Cárdenas put the strength of the government of Mexico and of the Revolutionary Coalition behind the effort to create such an organization. On the basis of the decree, work went forward immediately to organize local groups in the many *ejido* communities throughout the country and then bring these together in state organizations. In each state there was to be a League of Agrarian Communities and Peasant Unions (*Liga*).

It was out of the formation and unification of these *ligas* that there developed the National Peasant Confederation (CNC). Under organizational changes which Cárdenas arranged, the CNC was incorporated into the official party as the peasant sector. The move was designed to keep labor and peasant organizations separate while at the same time strengthening each in its own field.[1] As indicated, the CNC claimed as its special area of organization the peasantry living in *ejido* communities. In addition, the scope of the CNC was recognized as encompassing rural wage laborers and persons forming their own small plots.

The CNC is best visualized as an executive committee functioning at the head of a series of executive committees organized in a vertical-horizontal pattern reaching from the national level to the state level and on down to the local *ejido* communities. The top organizational unit at the state level is the executive committee, which constitutes the working machinery of the state *liga*. Under each *liga* there are several regional committees. The regional committees themselves bind together different types of locally organized units.

There are at least six types of locally organized units which form the basis of the CNC with its claim to act as the special organized

[1] Daniel James has a good discussion of the background of the formation of the CNC in *Mexico and the Americans* (New York, 1963), pp. 265–267.

representative of the agrarian aspect of Mexico's Revolution. Among the local groupings there are first of all, the "executive agrarian committees" which are formed to help groups of peasants who are petitioning for grants of land under the land distribution programs. There are then commissariats of *ejido* communities elected as the community government of the *ejido* by the *ejidatarios*. Local organized units may also include members of "agricultural colonies." The members of the "agricultural colonies" are people who have solicited expropriated land from the government and received it under an arrangement by which each member of the group pays the government for the plot he receives rather than receiving it free of charge without proprietary rights, as in the case of the *ejido*. Members of the "agricultural colonies" have private plots that range anywhere from one or two hectares up to fifty. Another type of group is the "urban colony." "Urban colonies" are frequently found within *ejido* communities where the younger generation of the community has demonstrated need of land to build houses in order to form homes of their own. The land for these houses within the *ejido* community is received as a government grant. In addition, local groups affiliated with the *liga* and the CNC may include small property owners who have formed themselves into a union. These small property owners seldom have pieces of land that exceed fifty hectares. Finally, there are unions of workers formed in connection with industries related to agriculture such as sugar, coffee, cotton, bananas, and other crops that require an accompanying processing industry.

Each local group has its own executive committee, and where the boundaries of a regional organization of the *liga* do not coincide with those of a *municipio* there will be a municipal delegate who acts as a kind of coordinator for these groups. Representation of the rank and file in the highest councils is indirect. There are local organization meetings which send delegates to municipal or regional meetings. From the regional level the delegates chosen, usually members of the regional committee, will gather together to choose the members of the *liga* committee. It is well known that members of the *liga* committee are usually but not always chosen with regard to the wishes of the governor of the state.

Patterns of Conflicts and Articulation of Demands

The organizational framework of the CNC has had three major functions. It has been assigned the task of mobilizing support among the peasantry in order to guarantee the peaceful succession to public office of the candidates named by the leadership of the Revolutionary

Coalition. Secondly, it has been charged with defending interests of the peasantry in dealing with government officialdom. In the third place, this network of committees is supposed to find solutions for internal problems which create divisions among the peasantry and discontent which might undermine the support which the regime is able to draw from the peasant sector.

There are several types of conflict which are evident within the CNC's organization. First, there is the situation in which a large landholder wishes to gain control of the organizational machinery of the CNC, usually at the level of a regional committee, for the purpose of securing his own holdings against petitioners for land. Another purpose of the large landholder might be to bring about a resurvey of the land adjoining his property in the hope of finding some difficulty with the boundary which would result in the expansion of his holdings at the expense of an adjoining *ejido* or small private property plot.

A second typical situation of conflict centers around the effort of a municipal president to control local interest groups, particularly where the jurisdiction of a CNC regional committee coincides with the jurisdiction of the *municipio*. Control of the regional machinery of the CNC in conjunction with the governmental machinery of the *municipio* provides the prospect of influence as well as financial rewards which are difficult to overlook. In a rural *municipio* the CNC organization may well be the only organized interest. Control of that organization is an important step in the formation of a local machine on the basis of which a man can become the boss or *cacique* of the *municipio* for a long time. Through control of the regional committee of the CNC it is possible to become a factor in the selection of the *liga* at the state level. Thus, though a position as municipal president may slip away as the term of office ends and "no immediate re-election" bars the way to an extension in office, continued prominance in the CNC can provide acceptance in the high circles of decision-making at the state level.

Still a third conflict situation within the framework of the CNC involves domination of a local *ejido* community through "continuism" in the office of president of the *ejidal* commissariat. Not only the CNC is involved in such cases since the Department of Agrarian Affairs and Colonization, the Department of Agriculture and Livestock Husbandry, and the Ejido Bank all have, in addition to the CNC, some formally mentioned role with regard to *ejido* administration under the Agrarian Code. In situations of conflict, however, in which one man perpetuates himself at the the head of the administration of the *ejido* community to the detriment of other members of the community through fraud or arbitrary action of some sort, the organizations most concerned are the CNC and the Department of Agrarian Affairs and Colonization (DAAC). Since the name of this latter agency has been changed from time to time, it will be referred to on occasion as the federal agrarian office.

In becoming president of an *ejido* commissariat the prestige and influence which a local resident has among his neighbors are significant considerations, but so also is the standing which the prominent individual has with the chief-of-zone of the federal DAAC and with the officials of the regional committee. It is important, of course, that the man himself is willing to give up a certain amount of his time to take on the responsibility of occupying the top office of the *ejido* community. Many are unwilling to devote time to this type of activity, and for that reason alone "continuism" itself is not ordinarily a cause for disturbance within the *ejido* community. However, "continuism" coupled with use of authority which deprives others of their rights can lead to a crisis situation.

In one case examined by the author an *ejido* president not only had been re-elected a number of times; he had built support for himself through cultivating factions within the *ejido* community. With this support in hand and the community divided it was possible for the *ejido* president to deprive a number of *ejidatarios* of portions of their rightful plots of land and also to embezzle the tax money which he, as president of the *ejido* commissariat, was supposed to collect from the *ejidatarios* to pay to the state and to the federal government. The experience of the *ejido,* Ignacio Romero Vargas, provides a useful case study in the problems of abusive "continuismo" at the *ejido* level and some insight as to how the CNC and other organizations intertwine in dealing with such problems.

A Case Example: Continuismo and Its Possible Remedy

The *ejido* of Ignacio Romero Vargas in the *municipio* of Cuatlancingo is located about ten miles from Puebla, Mexico. The original grant of land for the *ejido* was 355 hectares. The people began their efforts to get the land in 1922. In 1924 the land was granted on a provisional basis, and on April 22, 1925, the *ejido* was granted with finality, *en definitivo,* by presidential decree.

The *ejido* of Ignacio Romero Vargas had been distinguished by the quiet, orderly character of its community life until a man by the name of Donato Bello became president of the *ejido* commissariat. His election marked the beginning of troubles for the *ejidatarios.*

Upon being elected, Bello began to build political support that would enable him to maintain control of the *ejido* when and if he might relinquish office.[2] Bello's support came chiefly from the *colonos,* sons of the original *ejidatarios* and others to whom had been granted parcels of land for the construction of houses on untillable ground within the circumference of the *ejido.* The *colonos* voted in *ejido* assemblies like other members of the community; but — lacking in farming plots of their own — they formed a kind of underprivileged group. Backed by the *colonos,* Bello controlled *ejido* elections and — upon relinquishing the presidency — was able to name one of his group, Fidencio López Pérez, president of the *ejido* commissariat. Through López Pérez, Bello continued to manage *ejido* affairs from behind the scenes.

The principal abuses of power and authority on the part of the Bello faction were two. In the first place they revised illegally a number of the agrarian certificates by which the government guarantees to each *ejidatario* the use of an assigned plot of land so long as the *ejidatario* lives and conforms with relevant stipulations of the Agrarian Code. Thirteen *ejidatarios* lost portions of their plots to the Bello group. Secondly, the *ejido* commissariat was intrusted with the collection and payment of the *ejidatarios'* state taxes, but too often when the *ejidatarios* paid their tax money it never reached the state officials. Six years after Bello first became *ejido* president, the Office of State Tax Collections (*Recaudación de Rentas del Estado*), advised the community that the *ejido* had consistently failed to meet its obligations, and that its debt to the state amounted to 3,598 pesos. Further, the Office of State Tax Collections announced its determination to attach *ejido* property with value equal to the debt.

A number of *ejidatarios* had become aware of the alterations in the agrarian certificates and were indignant about them. However, the abuses had been at the expense of a few, and the most of the *ejidatarios* had their own problems. They did not care to become involved in the complicated and sometimes dangerous area of politics into which steps against Bello would take them. But, when the news reached the *ejidatarios* that their tax money had not been paid by the commissariat and that their goods, houses, and equipment might be attached by the state government, there arose a specter of hardship sufficient to alarm even the most apathetic among them. A group was quickly formed that began to work for the downfall of the Bello faction.

A principal difficulty in replacing Bello, who had by this time once again assumed the *ejido* presidency, involved the positions taken by the zone chief, *jefe de zona,* and the *delegado* of the federal agrarian office

---

[2] Members of *ejido* commissariats are elected for a three-year term and may be re-elected by vote of two-thirds of the *ejidatarios* gathered in general assembly. A two-thirds vote of the *ejidatarios* may also oust the *ejido* officers for specified causes.

— the organ of the central government most universally connected with *ejido* affairs. When it became clear that these two officials would stand against any effort to displace the Bello faction, the group of discontented *ejidatarios* went to the committee of the *liga,* pointed out what was happening, and asked the secretary general of the *liga* committee to help them. The secretary general agreed to lend his aid on the basis of the long list of petitioners put before him and the proof of fraud in the way the Bello administration had mishandled the tax money. Enough people had saved the receipts verifying their payments for it to be shown that at least 1,450 pesos had been paid by the *ejidatarios* without any ever having been received by the state officials.

The secretary general of the *liga* went to see the governor. The situation at the *ejido* of Ignacio Romero Vargas was explained, and the difficulty of resolving the matter in the face of the position taken by the delegate of the federal agrarian office was pointed out. The governor then resolved to act in behalf of the dissident *ejidatarios.* He requested that the *delegado* be replaced. This was done, and early in October a new delegate arrived to take over.

With the stage set in this fashion the dissident group came out in the open and held its first assembly in the federal school, Benito Juárez, in the *pueblo,* Ignacio Romero Vargas. The auxiliary municipal president presided. A copy of the assembly record signed by all who attended went to the *liga* committee. To the record was attached a letter from the committee of *ejidatarios* who were the leaders in organizing the resistance to the Donato Bello group. The *ejidatarios* who spoke in the assembly reflected the indignation and wrath of all in attendance. The words of Everardo Vera López recorded by the secretary were much like those of his fellow *ejidatarios:*

> He in particular has not been affected [by the abuses of Donato Bello] but in no way does he agree with the disorder that the *ejido* representatives are carrying out agitating in this way a village which has always given signs of order and tranquility. . . . He condemns the conduct of Donato Bello . . . who continues despoiling [*ejidatarios* of their land rights], and he disagrees with the way money has been demanded of the *ejido* people without ever calling an assembly to explain to what use the money is put. [He says] this ought not to be, because the Agrarian Code does not authorize such vile tricks [*chanchullos*].

In their letter attached to the record of the proceedings, the committee for the protesting *ejidatarios* said:

> The existing system of oppression and tyranny [in our *ejido* community] is denounced. May this system imposed by Donato Bello

be terminated forever because never has been known in the past a time like the one which now embarrasses us.

We hope that once the investigation is terminated competent persons of recognized integrity in this *pueblo* will be substituted for the present commissariat of the *ejido* — and that those who have lent themselves to the tactics of Donato Bello may be excluded from all representation.

Finally, we ask that there be a measure of order, that the tranquility of this *pueblo* continue as always, that justice be done our comrades and that the due guarantees be given to everyone without distinction between those who are and those who are not *colonos*. With this will follow the peace we desire for our humble *pueblo* of Romero Vargas.

The effort to normalize the situation in the *ejido* community of Ignacio Romero Vargas was an extended one. An assembly was held in the presence of the delegate of the federal agrarian office in which were repeated the charges stated in the assembly of the previous day. Then, three days later on, there was another assembly in the salon of the same official, José T. Balderrama. Also present was Miguel Mendieta, financial secretary for the *liga* committee, who had been given the Romero Vargas problem as a special assignment. The question at hand was that of the tax money owed to the state. The evidence of fraud was reviewed, as was the state's position on the debt. As a result of this meeting the *delegado* ordered the Bello faction to appear before him within a week for the inspection of the *ejido* accounts. Instead, the Bello group went to the *liga* committee to complain of the tactics of the dissident group and to enlist the sympathy of the secretary general. The beleaguered *ejido* officers were only partially successful. The secretary general secured for them an extension of time. However, it was not an indefinite extension. On the contrary, the Bello group, i.e., the *ejido* officials, were ordered to present the *ejido* accounts without fail at the end of the time extension. At this point three weeks had elapsed.

When the appointed date came, the *ejido* officials again did not appear with their records. Instead, they went to the office of the federal *delegado* and asked for another extension. The official intervened to secure it for them.

Meanwhile an investigation of the manner in which Bello and his group had used their authority to alter the agrarian rights certificates of the *ejidatarios* was under way. Charged with carrying out the investigation was Joaquín González Rosas, agrarian organizer attached to the federal agrarian office. Miguel Mendieta, representative of the *liga* committee, also participated. The investigation was completed in a short time, and there was evidence that Bello and his following had endeavored to enrich themselves by illegally revising the certificates of thirteen *ejidatarios*.

Two months later the judgment of *ejido* accounts was carried out in the offices of the director of state tax collections. The *ejido* officials refused to come and bring their books, but the state gave the *ejidatarios* credit for the money they had paid on the basis of the receipts in their possession.

In view of the continued lack of cooperation on the part of the *ejido* officers, both the *delegado* and the *liga* committee asked the federal district prosecutor (*Agente del Ministerio Público Federal*), to take the case "because of the infractions of the law committed by the *ejido* officers."

Six months after the first assembly denouncing Bello there came a federal order which brought the expulsion of the members of the *ejido* commissariat for violations of the Agrarian Code and stipulated that their alternates (*suplentes*) take office.

The deposed *ejido* officials twice appealed to the second federal district court of Cholula for a writ of *amparo* to stay the federal order.[3] In both cases the writ was denied on the ground that removal of the plaintiffs from their positions on the commissariat of the *ejido* was in keeping with relevant legal provisions.

Still later, the *ejidatarios* of Ignacio Romero Vargas were convoked by the delegate of the federal agrarian office in order that they might elect a new commissariat and also a "council of vigilance."[4] The governor's representative and federal officers and the leaders of the *liga* were present. However, in spite of the important persons who attended the assembly, the situation with regard to *ejido* officers remained fluid and was not settled until fully a year after the initial assembly had been held. At such time another commissariat was elected, and a man by the name of José del Razo Espinosa became president of the *ejido* organization.

José del Razo Espinosa was a leader of the original group that solicited land from the government in 1922. As president of the executive committee that represented the group he had received the first certificate of agrarian rights when the grant of 355 hectares was

[3] The *amparo* is exclusively a federal writ which stays government officials from action that the courts feel is not in keeping with the federal laws and Constitution.

[4] The latter under the Agrarian Code is supposed to act as a check on the commissariat. In practice the effectiveness of the check depends on the situation in a given *ejido* community. Donato Bello had managed to control both the council of vigilance and the commissariat prior to the popular uprising.

definitely approved in 1925. He had served as president of the *ejido* commissariat for one regular three-year term. He did not play an active part in the political life of the *ejido* again until the Bello episode. At that time, as he expressed it,

> there . . . came a political situation that was insupportable to me because twelve widows and two blind persons as well as the whole community were being abused and despoiled. And this is how I came to return again to face the difficulties of responsibility.[5]

The *ejido* of Ignacio Romero Vargas returned to the tranquility that had characterized it before the era of Donato Bello, and as a reward for their struggle, the *ejidatarios* were pleased to find that other benefits accrued to them above and beyond their chief goal — the destruction of the Donato Bello machine. Indeed, the internal conflict in the *ejido* of Ignacio Romero Vargas in a sense put the *ejido* itself on the map. Officials began to take the *ejidatarios* into account in a way they had not done previously. Within a year of the episode's close the long-desired aid from the National Bank of Ejido Credit was received. There was a thirteen thousand peso loan, and the community formed a "society of *ejido* credit." As a result of the loan the members of the *ejido* were able to purchase the tractor they had wanted for so long.[6] The community also received a new and modern school. Financial aid from the state government made the project possible, although the *ejidatarios* also contributed their money and their labor as well. The governor graced the school's inauguration ceremony.

The *ejidatarios* of Ignacio Romero Vargas had greatly bettered their situation by acting together against poor and dishonest government in the community. The structure and operation of the system in which this *ejido* was but a very small unit had allowed the majority in the *ejido* community to prevail.[7]

Three centers of authority and power at the state level had been involved: (1) the federal *delegado;* (2) the governor of the state; and (3) the committee of the *liga*. An alignment of the latter two had produced a just arrangement according to the relevant provisions of Mexican law found in the Agrarian Code. It is possible that a still different alignment would have served the Bello faction. Although the *ejidatarios* of Ignacio Romero Vargas succeeded in deposing their

[5] Interview with José del Razo Espinosa at his home in Romero Vargas.

[6] When I visited Ignacio Romero Vargas in order to interview various *ejidatarios,* the tractor was resting proudly in its shed at the head of the main street of the village.

[7] L. Vincent Padgett, *Popular Participation in the Mexican "One-Party" System* (unpublished dissertation, Northwestern University, 1955), pp. 207–216.

delinquent officials, this should not be interpreted to mean that like situations can always be resolved according to the rule of law and the wishes of the majority.

Major Problems in Support and Control: The CCI

In all of the conflict situations discussed above the key seems to be unfair or inept handling of assemblies. Assemblies either are not held at the appointed time, or people do not take enough interest to attend, or the assembly is in some way structured so as to bring about the representation only of those who are in agreement with the person who wishes to expand or maintain his power. Since, under Mexican norms, the office — or at least control of it — is sometimes regarded as the office-holder's private property, it thus becomes very difficult in spite of procedural guarantees to displace someone who has rigged an assembly, especially, as in the case at Ignacio Romero Vargas, if the paramount chief has had long tenure.

The rigging of local assemblies and the consequent perpetuation of *caciquismo* are irritants which, in addition to failures in policy formation at higher levels and faults in administration, bring about unrest in the countryside.

When López Mateos took office in 1958 it was clear that the CNC was not maintaining a desirable level of support among peasants, agricultural workers, and others within its organizational sphere. Many rural people were not sharing in the prosperity of industrialization. Moreover, the militancy and determination of the CNC as a channel for effectively presenting the demands of the peasants seemed to be more lacking every year. In these circumstances demonstrations in the rural areas and even violence on occasion were followed by efforts on the part of minor figures among agrarian leaders to create new types of organizations which would have the militant spirit necessary to articulate demands of the rural people. Giving added impetus to the efforts of these men were certain general conditions throughout the country and some instances of great local deprivation. Foremost among the general conditions were the widespread number of droughts and disastrous cloudbursts suffered in 1961 and 1962. Also, throughout most of the country credit for agriculturalists was hard to come by, and middlemen dealing in agricultural products seemed to be making whatever profit there was. Meanwhile, the government kept pointing out that the distribution of land was continuing and had been extended under López Mateos. Government spokesmen stressed the theme of the rosy prospect of the future, an overall agrarian reform dedicated to total renovation — social as well as economic — of the way of life in the rural districts. There occurred, however, very little basic improvement in the living conditions for people holding small *ejido* plots and small private parcels. With the pressure growing from existing conditions an effort was made to carry out reorganization within the CNC, but the initial result was simply to encourage rebels in the countryside to go ahead and try to form their own organizations.

The upshot of the course of events was a meeting held in Mexico City on January 6–8, 1963, to which twelve peasant organizations sent delegates for the purpose of forming a new peasant confederation. They called the organization they agreed to form the Independent Peasant Confederation (CCI). It was not easy to assess in the beginning the sources of strength or dynamics of these new organizations which had federated themselves as the CCI. Clearly, though, the CCI was not a movement of the right wing of the Mexican political spectrum. It was associated with the National Liberation Movement (MLN), and the name it used most frequently to legitimize its aims was the name of Lázaro Cárdenas.[8] Moreover, the dynamic for the formation of such groups seemed to stem largely not only from general conditions in the countryside but from the existence of some special conditions such as regional drought or, as in the case of Baja California, the issue of the salinization of the soil brought about by the Welton-Mohawk Irrigation Project.[9] The state organizations of the CCI were dubbed state agrarian leagues (LAE), in contrast to the state level CNC organizations called *ligas*.

The state agrarian league of the CCI in Baja California provides a useful illustration for examination of the history of the CCI. The state organization in Baja first began to form on September 5, 1958 when a group of dissident CNC local leaders asked for an opportunity to use the assembly hall of the *liga* of the CNC and was denied that opportunity. The group then went to the office of the CROC and held its assembly. A new organization was formed, though there was not much concern for a national organization as yet. It was not long before presidents of many *ejidos* in the Mexicali area began to join the new state agrarian league and leave the old CNC *liga*. Where presidents of *ejidos* did not join the new organization there were formed within the *ejidos* other groups which affiliated with it independently. Rallies held by the State Agrarian League of Baja California were extremely successful and often had as many as 20,000 peasants turn out in attendance. The bitterness over salinization of the soil from polluted

[8] *Comercio Exterior,* Banco Nacional de Comercio Exterior (Mexico, January, 1963).

[9] This federal project in the state of Arizona loaded the Colorado River with salt prior to its entry into Mexico for use as irrigation water in the cotton area around Mexicali in the state of Baja California Norte.

Colorado River water as well as countless other lesser irritants helped produce the overflowing crowds at the frequent rallies. The league never lost an opportunity to maintain that it was carrying on the true agrarian tradition in the Baja area, a tradition which had been abandoned by the CNC. Finally, in January, 1961, the league was large enough to purchase its own building and lot for 125,000 pesos. It continued to appeal to small farmers and *ejidatarios* through attacks on the role of middlemen in agricultural sales and credit practices of private lenders and of the Ejido Bank. Particularly, the Baja California state agrarian league squarely headed the attack and articulated the resentment in relation to the saline content of the Colorado River mentioned above [10]

Interestingly enough, Mexican officialdom tolerated the new agrarian leagues. Representatives of the government and, on occasion, a representative of the President of the Republic, came to the large gatherings to hear the criticisms which the members of the state agrarian leagues had to make of both federal and local government in connection with official handling of agrarian problems. Some government sources made the point publicly that the state agrarian leagues were doing the country a service in articulating discontent which had too long been suppressed or glossed over. The federal government's position clearly was that it could get along with the CCI in spite of long-standing ties with the CNC. By 1965, however, some of the local situations that had given rise to the formation of the state agrarian leagues and ultimately the formation of the CCI began to dwindle in significance. In addition, the overall political climate was less favorable for the CCI than it had been both on the domestic scene and in foreign affairs. In Baja California, for example, negotiations between the government of the United States and the government of Mexico regarding the salinity of water had progressed satisfactorily. Eventually, as the sources of complaint began to ease somewhat, enthusiasm for the new agrarian leagues also lessened.

It became clear that the state agrarian leagues in Baja California and elsewhere were having a hard time collecting funds from the peasantry. Without positive support from the government — something clearly different from mere toleration — it was doubtful that the CCI could continue to operate effectively. In the outlook for the future the CNC, slightly reformed, loomed a good deal larger than the CCI. The movement from below, while not devoid of a certain political capability, showed signs of weakening. Direction from above appeared likely to triumph once again in the form of a strengthened CNC.[11]

[10] *Brecha: México es primero,* Organo de la Liga Agraria Estatal de Baja California, CCI, No. 4 (Mexicali, B.C., January 27, 1964).

[11] *New York Times,* January 10, 1965.

✦ 5 ✦

The Middle Sector and Related Organizations

The National Confederation of Popular Organizations

The National Confederation of Popular Organizations (CNOP) was founded on February 7, 1943, in Guadalajara, Jalisco. Mexican politicians speak of it as the "organized middle class," or "the organized middle class on the march." Formation of the CNOP marked the beginning of ascending political fortunes and more effective representation in the political system for many interests that had before remained on the periphery of the Revolutionary Coalition. Unlike the peasant and labor organizations, the organized middle sector of the Revolutionary Coalition is not rooted in the traditional issues of "revolutionary" conflict. Nor are there provisions of the Constitution or of statutory and decree law which raise on high revolutionary goals defined in terms of the CNOP. In spite of these considerations, however, the superior education and technical training which characterizes members of the CNOP place it in a political position which overshadows the mass groups of peasants and labor with their long-established claims upon the Revolution.

The structure of the CNOP like that of the labor confederations and the CNC has been influenced by the federal arrangement of government. The rules of the confederation state that the "[CNOP] recognizes as the basis of its political and social organization the municipal union or group of individuals that are engaged in the same type of work within the limits of a *municipio*. . . ."[1] Five municipal unions form a municipal league (*liga municipal*). The municipal

[1] Confederación Nacional de Organizaciones Populares, *Bases constitutivas, declaración de principios y estatutos* (México, 1947), Art. 5, p. 17.

123

leagues are bound together in a federation at the state level with the committee of the state federation linking the municipal leagues with the central committee of the CNOP at the national level. The municipal union has an executive committee elected in an assembly of union members. The executive committee of the municipal league is elected for a three-year period in an assembly of representatives from the municipal unions.[2] The committees of the state federations are selected by representatives from the municipal leagues and serve three years. The central committee of the CNOP is named for a six-year term by the national assembly. Rules of organization have provided for councils — national, regional, and "technical." The councils have met annually and biennially during the periods between national and state assemblies. The role of the councils has been similar to like bodies in the confederations of organized labor, i.e., the councils have served to inform the federation and confederation executive committees of local problems on the one hand and on the other to increase the degree of cohesion among elements of leadership.

The CNOP and the many groupings over which it has come to preside have been set apart from agrarian and labor confederations in two principal ways. First, no special legislation or legal code, such as the labor code or the agrarian code, has formally institutionalized the links between the CNOP and the machinery of government. In other words, there has been nothing in Mexican legislation affecting the pattern of control in the organizational sphere of the CNOP in a manner analogous to the *Nuevo Código Agrario* with reference to the organization of the peasants or the *Ley Federal del Trabajo* on labor. In the second place, the organizations affiliated with the CNOP have been extraordinarily diverse in character. The statutes of the CNOP have indicated this heterogeneity:

> *La Confederación Nacional de Organizaciones Populares* is composed . . . of the following organized nuclei: (a) small agriculturists; (b) small industrialists; (c) small merchants; (d) artisans; (e) members of cooperative enterprises; (f) professional men and intellectuals; (h) youth groups; (i) women's clubs; (j) diverse groupings.[3]

The principal national groupings that have been gathered into the CNOP also mark the varied nature of its composition. Five groups stand out: (1) The National Cooperative Confederation; (2) The Federation of Unions of Workers in the Service of the State; (3) The National Union of Teachers; (4) The National Confederation of

---

[2] CNOP, *Bases Constitutivas,* Art. 58, p. 40.
[3] CNOP, *Bases Constitutivas,* Art. 2, pp. 15–16.

Small Agricultural Property; (5) The National Confederation of Indian Youth.

The central committee of the CNOP serves as the Secretariat of Popular Action for the Central Executive Committee of the PRI. The secretary general of the CNOP consistently has been elected the "popular" secretary for the party while operating from the headquarters of the CNOP rather than from the party's central offices. The organization of "popular" groupings has been more adaptable to such an arrangement because — unlike the situation in other organized sectors — all the important groupings have been brought under one roof.

The circle of groupings termed "popular" has been broadened greatly since the CNOP was organized in February, 1943. During the subsequent years the growth of organized support for the "revolutionary" regime was relatively much greater in the CNOP than in the agrarian or labor sectors. The prestige and influence of the CNOP in "revolutionary" circles has constantly expanded. Part of the reason for this success has been a high quality of leadership.[4] Confederation leaders have been tireless and competent organizers who have endeavored to bring into the fold any cluster of individuals having an interest in common. In addition, subsequent to 1947 two groups now forming the backbone of the confederation, the FSTSE, or bureaucrats' union, and the teachers' union left the CTM and moved in with the CNOP. Finally, support from President Miguel Alemán, 1946–1952, helped a great deal. By 1953 the CNOP claimed a total membership through its affiliated organizations of "approximately" one million persons. By the latter 1950's its membership in Congress and other elective posts roughly doubled the highest figure from any other organized sector of the Revolutionary Coalition. Moreover, if the CNOP is really the Mexican middle class "organized," as Mexicans commonly refer to it, then the division of electoral posts weighs correspondingly more against other sectors, since middle-class persons with middle-class values frequently become the elected representatives of labor and peasants.[5]

The CNOP was created for the purpose of bringing into the circle of "revolutionary" groupings people with interests not readily sus-

[4] Higher quality leadership in part refers to the fact that there is a higher percentage of persons holding professional degrees in the popular sector than in any other sector. Persons holding professional degrees not only have the great prestige which such degrees are assigned in Mexico but also emerge from the universities with political contacts already well developed due to the great emphasis on political action in Latin American universities — a matter in which Mexico is no exception.

[5] Robert E. Scott, *Mexican Government in Transition* (Urbana, Ill., 1959), pp. 89–90.

ceptible of inclusion within the organizational pattern of the CNC and the labor confederations. As indicated above in practice this has meant great diversity in composition. The professional man, the wealthy businessman, the small shopkeeper, the artisan, and the very poor day laborer have all been welcomed into the fold by the CNOP leaders.[6] In order to accommodate such contrasting groups and keep them as enthusiastic supporters of the Revolutionary Coalition, the CNOP has had to render its membership tangible benefits great in variety and quantity.

The popular sector is described by leaders as "eminently political" in its orientation. A report by one secretary general offered some concrete examples of how the popular sector leaders carry on their "eminently political" activity, i.e., how large groups of people, extremely heterogeneous in their cultural background and interests, have been drawn into the CNOP constituting a popular base of support from which to launch claims for more and more public electoral offices:

> We petitioned and [the governor] granted us a special audience Wednesday of every week. In this *audiencia* the popular groups from all over the state advised by the federation [*de Organizaciones Populares del Estado de Veracruz*] presented fully their petitions and problems to the governor. To [the governor's] consideration have been submitted 751 memorandums requesting among other things: teachers for schools, lands for the creation of *colonias urbanas* and sports [or recreation] fields, scholarships for poor students, pensioning off of public employees, introduction of potable drinking water, sanitation works, cooperation for festival ceremonies of a cultural-civic nature, etc.
>
> We recognize that thanks to the generosity of [the] governor . . . and his closest co-workers . . . the majority of the petitions were favorably received. With the aid of [these officials] and through the efforts of our federation, four hundred humble families of the city of Veracruz, grouped in the *colonia,* Ing. Miguel Angel de Quevedo, were favored in their just desire to construct their own homes because we arranged an agreement . . . [by which] they could acquire the necessary lots at the very low price of 1.35 pesos per meter . . . [and the families] were given up to twelve months with the easiest possible installments in order to make the corresponding payment.[7]

[6] The ensuing discussion applies only indirectly — if at all — insofar as two of the important affiliated groupings of the CNOP are concerned. The National Teachers' Union and the Federation of Workers in the Service of the State have certain legally formalized connections with government not common to other groupings affiliated with the confederation.

[7] In an interview with the secretary general of the CNOP of Veracruz the author was given other illustrations of the eminently political activity.

Generally speaking, the petition mentioned in this quotation is representative of the demands made by CNOP leaders throughout the country on the part of their members. In addition, however, it is necessary to keep in mind that the CNOP is dominated by professional people who are often also propertied people. Thus, the CNOP tends to stand against any raise in property and income taxes. It also promotes the cause of the rural property owner in relation to demands for expropriation on the part of landless peasants, and it stands for increased emphasis upon urban improvements and investments, and investment in the industrialization process as opposed to larger allotments of government money for credit to those on the *ejidos*.

A series of informal understandings with persons in government have been necessary in order to secure services and benefits expected by the ordinary members in return for dues paid and effort expended in mass demonstrations for public functions. It has been expected that rewards be not only psychic but material as well, and in this latter connection the benefits and services have been indispensable. Leaders unable to produce have been left without a following, for persons have had nothing to lose in dropping from the roll of a CNOP grouping incapable of producing advantages to offset the obligations of membership. In this respect the CNOP member has been in a considerably different situation from the peasant of the *ejido* community or even the member of a labor union; for, in the case either of peasant or worker, membership in the *ejido* or the union has been formalized in public law in contrast to the non-formal character of membership in the CNOP.

For the above reasons the interpersonal relationships of confederation leaders and government officials have been — if possible — even more crucial for the CNOP than for the peasant and labor confederations. In this connection the gradual disappearance of the generals and pistol-carrying school of old-time "revolutionaries" and their replacement in public office by men with considerable academic preparation has been central to the expansion of the influence of the CNOP, for those who have headed the confederation have been men of professional middle-class background better fitted to achieve firm friendships with the new style, university-trained "revolutionary" than the old rough and tumble variety.

Confederation leaders push harder than do most leaders in other organized social segments in order to maintain a continued drive toward consolidation and expansion of the extensive gains that have been achieved. Chiefs of the CNOP have assumed that they cannot rest assured of the permanence of their work until stabilization of leader-rank and file relationships on the one hand and of leader-public official relationships on the other hand has been attained. Until such time as this goal may be reached the men who hold positions of responsibility in the CNOP organization will probably continue to operate at a furious pace.[8] The rewards of success have been obvious. Nearly all persons of ministerial rank claim political connections with the CNOP and so do the majority of members of the Chamber of Deputies and the Senate. These are the people who have greatest access to the President and who most clearly influence the policy of the Mexican government today.

In summary, CNOP leaders have had to work at politics around the clock. Failure to do so has meant inability to produce expected benefits for the members. Lacking in this connection, a "leader" has found himself in the embarrassing circumstance of being a leader without followers — a drum major without a band. Such persons will be recognized neither as politicians nor as leaders. Long hours and great activity form the basis for the continued vitality of the CNOP.

The Federation of Civil Servants' Unions

The single most powerful organization within the CNOP is the Federation of Unions of Workers in the Service of the State (FSTSE). The FSTSE developed from an earlier organization, the FNTE (National Federation of Workers of the State) which was one of the founding organizations of the Confederation of Workers of Mexico (CTM) in 1936. President Cárdenas later obtained passage of a law entitled Statute of the Workers in the Service of the State which spelled out the legal position of the organized bureaucracy and enabled bureaucrats to reform their union and make it into the present day FSTSE with autonomous status. Later, during the government of Miguel Alemán the FSTSE affiliated with the CNOP.

The FSTSE encompasses thirty-one unions throughout the major departments of the executive, legislative, and judicial branches of government as well as governments of the territories, the federal tourism department, and the national university (UNAM). In all, the persons affiliated with the FSTSE through its member unions number approximately 350,000. Many benefits to the membership are made available through the Institute of Security and Social Services for Workers in the Service of the State (ISSSTSE). The ISSSTSE, with over one billion pesos in reserves, provides an extensive program of medical, hospitalization, and pharmaceutical aid as well as pension plans, numerous low-rental housing projects, low-cost housing for

---

[8] CNOP headquarters begins to hum about 11:00 A.M., and is the scene of intense activity until after midnight. Other confederations as a rule close up shop about 8:00 P.M.

purchase and short-term loan arrangements to free members from usurious interest rates.

The FSTSE has a loyal, well-disciplined, and well-informed membership. The enthusiasm of the group, which is clearly manifest in the large numbers that turn out for political demonstrations, stems in part from the relatively well-developed political consciousness of the people involved and also from extensive benefits received through the programs of the FSTSE in conjunction with the ISSSTSE. The result of loyalty based upon benefits received is cohesion and activism in the rank and file which makes the leaders' pronouncements authoritative in the CNOP or any other group or alliance with which the FSTSE has close ties.[9] Bureaucrat leaders speak for the best organized group in the popular sector which, as indicated above, has become the most influential of the sectors. Bureaucrat leaders often hold top positions in the legislature as in the case of Sánchez Mireles and others less well known. When there is a division of opinion in the popular sector these are the deciding voices. It is their organizational strength which makes the case.

Organized Groups in Industry and Commerce

Two groups which do not fall within the organized sectors of the Revolutionary Coalition but which do have extensive influence with the governments selected by the coalition are the Confederation of Chambers of Industry of Mexico (CONCAMIN) and the Confederation of National Chambers of Commerce (CONCANACO). Although not within the organizational framework of the party nor formally affiliated with it, these groups do have a semi-official status in that their membership and organization are provided for in public law.[10] All but the very smallest commercial and manufacturing enterprises are legally required to affiliate with some member chamber of one of the parent organizations.

The idea of grouping commercial and industrial enterprises into chambers which in turn could be confederated with a national directive committee to speak for them stems from early Mexican experience when individual businessmen used to contribute to the political efforts of some individuals in the hope that there would be rewards commensurate with the contribution should the office seeker succeed in climbing to the position he wanted. The constant pressure exerted

---

[9] Romulo Sánchez Mireles, El movimiento burocrático," in *México: Cincuenta años de revolución* (Mexico, 1960), II, pp. 289–305.

[10] The Minister of Industry and Commerce has supervisory capacity over these organizations. See William P. Glade, Jr. and Charles W. Anderson, *The Political Economy of Mexico* (Madison, Wis., 1963), p. 94.

upon official incumbents by persons who felt their contributions afforded them the right to seek favors led eventually to the adoption of the idea of chambers (*cámaras*). Under such an arrangement it was possible to classify enterprises under public law so that businesses of a like nature could be grouped into one overall classification with an executive committee to act as the sole bargaining agent for that classification of enterprises. Membership was made compulsory, and it became possible for government ministries to deal with types or categories of business rather than with individual businessmen. In this way the government officials were afforded the means of learning the needs and demands of specific types of business before announcing legislative proposals. Though by no means foolproof, this arrangement has prevented much embarrassment and disappointment on both sides, as each *cámara* decides upon specific policy demands for its members.

Frequently demands are phrased in the form of proposed laws in anticipation of legislative initiative from the government. Most *cámaras* or groups keep a staff of specialized lawyers to draft legal proposals — either as initiatives or as counterproposals to government initiatives. The strategy, of course, is to show that the proposal of the *cámara* or the confederation is drawn to serve the general interests of the Mexican public. Particularistic factors enter into arguments, but the argument for the general interest, the argument in universalistic terms, must also be made.

The government more and more finds it useful to consult with the different *cámaras* in relation to official decision-making. These consultations have become more or less institutionalized. Specific economic interests are discussed in relation to questions involving many areas of industry or many areas of commerce. In addition to spokesmen for the CONCAMIN or CONCANACO, representatives of the individual *cámaras* are also invited to participate. The model principle that government will deal with the *cámara* or the confederation of *cámaras* instead of individual businessmen or firms tends to be the rule, but it is also true that there are occasions on which firms or businesses ask for special privileges for themselves and not for their business category in spite of the institutionalized norm against this practice. Negotiations conducted on the basis of the relations between a government official or agency and an individual business or entrepreneur, however, have tended to diminish, while negotiations conducted on the basis of the collective *cámara* have become the general pattern.[11]

The CONCAMIN and the CONCANACO have become increasingly important in Mexico since 1950. Of particular significance also is an

[11] Frank R. Brandenburg, *Mexico: An Experiment in One-Party Democracy* (unpublished dissertation, University of Pennsylvania, 1955), p. 300.

outstanding sector of the CONCAMIN called the National Chamber of Manufacturing Industries (CNIT). The CONCAMIN and the CNIT are clearly not the same. The CONCAMIN includes the CNIT, but the CNIT has a somewhat different orientation from the CONCAMIN. The CNIT has been the spokesman for Mexican industrialists and particularly the instrument of a new group of industrialists that arose in the latter 1930's and early 1940's. This new group, the CNIT, was not formed until April, 1942.[12] In terms of its name one would think that the CNIT would include all manufacturing firms. Actually, however, it has been limited because some of the most important manufacturing industries that have been longer on the Mexican scene have their own associations or *cámaras;* this would be true in textiles, shoes, paper, and soap. The CNIT, however, from the beginning included the basic iron and steel, beer, tobacco, food processing, and cement industries. Though important in the Mexican economy as a whole, these were certainly only a small fraction of the overall membership of the CNIT and even a smaller fraction of the general membership of the CONCAMIN.

Most of the firms belonging to the CNIT began as new and rather small firms in the latter 1930's or early 1940's. Often firms that occupied prominent places on the Mexican manufacturing scene in the 1920's and early 1930's did not join the CNIT. The newer and smaller firms first began to appreciate the importance of their numerical advantage within the CNIT in the mid-1940's and eventually were able to make the CNIT primarily an organization for their own use, their own vehicle.

As indicated above, the new group that succeeded in getting control of the CNIT and, to a large extent of the CONCAMIN, was composed largely of owners of small manufacturing plants. These came into being during the Second World War when there was a demand for articles no longer available from foreign sources. One of the important characteristics of the group was that they tended to use Mexican capital, something which set them apart in outlook from some new industries on the Mexican scene in which American capital was participating. This new group was unable to develop good relations with the principal private financial institutions of Mexico and therefore found it expedient to use the government as a major source for necessary capital. Still another characteristic of the new group was their determination to prevent competition between their products and those of the advanced industrialized nations.

The new group was determined to obtain maximum protection for all

[12] For a more complete description see Sanford A. Mosk, *Industrial Revolution in Mexico* (Berkeley, Calif., 1950), pp. 21–52.

industries and this has continued to be its approach as it has sought to line up support of all Mexican industrialists for a general program of protection. The new group was successful in obtaining its objectives of protective tariffs and government investment funds because it was vigorous and because it had aggressive leadership. Although the leaders were not many in number they were extremely articulate. They were prolific pamphleteers, and they mastered the art of propaganda. Their conclusions were simple categorical statements, frequently repeated. They were very successful in getting a favorable press in Mexico.[13]

For a long time after the new group appeared on the scene, older industrialists in Mexico, leading bankers, and merchants of particular importance in the CONCANACO (Confederation of National Chambers of Commerce) continued to do business in a common atmosphere of cordial relations. These elements reacted negatively to the approach of the new group as it sought new sources of capital from government and protection for infant industries, but the older groups simply did not have as effective a vehicle for propagating their views as was the CNIT for the new group.

CONCANACO became perhaps the most effective spokesman against the CNIT and to some extent against the CONCAMIN (Confederation of National Chambers of Industry of Mexico). The ties between the bankers, the large merchants and the old industrialists continued to be manifest in the pronouncements of CONCANACO for some time,[14] but the situation began to change and the opposition became more moderate about the middle of the 1950's.

One of the important features of the new group-CNIT approach has been the view which it has taken toward organized labor. Its tone has been conciliatory, and it has shown on the whole a willingness to negotiate grievances. Above all there has been an open recognition that labor is bound to have and should have a stake in industrializing Mexico.

Also significant has been the comparative attitude of the new group in the relationship between industry and government. The new group and government have worked together to implement a program of industrialization for Mexico, something that has involved more than

---

[13] Sanford Mosk, pp. 21–22.

[14] The CONCANACO, as indicated above, stands for the Confederation of National Chambers of Commerce. Membership is organized in locals based upon geographic location. The membership in the CONCAMIN, on the other hand, is based upon types of industrial activity. ". . . CONCANACO seemed to [be] less concerned with import restrictions and more concerned with governmental interference in domestic markets." Raymond Vernon, *The Dilemma of Mexico's Development* (Cambridge, Mass., 1963), p. 166.

just producing some general plan for industrialization. The new group early had in mind a process of continuous and intimate contact between various government agencies on the one hand and industrial groups on the other. The new group saw the various *cámaras* of industry — particularly the CNIT and the CONCAMIN — as the means for achieving such close collaboration.

In the large and complex system of Mexican trade associations the pronouncements of the leadership do not always reflect the temper of the businessmen members. Frequently an association leadership will take an extreme position beyond any that the ordinary member would be willing to support in order to gain concessions from the government.[15] It is also true that these trade associations are sometimes taken over by a few energetic and extreme men who are able to dominate the membership. In some cases an association has a situation of such great internal conflict that there is no possibility of an adequate statement of the association's interests. The general style does not differ greatly from that of any relatively free country, but the official tie with government probably limits and channels the actions taken while at the same time allowing considerable freedom of choice.

There has been a marked shift in the ideological position of Mexican businessmen since the early 1940's. At that time CONCANACO took the position that any government interference in the activities of private concerns could only be regarded as obstructive and negative. While the CONCANACO maintained its position in favor of foreign capital and relatively free trade the CNIT was able to make its weight felt in the circles of the CONCAMIN. The CONCAMIN tended to concentrate its efforts upon getting more protection against imports as well as government credits needed by manufacturers. However, while the CONCAMIN wanted government help, it did not want government in the field of direct production. The CONCAMIN felt that the job of industrializing the country should be basically for private enterprise but that the state had an obligation to interfere or intervene when requested by the *cámaras* or even individual industrialists in order to give protection and some types of assistance. Basically the emphasis upon protection for industry, upon tax exemptions for new types of products, and upon export subsidies for manufacturers increased.

The CNIT, with its leadership from the new group of industrialists, went beyond the position which it could bring the CONCAMIN to take and endorsed an accelerated land reform, more extensive social security, and stronger unions — even direct government participation in some industries. However, the CNIT position, though advanced, did

15 Vernon, p. 163.

not until recently extend to support an overall "revolutionary" ideology. There was little evidence of recognition of the great importance of the agricultural masses and organized labor as basic to the Mexican economy in their role as consumers.

Since the mid-1950's the lines between CONCANACO and CONCAMIN have grown more obscure, and the official pronouncements of both have more closely approximated statements of the CNIT. Thus, the CONCANACO leadership has begun to speak to the members about sharing their time and resources to raise the standard of living of the masses — the importance of taking an active part in the general improvement needs of the society. Leaders of the CONCAMIN have apparently come to the conclusion that there is no longer any debating the right of government to intervene in economic affairs, and they take the position that the major objective of private enterprise should be the elevation of living standards for the masses. Moreover, CONCANACO, an organization that once defended foreign investment in Mexico, has begun to show more and more uneasiness about direct foreign investment in commercial activities, though it has not yet come to the point of criticizing foreign investment in industrial projects.

In other words, in the 1960's it has become difficult to distinguish the positions of CONCANACO and CONCAMIN one from the other. Along with the CNIT, they argue that private foreign investment should be based upon considerations of Mexican development, and that private foreign investment has to be controlled by Mexicans and not from abroad. Statements by CONCANACO and CONCAMIN on private foreign investment are milder than those of leadership of the CNIT, but there are no basic differences, and the result of this closing of ranks is clear in Mexican government policy with regard to protection for domestic industries, controls on private foreign investment, and nationalization of such great enterprises as the electrical industry.

In the author's opinion the CNOP, its related organization the FSTSE, the CNIT, the CONCAMIN, and the CONCANACO are all part of a pattern, politically speaking, though their relationship may not be clear at first glance. They represent widely varied sectors of Mexican society, but essentially they all have an outlook which is conservative within the framework of "revolutionary" values, i.e., within the framework of the regime. In Mexico, conservative bias has meant concern for urban problems, urban development, industrialization, and preferred positions for professional people and government employees, with the result that the importance of the rural problem is reduced in the eyes of Mexican policy-makers. The members of these organizations are the people who benefit most from the overall policy of industrialization that became predominant at least as early as the administration of Miguel Alemán. They are the least likely to support programs designed to bring backward rural areas quickly into harmony with the advances of modernization.

6

The Presidency

Presidential Nominations and Elections

Nominations and elections need to be viewed in the perspective of one political party's dominant position. Both the part the elections play and the way they are carried out differ markedly from two-party or multi-party systems. Rather than having an aggregating function involving interplay between two parties or among several parties, the interplay of interests and the accommodation of competing demands that might normally mark the campaigning of candidates representing various parties takes place largely within the Revolutionary Coalition, the institutional manifestation and electoral symbol of which is the Institutional Revolutionary Party (PRI). The focus within the Revolutionary Coalition is upon nominations for posts in the executive, with the competition somewhat less keen for legislative positions.

The many campaign trips to all corners of the country made by the president-designate — the presidential candidate of the official party — are in large part a device for reaching people to create a favorable impression that will increase support for the regime. Such journeys also permit the candidate to study the most pressing problems and demands in all sections of the Republic. On these trips conferences of national leaders, community leaders, businessmen, politicians, and technicians are held in the principal cities and even in some of the outlying towns to discuss the problems of a given region. The conference device probably does a great deal, not only to improve the candidate's knowledge of a given regional situation, but also to broaden his understanding of the personalities involved in the various regions and localities of the country. In addition there is an opportunity to evaluate the capabilities of the staff chosen to arrange the meetings.

The effort to reach the Mexican people at campaign time finds no village left unvisited.[1] Though the candidate himself cannot possibly visit every population nucleus in Mexico, his representatives go out to all villages. The campaign teams bear posters with the candidate's picture and carry audio-visual equipment to show the candidate and project excerpts from his campaign speeches. An effort is made to bring the personality of the candidate home to Mexicans everywhere so that support will be strengthened as people are given the sense of "knowing" their next President. At election time the newspapers carry many accounts of these election teams of young PRI supporters barnstorming in the remote villages of Mexico. Such efforts were first made during the time of Lázaro Cárdenas and have continued. They are designed to bridge the gap between the still extensive sections of isolated rural Mexico and those other parts of Mexico now linked with the communications and transportation networks. The problem of the urban politician in his attempt to carry on a dialogue with rural people is familiar to every student of developing countries. The Mexicans make an outstanding effort to solve this problem.

The campaign trips also afford the president-designate an opportunity to test the sentiment throughout the country, and change the emphasis on one or another program in accord with that sentiment. Thus, if the cost of modernization seems to weigh too heavily on one socio-economic group, causing disaffection in the membership, the candidate, sensing this discontent, can shift his stance on relevant issues. For example, the problem may well be redress of the balance between benefits for countryside over against cities, emphasizing the modernization of the countryside as well as the industrialization of the cities. The point here is not so much that the president-designate shifts positions from one section of the country to another, a tactic used in many countries; it is rather that the president-designate attempts to promote a dialogue with influential persons in all sections to evaluate the political feasibility of his policy line. Since radio and television are declared by law to be non-political these changes in line and in emphasis are more easily carried out.

The person who is considered available (*presidenciable*) usually has been a cabinet officer. Cárdenas and Ávila Camacho were respectively Minister of War and Minister of Navy before their nominations. Miguel Alemán, Adolfo Ruiz Cortines, and Díaz Ordaz were Ministers of Interior (*Gobernación*). López Mateos was Minister of Labor.

---

[1] "The name, Díaz Ordaz, and his austere, strongly Indian face are today familiar in the most remote reaches of the country." Martin C. Needler, "Changing the Guard in Mexico," *Current History*, 48 (January, 1965), p. 29.

From these cases it is clear that the constitutional provision commanding a cabinet officer to separate himself from office six months ahead of the election date does not restrict presidential aspirations of cabinet officials in any significant way.

The important consideration for a candidate is the degree of his acceptability to the presidential incumbent. Acceptability operates both at the level of consideration of personal relations and on the level of political convictions of the potential candidate, i.e., his probable choice of policy alternatives. Physical appearance and health make a difference; neither should be clearly negative. A man must have a reputation for an energetic approach to his tasks. It is helpful if the aspirant's wife has a moderate interest in public affairs. It is definitely a drawback to have a wife who is foreign born, particularly if the country happened to be the United States. Ezequiel Padilla, losing presidential candidate in 1946, is an example in this latter connection. No presidential nominee in the past two decades or more has leaned strongly toward or away from religion. Most presidents have come from a lower middle-class background. In such circumstances there is not too much wealth nor too little to provide some education, and from such a social stratum can come a man who has some feeling for the masses as well as some understanding of the expectations of the affluent.

Presidents tend to be chosen from large and economically prosperous states. Since the time of Lázaro Cárdenas these states have been on or near the central *mesa* of Mexico. Another consideration is training in practical politics and government. Alemán and López Mateos were campaign managers for their predecessors. Since the time of Cárdenas, presidents have always had experience as governors or senators, although not immediately before nomination. Successful candidates for the Revolutionary Coalition's nomination have always served as head of some ministry.

It is important that the successful candidate for the nomination be well known nationally and acceptable to all of the major groups which in one respect or another have a voice in the highest circle of decision-makers around the incumbent president. A successful player in this most strenuous of all Mexican political contests must not be too closely identified with any single major interest association and must avoid extremes. It pays to be moderate enough so that neither of the major wings of the party will oppose the nomination on the grounds of too close alignment with the other wing.[2] The trend since 1946 has run ever more strongly against pre-candidates who have worn the

[2] See Frank Brandenburg on wings of the party. Frank Brandenburg, *The Making of Modern Mexico* (Englewood Cliffs, N.J., 1964), pp. 131–136.

general's uniform. Civilian Presidents for the time being, at least, have become the vogue in Mexican politics.

The President of Mexico is the dominant factor in the selection of a man to succeed himself. Even though he must contend with some of the expectations of the two wings of the Revolutionary Coalition as well as many conflicting wishes and demands from diverse interest groups, the final decision as to the most available man must be made by the incumbent chief executive. Over the years the decision-making process of which the presidency is the core has compiled a generally successful record in picking men of competence, energy, and political ability as occupants of the presidential office.

One of the most difficult jobs facing the president-designate is the responsibility of making sure that there are people in the Congress on whom he can rely. Nominations to the Congress are sought by many individuals, and there are not nearly enough positions to go around. There is added influence, access to the President, prestige, and some income connected with these positions, and they need to be parceled out carefully as coveted prizes. These choices are made more often by the president-designate, the nominee of the official party, than by the incumbent. There are at least three types of persons from whom the president-designate takes suggestions for nominations to the Congress. The first type are those who form the inner circle around his own person; the second are the leaders of the major interest groupings; and the third is made up of the governors of the states. When choice of a pre-candidate involves a conflict, the ability of the president-designate to avoid offending members of these three groups provides a major pre-election test of political capacity.

Internal Rivalries

The most important political and constitutional office is that of the President of the Republic; consequently the major scramble for nomination to office within the Revolutionary Coalition centers around the presidency. The organizations of the PRI's three sectors as well as many non-sector organizations related in some way to the party become involved in rivalries which reach the highest peak of intensity. Because rivalries are so intense, the man in the presidency, as election time rolls around, usually seeks to put off the time when actual electioneering (*futurismo*) by presidential hopefuls in the cabinet begins. Once electioneering does begin, the incumbent seeks to postpone the announcement of the selection of a president-designate, since everyone will turn to that man in an effort to win his favor. The difficulty for the President is that the announcement of his successor encourages men in politics to neglect their immediate administrative responsibilities to seek as a primary goal the establishment of a close relationship with the future President. Thus the President seeks to avoid giving the final nod of approval necessary for the naming of his successor until the last possible moment.[3]

The role of the presidential incumbent during the pre-nomination period is difficult. There is a pressing necessity to balance achievements of his administration against the difficulties created by the intra-family struggle for the presidential nomination. Each person who fancies himself a candidate for the nomination puts in action a whispering campaign calculated to undermine his closest competitors. Such rumor-mongering does not have the best effect on public regard for the incumbent President's administration since many of the unfavorable rumors run against its members. Frequently, the rumors also question the economic condition of the country in regard to its balance of payments, store of foreign currency, and other vital matters.

In the campaign for the presidential nomination as Revolutionary Coalition candidate, pre-candidates seek to establish the impression of great popular support by stimulating and welcoming the formation of supporting organizations and committees. Such groups seldom explicitly reveal their true objectives. It is considered better strategy to campaign in terms of support for patriotic causes, or, on occasion, economic interests. In addition, there are genuinely independent interest organizations which spring up in an effort to make use of the pre-nomination confusion to achieve their own goals.

A high point in the pre-nomination activity occurs on the occasion of the President's State of the Union message on September 1 of the year preceding the general election. All categories of politicians — governors, senators, deputies, commanders of military zones, regionally prominent leaders — come to Mexico City ostensibly to hear the President; they are, however, more concerned in looking up their best sources of information in order to find out who is on the inside track for the presidential candidacy. Each politician seeks to visit as many as possible of the potential winners in the nomination race. Government offices, the central offices of the PRI, favorite restaurants, and hotel lobbies hum busily reflecting the stepped-up interaction in the Revolutionary Coalition.

After the State of the Union message it becomes more difficult than ever for the President to avoid the final act of approving a successor. By late fall of the year prior to the general election businesses begin to slow down, and soon interest is at a peak as ordinary folk manifest their excitement through a growing willingness to place bets concerning

[3] Robert E. Scott, *Mexican Government in Transition* (Urbana, Ill., 1959), pp. 197–199.

the outcome of the nomination race.[4] The necessity of bringing the successor into the open is increased because of the threat of economic slowdown as businessmen delay decisions on inventory and investment. In the most recent decision, López Mateos was able to withstand the pressure only two months following his State of the Union message. The first declaration of a major interest organization in favor of Díaz Ordaz came from the CTM federation of the state of Nuevo León on November 1, 1963. By November 3 the opening salvo had become a barrage of high-powered endorsements from the labor sector, and the issue was no longer in doubt.[5]

With the exception of the PAN, the party which tries harder than any other to give the PRI competition, other parties strangely enough seem to interest themselves in jockeying for position from which

[4] Brandenburg has provided a more detailed description of the decision-making process involved in the presidential succession than can be found elsewhere. There are at least nine discernible stages in the process. The first three encompass the designation of a president-elect and the ensuing scramble to climb on his bandwagon. The process is initiated by inquiries from the presidential incumbent as to the relative acceptability of several individuals, usually cabinet ministers. The President consults the few individuals who advise him most closely on policy and a slightly wider circle including cabinet officers, leaders of major interest groups in the Revolutionary Coalition and spokesmen of powerful economic interests outside the revolutionary circle.

When a consensus has been reached, and the time appears propitious to the presidential incumbent, the Minister of Interior (*Gobernación*) is informed of the choice, if he has not been included in the decision-making circle, and the president of the PRI is also told at this point. The public announcement comes from one of the major interest groups of the Revolutionary Coalition. The privilege of making the announcement is awarded by the president-designate himself (*el verdadero tapado*).

The announcement of the choice is the second stage of the process which is followed immediately by a third stage (*irse a la cargada*) in which every power seeker and politically articulate person affiliated with the Revolutionary Coalition strives to outdo the others in praising the future President. Shortly, thereafter a fourth step provides the official nomination of the new man at a giant rally of the PRI in Mexico City. After many speeches, the one and only real candidate is accepted unanimously by the nominating convention.

The fifth, sixth, and seventh stages are respectively the campaign, which serves many purposes other than vote getting, the general election, which the PRI candidate always wins by a wide margin, and official acceptance of the vote which is conducted through formal agencies dominated by the Revolutionary Coalition. Eighth and ninth steps include the choosing of a new presidential administrative team for the future President with all the patronage belonging to each office and the final step of weighing carefully the timing for the announcement of these appointments in order to obtain the best political effect. Brandenburg, pp. 145–150.

[5] Florencio Zamarripa M., *Díaz Ordaz: Ideología y perfil de un revolucionario* (Mexico, 1964), pp. 14–15.

to attempt to influence the choice of the PRI nominee. Parties such as the PPS and the very small PARM attempt to achieve specific goals through supporting the pre-candidate of the Revolutionary Coalition whose views come closest to that of the small party involved. This kind of activity appears to be regarded by the Revolutionary Coalition and the officials of the PRI as perfectly compatible with the interests of the dominant party, since the minor parties, in working to affect the nomination, seldom exert much influence but do derive the psychological benefits of participation in the system.

Since 1952 attention among top decision-makers has focused primarily upon nominating a man capable of balancing the right and left wings of the Revolutionary Coalition, the Alemanistas and the Cardenistas. In addition to the general division between Right and Left there are also many interest groups with specific narrower goals which must be considered and to some extent satisfied. The problem is to select the candidate who will be, as President, moderate and flexible enough to adjust his program to the nation's major needs while at the same time accommodating the most important conflicts between Left and Right and satisfying the outstanding demands of the most significant interest groups. The success of the revolutionary tradition in assimilating a wide variety of interests and many shades of political opinion has now raised the problem of acquiring a skilled compromiser to lead the nation.

The diverse wings of the Revolutionary Coalition are strong, in part because each represents a main current in the stream of revolutionary thought. The Cardenistas favor benefits for small farmers and other mass interests, to be realized by socialistic means if necessary. For the Alemanistas, the push for industrialization is most important, with a strong emphasis upon private ownership mixed with government assistance. The whole approach of the Alemanistas to Mexico's problems is somewhat reminiscent of the Calles formula of an earlier day. However, neither the Alemanistas nor the Cardenistas has an ideological position so clearly defined that it excludes the other group. Furthermore, the lines between the two are often blurred because of personal ties which have little to do with the socio-political goals. Neither wing far outweighs the other, for the Cardenistas, while they have a larger popular membership, are not so well organized as the Alemanistas nor as well financed. One thing is certain, the existence of the two conflicting interpretations of revolutionary goals accompanied by major coalitions on Right and Left have made it necessary as well as feasible for Presidents to assume a middle-of-the-road position in order to maintain the broader coalition which encompasses the two wings.

One reason that a President can take a middle position with regard to the two wings of the revolutionary group is that even for people on the extremes there exists consensus with regard to a core of revolutionary values. There is the common memory of participation in a common movement and the common interest in a better Mexico to be developed on the basis of a tradition encompassing positions both of Right and Left. Particularly, there is a recognition of the value of compromise in order to keep the Revolutionary Coalition intact. Willingness to give way on certain points in order to gain others is a valued characteristic. It is this attitude toward accommodation, the high value placed upon conciliation rather than force, which makes it possible for a Right, a Left, and a Center to coalesce in support of a hierarchical control structure.

The President's Role

Institutionalization

The problem of transferring power from one leader to another in Mexico's highly charismatic pattern appears to have been relatively well worked out by changing the outward symbols of charisma from the individual leader to the office he holds. It is the office which commands the respect, clothes the leader with dignity, and endows him with charismatic qualities. Thus over the years there has evolved a situation which is less personal and more mechanical and procedural, a fortunate development in this case. Of course, some personal identification carries over for some Mexicans, but the difference is that the recipient of such loyalty tends to be himself a product of the system rather than its major originator and supporter. In this arrangement a new person takes office every six years. He is clothed with viceregal dignity and power, and at the end of his term is replaced by another individual who by reason of the office receives the same attributes. Thus are the powers of the office institutionalized.

The President is chief of government and nearly always head of the Revolutionary Coalition. In these roles recent Presidents have been highly successful in balancing competing interests in a situation featuring the rapid proliferation of organized groups. This success would not have been possible had the President alone had to gather the information and make the decisions necessary to the balancing process. Fortunately for Mexico and for the stability of the system, Presidents have seen the necessity of increasing staff and delegating responsibility, a development which has culminated in the establishment of an Office of the Presidency to provide the staff assistance necessary to effective action in all areas of political activity. The situation today presents a marked contrast to the lack of administrative and political talent backing up the presidency in the 1920's and early 1930's.

The institutionalization of the presidency has created a situation in which the office automatically provides great authority and power while at the same time putting a premium upon a degree of moderation and mildness in the political style of the President in order to balance successfully contending pressures. The office itself, however, gives its holder such strength that even a relatively mild man seems to be able to stand independently of his predecessor, even a dynamic predecessor. The normal condition seems to have become one of an ex-President's leaving his successor alone to carry out the duties of his office as best he is able, and in support of this rule there is the understanding that no ex-President is to be punished or harried. Whatever differences may exist between the outgoing President and his successor are worked out privately, a fact which in turn tends to legitimize the presidency in the eyes of Mexican citizens.

The presidential incumbent of today with an institutionalized office to clothe him with charisma does not need in himself the dynamic characteristics necessary a few decades ago. Some of the men, lacking such characteristics, were run by others from behind the scenes. This is not the case today. Mexican Presidents for some time now have demonstrated their own independence while at the same time they have been different personally from the old *caudillo* type. The presidential political style of recent years has been characterized by a bland approach which seems useful in maintaining equilibrium among many diverse interests within the Revolutionary Coalition.

The comparison of the type of politician who held the presidency in earlier decades with Presidents of more recent times is striking. There have been thirteen Presidents since 1920 — five of whom were generals, two leaders of armed forces without a corresponding military rank, and six civilians — but four of those six civilians have held office consecutively in most recent times. When Miguel Alemán left office in 1952 he was the first civilian executive to have completed a full presidential term since Benito Juárez. Since Alemán, Ruiz Cortines, López Mateos, and now Díaz Ordaz (all civilians like Alemán) have used the political and constitutional powers at their disposal to balance contending interests, provide greater stability, and to achieve a higher level of productivity for the nation than strong-man Presidents such as Obregón, Calles, and Cárdenas could do under the conditions existing at the time of their leadership.[6]

[6] "In sum, the presidential function does not now make the same demands upon personalistic leadership to evoke singular and immediate emotional response by followers in the heat of battle that it once did." Robert E. Scott, *Mexican Government in Transition* (Urbana, Ill., 1959), p. 148.

The civilian Presidents since 1946 have had a number of characteristics in common, but outstanding among these is the determination to deal with serious trouble before it can get out of hand. Thus, in Alemán's case a major oil refinery strike tested his will, and the strike was successfully broken, demonstrating the capacity of the man who governed. Ruiz Cortines, when he first took over, proceeded to attack corruption on a grand scale, even though it hurt many friends of the former President. He also successfully avoided a threatened general strike in July, 1954, demonstrating his capacity to deal with serious challenges effectively. López Mateos had to face a major wildcat strike among railroaders in March, 1959, after taking office in December, 1958. Swift and efficient action proved he could control the situation. A number of major leaders were imprisoned, and the strike was effectively broken.

Modern society demands orderly government. Because of the complex social and economic relationships involved there must be mechanisms which can provide access to policy-making for all the major interests participating in national life. There also must be a relatively satisfactory level of assurance among the populace that public policy will be more or less predictable and equitable for all articulate elements. In order to provide such a situation the presidents of Mexico have sought uniformity of rule application on the part of key government agencies so that the day-to-day needs of average citizens are met. In seeking uniformity in procedures from his departments and ministries the President limits his own capacity to act arbitrarily. Nevertheless, the directing hand does come from the President, and the presidency does need to have a decision-making apparatus which can adjust to the ever expanding needs of the country in order to provide effective political controls. Involved in this teamwork to provide the political controls and the staff which the President needs are the heads of the executive departments, the heads of the major interest groups, both in and out of the Revolutionary Coalition, heads of some non-governmental bureaucracies and the high officials of the PRI.

Formal Elements of the Presidency

The strength of the Mexican presidency is based in part upon constitutional powers. Included in this field are a broad power of appointment and removal, fiscal powers, the capacity to initiate and veto legislation, and control of the military. Finally, and perhaps most important, there is a tradition of presidential supremacy in the grand manner of the colonial viceroy.

Election is by direct popular vote. In order to be chosen, an individual must be male, 35 years old by election day, and a native-born citizen who is the son of Mexicans themselves citizens by birth and must have resided in the country a full year (official missions excepted). A presidential candidate cannot be a minister of a religious sect nor have any ecclesiastical status. Anyone who wants to be President and who is in the military, in the national cabinet, or holds the governorship of a state or territory must retire at least six months prior to election day. Mexican Presidents may never be re-elected. Should a President become too ill to carry on, or if he should die in office, an interim President is appointed by the Congress.

The President of Mexico has a wide variety of ceremonial activities connected with his office. Scarcely a day goes by but he is involved in the dedication of some new public building or public work, whether it be a highway or a new sewage plant. Often such dedications are occasions for fiestas in the countryside at which the President, surrounded by a large group of his co-workers, appears before the people in a kind of holiday atmosphere in order to speak to them of the on-going Revolution and its accomplishments. Conventions of farmers, workers, or professional people all provide occasions for the appearance of the President, as do gatherings on patriotic days. Finally, there are the visiting dignitaries to be met, educators and scientists and public benefactors of all kinds to be congratulated.

Presidential power in relation to the military is extensive. Not only are there powers of appointment but there is also the authority to order troop movements relating to internal security and external defense. The power over internal troop movements in a country such as Mexico, which has had little necessity to defend its borders, looms much larger than does the defense function insofar as the armed forces are concerned; and in it is reflected one of the central facts of domestic politics. The specific role of the military in Mexico over recent decades has given rise to the impression that the military is no longer as important a mainstay of the presidency as it once was.[7] The next ten years ought to decide.

With regard to legislative functions, it should be emphasized that initiation of legislation is carried on almost entirely by the President. Though legislators have the right to initiate bills, they seldom do. In addition to the President's vast field of action with regard to the initiation of legislation and his work to secure its passage there is also a presidential veto power which never comes into play in practice because the legislature does not amend bills without prior consultation with the executive, thus eliminating the necessity of employing a veto. The veto remains, however, as a legal means at the disposal of the President.

[7] See Martin C. Needler, "The Political Development of Mexico," *American Political Science Review*, 55 (June, 1961), p. 311.

Following passage of legislation, there remain under Mexican law a number of important functions for the President to carry out. He must promulgate the law, which is an act recognizing the authenticity of the existence and regularity of the legislation. Publication of the law in the official gazette of Mexico, the *Diario Oficial,* is also a presidential act carried out in company with other administrative officers. After promulgation and publication a *reglamento* must be issued. The *reglamento* is a form which in fact constitutes a kind of sub-legislation through which a number of basic rules giving effect to the more general provisions of a statute are laid down. The *reglamento* is a traditional step in governmental procedure which continues despite the fact that it is not provided for in the Constitution. A valid *reglamento* has the same force of law as has the statute to which it refers. Presidents have also acted to legislate through the decree power, but this is an emergency power upon which it has not been necessary to rely since the Second World War.[8]

Congress is subordinate to the President.[9] As long as the official party carries out its functions of liaison and political communication effectively, and as long as the President successfully balances interest conflicts with regard to special goals of the various organizations, there is every reason to expect that legal approval for the acts of the President can be obtained from the Congress without question. There have been periods in earlier days, notably during the presidency of Ortiz Rubio, when these "if" conditions were not satisfied, but recent decades seem to indicate a high and fairly stable level of performance in taking care of such requisites. The presidential capacity to keep

[8] William P. Tucker, *The Mexican Government Today* (Minneapolis, Minn., 1957), p. 108.

[9] Those who arrive in the legislature fit into the hierarchy of power and influence at a step just below the cabinet ministers and governors. At the highest step of the pyramid, of course, is the President of the Republic and his closest advisors as well as a few other individuals who lead the wings of the coalition and together with the presidential group form the inner circle of the most powerful. It is indispensable to think in terms of degree in distinguishing the powerful from the power seekers and others of even less significance in the system. In making distinctions concerning the degree of power and influence one must take into account also the degree of support which different individuals and groups are able to offer or the dependence which the most powerful have upon these lesser groups and figures for a rendering of support. It is at this point that an overly simple view of presidential power may result in a distorted impression. For it is possible to assume so much power in the President and the inner circle of the Revolutionary Coalition that no significance attaches to people at other levels, such as legislators, who through their political militancy or activism provide the dynamic, the input of active support necessary for the system to function. For an interesting schematic suggestion of power structure see Robert A. Dahl, *Modern Political Analysis* (Englewood Cliffs, N.J., 1963), p. 56.

Congress in line holds true both for legislation and for appointments. In fact, the legislature as an immediate and effective check upon the presidency lacks significance.[10]

With regard to the powers of a judicial type the President has authority to appoint judges and seek their removal by Congress. The President may also intervene directly in this area of activity through his capacity to grant pardons. The courts are in a large part dependent upon the presidency, but there are areas in which the judicial rule corresponds in some measure to the constitutional and legal provisions. For example, Pablo González Casanova has shown that the Supreme Court has come into conflict with the President in a number of cases and ruled against him. There are recorded 3,700 conflicts of this type from 1917 through 1960. In these conflicts, most of them involving the *juicio de amparo* — a writ calling for a stay of government action, just over 1,000 were decided against the President in behalf of those requesting suspension of action ordered by the Chief Executive. However, González also shows that favorable action usually has resulted in the case of economically powerful persons or groups.[11]

Of course, Mexican courts do not pass upon the constitutionality of the law itself. Rather, they act in terms of decisions on specific questions of law in a given case. The most important appeal from governmental acts claimed to be unconstitutional operates in terms of the *amparo* which is available only through national courts.[12]

[10] Scott has provided a good example of legislative dependency. See Robert E. Scott, "Budget Making in Mexico," *Inter-American Economic Affairs*, IX, 2 (Autumn, 1955), pp. 3–20. There are aspects of the legislators' role, however, which do merit more attention than is customarily given. For one thing, there is a significant amount of open discussion in the Congress in which the small number of opposition members are allowed to take part, and the merits of bills are discussed in these sessions. It also is true that the legislators of the PRI seldom attain their posts without long service in government, interest group bureaucracy, or both. Their function as political communicators and mobilizers of support would seem significant in light of their career records.

[11] Pablo González Casanova, *La democracia en México* (Mexico, 1965), pp. 19–21.

[12] *Amparo* has some elements of the writ of injunction and some of habeas corpus as known in Anglo-American law. Cases in *amparo* rise from acts of government agencies at any level which are claimed to infringe constitutionally guaranteed rights. *Amparo* can also arise from the claim that a national law has invaded the sovereignty of a state, or that state laws have invaded national jurisdiction. Perhaps most important with regard to *amparo* are the personal procedural rights which it is designed to protect, although these do not reach to political matters, as the courts define political matters. To a certain extent precedent operates in the case of *amparo*, since five similar decisions on a point of law by the Supreme Court create a fixed application in *amparo* proceedings.

Amparo is applicable only against acts of government authorities, but in spite of this fact the number of writs of *amparo* has increased rapidly. The increase in the number of writs of *amparo* would seem to indicate there are many types of cases in which people can expect satisfaction through the courts in dealing with the government. In fact it is on the point of the constantly increasing number of *amparo* cases before the courts that the case for the courts as a limiting device with regard to agencies of government seems to turn.

Since *amparo* does not include political matters as defined by the courts, if a petition seeks relief from a major policy decision of the President or one of his close official collaborators, it is unlikely that a decision will emerge granting the writ. Early in the administration of President Ruiz Cortines a commercial motor carrier operating in Jalisco and other western states asked for *amparo* against a decision of the Ministry of Communications and Public Works. The minister became involved in a controversy with the judge hearing the case. The judicial decision was for *amparo*, but the minister maintained that he was not going to abide by it. After several days of discussion prominently covered in the newspapers, a solution was found — the judge resigned.[13]

Central Control

Mexico is nominally a federal system, but the Constitution in this respect is observed more in the breach than in practice. Presidential control of state governments is based upon a wide variety of legal-constitutional instruments, which in turn are backed by sources of power, political, traditional, and economic in character. Major constitutional powers would include Article 89, Section 4, and Article 76, Sections 5 and 6 of the Constitution of 1917. The former has to do with the legality of state elections, the latter with the capacity to intervene and declare null and void the powers of a state government. Since 1952, the use of these constitutional powers has not been much in evidence. Instead, less explicit considerations such as availability of grants-in-aid, control of police, support from the military, and co-operation from interest groups controlled from the national level all place a kind of pressure on a governor which demands his resignation in the event that he becomes unacceptable to Mexico City. Despite this dependence upon the national chief executive, however, governors and state politicians in general seldom feel the direct pressure of the inter-ventor threat. Unless a President is unusually aggressive, and this was not characteristic either of Ruiz Cortines or López Mateos, the

[13] The judge involved was an esteemed writer on Mexican jurisprudence, Ignacio Burgoa.

governors are likely to be allowed a free hand in the spending of state funds and selection of personnel for state elective and appointive offices. Only if decisions in matters of this kind begin to result in manifest political unrest on the part of major interest groups will a governor begin to experience close observation from Mexico City and know the threat of intervention. In summary, the state administrations usually act in close collaboration with the national government in matters of joint interest and receive national government support and a relatively free hand in the administration of state affairs.

The fact remains, however, that the President is the ultimate power in state politics. He has authority to intervene to replace personnel of state governments with those who promise greater service in satisfying the President's policy needs. Under Article 76 of the Constitution, the President, acting through the Senate and the Ministry of Government, is able to declare that the constitutional powers of a state have disappeared and appoint a provisional governor pending new state elections.

The power of the President as head of the central government is clear in relation to state governments in the area of public finance. The federal government takes in more than 80 per cent of income for all governments and the income of the state governments seems to be decreasing. Moreover, in some cases, over 30 per cent of the small income available to the states came from subsidies or loans through some federal agency in the period 1950–1960. Federal sums may fluctuate as much as 100 per cent in the case of a given state. Obviously the states depend enormously on the President in carrying out state development plans. The amount seems to go up particularly in accord with the strategic position of a governor during a presidential succession year, or whether it is the first year in office for a governor with whose success the President feels especially identified. Governors will usually receive more support for their state governments if they have been selected by the President in office rather than being carried over from a previous presidential term.

At the level of the basic local unit of government in Mexico, the *municipio,* the pattern of centralization is even more pronounced. Each state has a municipal law which holds true for all *municipios* in that state. In thirteen states the governors can depose municipal authorities at will under the states' municipal laws, and in the other states the facts of political life make for a similar decision. Thus the governor, who takes office on the basis of presidential choice in the one-party system, in turn commands the municipal authorities.

The facts of municipal dependence are based, as in the case of state governments, largely upon financial considerations. The federal government pre-empts most of the tax sources with the state governments taking almost all that is left over so that for all *municipios* the percentage of public funds available runs below 5 per cent. This means that annual average income of *municipios* throughout Mexico stands at about $22,000 dollars with the average in poor states such as Oaxaca at about $1,166 per annum. Some *municipios* may have to run on a budget as low as $40 per year. Clearly the condition of municipal services suffers under such circumstances.

As the author discovered in a study of Tijuana, Baja California, any public works improvements have to be made through intercession with the state government and, more often, the federal authorities. Basic services, such as police protection, are often provided through aid of the state if they are provided at all.

The present state of affairs was reflected in some of the resolutions of the Fourth National Congress of City Councils (*IV Congreso Nacional de Ayuntamientos*) held in 1959 which requested that *municipios* be allowed to name their own officials and that federal prosecutors be limited in their capacities to intervene in the official tasks of the municipal presidents.[14]

Transfer of power from one governor to the next is primarily a matter of presidential control. Occasionally the President defers to the judgment of regional strongmen, such as Lázaro Cárdenas in the state of Michoacán or the leaders of the Ávila Camacho family in the state of Puebla, but this is not the rule. The normal consultative procedure prior to a decision on the gubernatorial succession involves of course the President's most intimate advisors but probably also includes prominent interest group leaders, the incumbent governor, spokesmen for major economic interests outside the Revolutionary Coalition, military zone commanders, and at times representatives of opposition parties. The men they will be discussing are persons who have accomplished enough politically to be eligible for a governorship by having become a senator, a military zone commander, a cabinet minister, or a federal deputy. In a survey of governors over the period 1946–1960 conducted by the author it was found that more governors had held a federal deputyship previously than any other kind of post.

As indicated above, governors dominate state politics in an immediate sense, although the President ultimately controls. Limitations on a governor's discretionary powers with regard to decision-making stem not only from his relationship to the President but also from the necessity of dealing with the bureaucracy of the PRI and the leadership of many interest groups which help to make up the Revolutionary

[14] González Casanova, pp. 21–26.

Coalition. The interest groups, of course, are in close contact with the leadership at the national level, and the national leaders depend for their success upon the good will of the President. In this relationship the President is able to use interest groups in case there is lack of cooperation on the part of government officials at the state level. However, it is important to remember that the interest organizations may find a state official preferred by the presidency over their own leadership in case of a conflict of goals, so that only in particular cases can interest groups actively pursue specific goals independently or in spite of the state or local executive bureaucracy and its leadership.

The capacity of the President to intervene in both state and national affairs places the leadership of all major interest groups at his mercy in the short run, although ultimately the regime needs their loyalty and that of their membership. Success or failure in achieving a satisfactory response to the demands of members depend upon relations with the chief executive. For labor, the key is the executive power to declare a strike legal or illegal. For groups in the agrarian sector it is the executive power with regard to roads, irrigation projects, control of *ejido* events, and control of credit. For business groups, it is the executive power over state and municipal indebtedness and taxation. The capacity to distribute patronage is particularly important in terms of the President's control of the popular sector organizations whose members frequently depend upon government employment. In all of these dealings with organized interests the President need not provide optimum satisfaction for the membership; there need be only some vestige of improvement on major issues to which the leaders can point as an achievement; the leaders themselves expect rewards in the form of more remunerative government jobs.

Foreign Affairs

In no area is the leadership of the President more clearly assured than in that of foreign policy. The Constitution and other laws of the land as well as the expectations of the Mexican people assure his prerogatives in this field, as does also his key position in the Revolutionary Coalition. Thus it is the President who sets recognition policy and who ultimately decides to approve or disapprove treaties. Along with the Congress he is empowered to make a formal declaration of war, and he commands the armed forces. Political refugees must look to the President for asylum, and it is the President's order which brings expulsion of "undesirable" foreigners. The whole area of economic foreign policy — devaluation of the currency, trade agreements, tariff schedules, and many similar policy questions must be decided in the end by the President.

In carrying out his policy decisions, and to some extent in making them, the President relies upon several groups for help. There is, first of all, his professional diplomatic service headed by either an outstanding career man or an outstanding Mexican intellectual. Advice also comes from the Ministry of Government in affairs having to do with extradition and asylum. The Bank of Mexico, *Nacional Financiera* (the Central Industrial Development Bank), and the *Banco Nacional de Comercio Exterior* (the National Bank of Foreign Commerce) all are used as sources of information and opinion on the basis of which to make foreign policy of an economic character.

There are certain basic principles which have long been the cornerstones of Mexican foreign policy to which the President must adhere in choosing from the alternatives available. The first of these is the doctrine of national sovereignty which in practice means that states other than Mexico have no authority over Mexican residents — that the Mexican state is the supreme authority in Mexican territory. Other principles are corollaries of the first. There is, for example, the principle of juridical equality which the President must uphold. From the principles of national sovereignty and juridical equality follows naturally the concept of self-determination. Particular emphasis is placed upon the right of each country to develop the forms of government and economic activity which seem best to fit the needs of the people of that state. The people of a particular nation are the only ones who have a right to decide the nature of their society. Finally, a fourth cornerstone of Mexican policy which clearly follows from the others is the principle of non-intervention. Several decades ago, when Mexico was in the throes of revolution, one of the leaders, Venustiano Carranza, denounced any kind of intervention or occupation of foreign territory for any reason no matter how elevated the motivation. This has been Mexico's position ever since.

Absolute non-intervention is the watchword. No Mexican President is free to overlook this principle, which explains why Mexico has a consistent record of voting in regional and world organizations in favor of an absolute hands-off policy in treating the internal political affairs of any state. Closely related in this connection is Mexico's Estrada Doctrine which calls for automatic and immediate recognition of any new government. Other principles playing a lesser part in presidential decisions concerning foreign policy include peaceful settlement of disputes, collective security, membership in regional and world organizations, and pledges to promote human rights.

The manner of application of these principles is not always clear to the President and his advisors. Choices have to be made of policy alternatives concerning problem areas such as Cuba and the Dominican

Republic. In both of these critical situations Mexico's President has sought to avoid a complete rupture between commitment to the traditional four cornerstones of policy and the position of the capital suppliers who are indispensable to continued Mexican economic development. These suppliers of capital are for the most part from the United States. They are either private enterprises providing direct investment or United States government-sponsored lending organizations.

In the case of the rise of Fidel Castro, Mexico's position was clearly opposed to the United States on all questions of sanctions. For a time, 1959–1961, the Mexican position in fact became pro-Castro to the point that United States investment sources became harder to tap. This caused a modification of the Mexican posture. Mexican pronouncements on Cuba became more neutral, but there was no substantial shift in the positions of either government. The United States continued to demand a stronger inter-American stand against Cuba, and the Mexicans steadfastly opposed each United States proposal on the grounds that the Cubans had made a choice and should be allowed to go their own way.

When the Dominican crisis arose in the spring of 1965 and United States troops poured into the Dominican Republic to "save it from a Communist coup," the Mexican response was instantaneous and uncompromising. The Mexicans believed the sovereignty of the Dominican Republic had been infringed — in fact that every cornerstone of Mexican policy had been violated. The technique of the Mexican President for expressing the official view was interesting and typical. No comment of note issued from the presidency itself, instead all Mexico's living ex-Presidents as well as many prominent figures of the Revolutionary Coalition or the revolutionary past issued strong statements to the Mexican press condemning the position of the United States and lauding the non-interventionist policy of President Gustavo Díaz Ordaz.[15]

Other questions which have confronted the Mexican Presidents of recent years have concerned policy toward American investors, the reduction of saline waters which have been dumped by the United States into the Colorado River damaging Mexican irrigation systems, treatment of Mexican migrant workers, the limit of territorial waters affecting the activity of United States fishermen off Mexican coasts,

---

[15] The author, who was in Mexico during this period, can vouch for the fact that the official Mexican posture did not result in a hostile attitude toward individual United States citizens. There was no mob hysteria against the United States, but the position of the government was unequivocal in its hostility toward official United States moves.

and the control of the small piece of land known as El Chamizal near El Paso-Ciudad Juárez. Most of these questions have been successfully resolved or are in the process of solution. The important point is that credit for a solution favorable to Mexico as well as the blame for unsolved problems is laid at the door of the President. In the end it is the President who determines the nature of relations with the United States as well as the success of Mexico's bid to lead fellow Latin American countries on many issues such as the stand of the Organization of American States in the Dominican crisis and resolution of problems concerning trade barriers among Latin American countries.[16]

The Nexus of Interest Aggregation

The presidency is the single most important aggregating agency in the Mexican political system, and it is for this reason that a characteristic of the role must be strong political leadership. In fact the need for leadership is so great that no President is free to take actions which would reduce his own paramount position. For example, it would be a violation of the role to treat a legislative body as equal. In this sense it is impossible for a President to free himself of the necessity to act in accord with the values that condition the working of the system. This does not mean that personal tendencies, preferences, and attitudes of each individual incumbent do not influence the tone of a given administration. It is suggested, however, that the preferences and attitudes of one man — his vast personal power — no longer suffice to describe the nerve center of Mexican politics. Instead of a personal rule, it is the office with its institutionalized forms and institutionalized rule which constitutes the nub of the political environment.

The President, as the central aggregating factor in Mexican politics, forms the nexus of a network of interest associations and other types of political organization. The capacity of the President to work through the presidency in order to direct the system and aggregate demands successfully and in sufficient degree depends upon two major considerations. The first is acceptance of the legitimacy of the Revolution and its political machinery by the majority of Mexico's politically

---

[16] The twists and turns of Mexican policy toward direct investment from the United States as well as the intricacies of Mexico's balance of payments have been avoided due to the author's conviction that such matters should be treated by the professional economist. For more comprehensive treatment see Brandenburg, pp. 318–340. A discussion of the basic tenets of Mexican foreign policy is to be found also in Jorge Castañeda, "México y el exterior," in *México: cincuenta años de revolución* (Mexico, 1961), III, pp. 267–287.

articulate. Secondly, the President has a wide variety of resources which can be called up and brought to bear should opposition arise. Such resources are of many types — legal, political, popular, traditional, and economic.[17]

Mexican interest groups and associations are often interconnected and tend to be arranged in hierarchical order. The leaders of these groups and associations interrelate with each other, and their loyalties intertwine, but always in ascending order culminating in the President. The President, standing at the top of the hierarchical arrangement, is able to maneuver one group or one leader against another in order to achieve the balance of forces necessary for political stability. In this situation no regional leader, nor even any high-ranking political figure at the national level can hope to remain influential for any length of time in his sphere of activity if he allows himself to stand in opposition to the majority of interests in the coalition, and the majority usually is with the President. One's position is likely to deteriorate rapidly if he allows himself to fall into a posture of conflict with the presidency. Ultimately, for any elected official, and particularly for governors and national legislators, the good will and support of the presidency is essential if demands of special interest organizations are to be balanced in relation to the needs of the general public in such a manner as to allow these officers an opportunity to appear successful in their respective roles as interest articulators.

Although the presidency stands at the central and highest point of the pyramid of power, there are secondary control centers which are also important and which are related to each other both horizontally and vertically. The organization of the official party and of all major interest groups has this horizontal as well as vertical aspect. "Horizontal" refers to the fact that the loyalties are not entirely monopolized by the presidency. There are also loyalties to state organizations and local organizations which tend to provide the major difference between a monolithic model and the more diverse and diffuse power arrangement characteristic of the Mexican political system. Another division of loyalty may occur between the interest organization and the governmental agency. Sometimes a division occurs between an interest group and a government organ on the one hand and the party on the other. While the paramount loyalty to the President remains, these sub-loyalties and divisions of loyalties offset the monolithic picture which a focus on the domination of the presidency may too easily provide.

[17] Frank Brandenburg spells out these devices in considerable detail. Brandenburg, pp. 163–164.

Decision-making and Consultation

Presidential government in Mexico, while emphasizing the authoritative character of the President's decisions and the power of his position, is nevertheless, as Professor Scott has pointed out, "government by consultation."[18] The political system has become too complex for the President to have personal contact with all upon whom he must rely for support and whose lives and political careers he affects by his decisions. Little by little, procedures and methods have sprung up by which people are able to consult at lower levels, preparing the way for a kind of consensus which only the President can articulate authoritatively.

Vital to the success or failure of a President is his choice of ministers. These men compose the President's administrative team and are major factors in carrying out interest aggregation and rule-making functions. The presidency rests in the end on a ministerial base which must be of high calibre if the various aspects of the developmental process are to move forward evenly. The kind of men whose capacities are vital to Mexico and the nature of their previous experience is somewhat clearer in terms of Table 3, based on some of the writer's research on recruitment patterns.

It is after discussions have provided a consensual basis that ministers directly concerned with a policy proposal, some of the top interest group leaders, and interested members of the coalition's inner circle sit down with the President to work out the final policy statement. The enforcement of the policy in detail in turn is worked out — with the exception of questions involving a major conflict — at levels lower than that of the presidency itself. The task of securing maximum cooperation and enthusiastic implementation falls to persons forming the President's staff in charge of conducting relations with the legislature, with the bureaucracy of the PRI, and with the leadership of major interest groups.

Policy demands which the President as the single most important aggregator of interests in the country must consider are presented by various means of political communication. Latently, messages come through whispers and conferences in guarded tones at lunch or in hallways or offices. Manifestly, or explicitly, they come through the press and other mass media, pronouncements of interest groups, speeches by the leadership of the PRI, statements by legislators and sometimes a public airing of views by opposition party members.

[18] Scott, p. 279.

Table 3

Selected Categories of Previous Experience of Cabinet Personnel in Four Administrations

	NDES	Other High	Inter-mediate	Deputy	Senator	Governor
	(%)	(%)	(%)	(%)	(%)	(%)
1946	15.5	43.7	50.0	25.0	15.5	18.7
1952	23.5	64.7	82.4	17.6	11.7	30.4
1958	28.0	52.0	84.0	0.8	16.0	0.8
1964	21.7	52.2	69.5	30.4	21.7	21.7

NDES — Ministers of Interior (*Gobernación*), Foreign Affairs, National Defense, Treasury, Agriculture, Education, Labor, Public Health, Public Works, Industry and Commerce, Water Resources, National Patrimony, Navy, Department of Agrarian and Colonization Affairs, Communication and Transportation, Department of the Federal District, Pemex, Social Security Institute, National Railways, Central Purchasing and Distributing (CEIMSA — CONASUPO), Tourism Department, President of the PRI.

Other High — Assistant Ministers, Chief Justice of the Supreme Court, Ambassadors, General Secretary of the PRI, Rector, UNAM, Chairmen of some special and most permanent commissions, Managers of federal banks and other positions of similar rank.

Intermediate — Bureau chiefs and officers of similar rank. Prosecuting officers, Federal District attorneys, Federal judges, Assistant managers of federal banks and other positions of similar rank.

Perhaps most important of all are the policy demands stemming from the major executive agencies of government which have their own vested interests in promoting their own programs.

The President, and recently the institutionalized Office of the President, must balance the competing demands coming from these various sources and develop overall policies generally acceptable to the articulate elements of the system. These articulate elements include both official and semi-official government agencies, political bodies such as the committees of the party, and the leadership both for regionally based groups and economic groups. It is also necessary to consider many organized commercial and manufacturing interests which are not identified in any formal way with the Revolutionary Coalition. Since it is not the function either of the dominant party or of the legislature in the Mexican system to aggregate authoritatively, the only other consultative organ which can perform this indispensable function is the presidency, i.e., the President operating through implementing mechanisms of the presidential office. The cabinet, as such, is not an implementing mechanism, i.e., the heads of major executive departments do not meet regularly and collectively with the President. The President meets with specialized committees for specific questions or with his ministers individually on problems pertaining to their own special area of affairs. The extent to which ministers or special committees are given latitude in making recommendations or even making decisions depends upon the individual President. There are narrow committees for narrow problems, and broad committees involving the membership of several ministers as well as interest group leaders to deal with broader problems cutting across a number of areas of concern. Generally, in these groups, the debate that takes place is not made public. Decisions are reached, and legislative initiatives are hammered out before Congress is consulted in any formal way as a body, although it should be pointed out that legislative committees do hold hearings and collect evidence.[19]

The important things to remember about presidential committees are that they are ad hoc, that they serve a specific purpose, that they die a sudden death, and that their formation is seldom given any significant publicity. Thus, for the student the important thing to know is that they exist, that they are constantly changing and that their impact on the President's final decision is probably known only to the President himself. Certainly such committees do not publish their findings, though they may have more effect than if they published a long report to be filed away for use on some indeterminate future date. In view of the Mexican *modus operandi* it is likely few of these committees ever produce a written document. They produce instead points of view and possibly a consensus.

It is imperative to keep in mind that the President selects the members of committees which he desires to form in connection with some problem, for example, a drive against illiteracy. He may choose several ministers whose particular efforts he wants devoted to the problem, some government economists, and some leaders from the business world. The usual technique is to announce the drive against illiteracy without specifically naming a committee or committee personnel. The President may only call them together once to ask their support and get their opinions. After that, the committee is forgotten. Other com-

---

[19] In this respect legislative committees carry on useful work in gathering information for the executive and in sounding reactions to possible proposals. This is an aspect of the legislator's role which is all too frequently overlooked in light of the fact that Congress does not exercise an effective veto on presidential initiatives.

mittees last longer, but the structure and temporary character are always the same so that no researcher, Mexican or of other nationality, discusses these committees in detail; he simply knows that they exist and that they appear and disappear with great ease and no fanfare. This way of doing things will come as a particular surprise to those who have devoted themselves to the study of government in the United States or England.[20]

Summary

The President of Mexico is not *elected* in any sense meaningful to Anglo-American readers. Rather he is *chosen* by a relatively few individuals who make their decision in terms of what they consider to be politically advantageous for themselves and politically acceptable to the articulate groups in Mexican society. The nature of nomination as the official party candidate, i.e., as the president-designate, differs in terms of procedure and to some extent in manner of participation from expectations of people on the United States side of the border in that it is a much more closed arrangement with fewer effective participants. In the same way the presidential campaign also differs from United States experience in the functions it performs. These differences in turn are related to the pattern of perennial electoral victory on the part of the official Revolutionary Party (PRI).

The role of the presidency is to some extent conditioned by the nomination and election pattern. This holds true in the sense that the nature of the Mexican presidential nomination and election places the nominee in the position of carrying out some presidential functions prior to assuming office. Thus it is usually the president-designate who must bear responsibility for confirming nominations for lesser elective posts which have been arranged in the first place by the party, its affiliated interest groups, or the inner circle members of the coalition. Also the primary responsibility for the image which the Revolutionary Coalition wishes to convey to the public of the type of regime under which Mexicans are governed shifts at election time from the incumbent President to the president-designate. The playing of the presidential role thus begins before a man ever becomes President.

Once he has taken office as President the man who is to govern Mexico for the next six years must never lose the father image which

---

[20] Policy news releases do not come out without careful advance preparation in the press. Usually this entails publication of some feature stories on the general subject, pronouncements by prominent government officials and a widespread discussion at all levels — national, regional and local — sponsored by the PRI and various of the most vitally concerned organized interests.

he first began to build for himself as president-designate. He must remember that his attributes as President, while institutionalized in large part, still carry with them personality characteristics which he must at least pretend to have. If he is a father, he is also supposed to be a benevolent father. Whatever is done for the masses, he does for them personally — he endows them or gives them public structures, sanitation plants, schools, and roads. By the same token, if he fails to provide these things, he has failed in his vital father role. It is paternal government, but it is only legitimate if it is benevolent paternal government. Thus there are great pressures to produce material and psychic rewards which are the penalty that a President must pay for standing at the heart of the political system as the center of the interest-aggregating apparatus.

In his role as the central factor in interest aggregation the Mexican President of the 1960's is confronted with an increasingly difficult problem. It is the problem of bearing responsibility for a growing multitude of actions on the part of government in a situation where personal capacity to check on these acts is limited. The paramount chief, in other words, must delegate an increasing amount of responsibility. Thus, as the power of government to act expands the President's capacity to channel those actions personally remains relatively constant. It is tempting to regard each expansion of governmental function as an expansion in presidential power, i.e., there is a tendency to perceive presidential power as *cumulative*. Thus one can generalize about the ever-increasing power of Mexico's President. It is possible, however, to view the growth of governmental activity as *distributive* insofar as the President *vis-à-vis* other government officers is concerned. In this sense, then, the Mexican President experiences a relative decline in power to act which presents the grand paradox of the presidential role in modern Mexico. For the role demands that the President accept responsibility for all governmental acts even though he cannot possibly be personally well informed on all facets of these activities. As he becomes in one sense more powerful, therefore, the President simultaneously becomes more dependent. It is the case of the leader and his staff described by Max Weber under the rubric "routinization of charisma," and it has been spelled out most clearly in recent years by Raymond Vernon.[21] As the major factor in interest aggregation on the Mexican scene, the President, nevertheless, faces the fact of his own personal incapacity to direct the

[21] "The presidents of Mexico have gradually been eased — or have eased themselves — into a political strait jacket. . . . In a real sense . . . the strength of the Mexican president is a mirage." Raymond Vernon, *The Dilemma of Mexico's Development* (Cambridge, Mass., 1963), pp. 188–189.

process adequately. Under these circumstances the vital importance of recruitment of the administrative staff of ministers and their immediate assistants becomes nearly the paramount function of the President in present-day Mexico.

7

Labor Policy

The Historical Backdrop of Major Labor Policy Areas

In placing the labor movement in the revolutionary tradition as well as in its logical position within the framework of the present regime, Mexican writers sometimes go back in time to the position of the lower classes in the Maya and Aztec societies of pre-Conquest days. Their point is that the Revolution of 1910–17 was a revolution to satisfy an ancient need for change not only in the area of individual and political rights, but also for the renovation of the economic and social order. Mexican labor organization and Mexican labor law, in accord with this historical view, have evolved from communal beginnings in the sense that the major laboring units in Aztec or Maya society (*calpulli*) are viewed as essentially cooperative in character.

After the Conquest, the medieval European concept of guild organization was introduced by the Spanish and became a factor in the development of modern Mexican values concerning the role of labor. Guild organization protected workers by setting standards, by providing access to government officials, by providing security in case of trouble, and by training new generations of skilled workers. Guilds were not set up to sharpen competition but rather to dull its sometimes painful edge. Guilds were based on skills, and often the law awarded monopoly privileges to one guild for the entire area of work involved. Of course, it is also true that most of the time the guilds benefited people who were first-generation Spanish and helped other persons only infrequently.

Aside from the guilds, Spanish legislation recognized and attempted to protect more humble day workers and Indians of town and country-side. One decree provided for a weekend of rest amounting to at least forty-eight hours. There were other decrees setting minimum wages

163

and maximum hours for labor at all levels, but legal stipulations of this type were not often successfully enforced except for skilled artisans.

As the colonial period wore on, the situation of the masses doing common labor came to be structured in terms of such institutions as the company or *hacienda* store. In the company store people received, rather than money, goods for which they were customarily overcharged. Other characteristic features of life for the common laborer were twelve- to fourteen-hour work days, abuse by foremen, debt slavery enforced by government officials, and a general misery and low level of living difficult for men in a modern civilized society to comprehend. Difficult conditions even among more highly skilled urban laborers sometimes led to disturbances. Something resembling a strike was reported in Mexico as early as 1788. As colonial days ended, there were rudimentary strike attempts and slowdowns in the factories as well as attempted rebellions in the countryside, though such occurrences still were not frequent.

When independence was won the situation turned out to be very little different from and in many cases not as favorable as it had been under the Spanish colonial rulers. The fact seems to be that the old oppressive institutions — the company store, the tiny wage, the bare subsistence level of living, and the incredibly long hours of labor — continued to dominate the situation of the lower classes. Roberto de la Cerda says that the situation was "worse than during colonial times."[1]

When the generation of the Reform met to frame the Constitution of 1857, one of the leading men of that period, Ponciano Arriaga, called attention to the fact that nothing had been done since independence to better in any material way the situation of artisans and workers in the cities or rural areas; but the men of the Reform generation made it clear in the Constitution of 1857 that their concern was reform primarily of a political-legal character rather than economic or social.

After the liberals of the generation of the Reform had fought a civil war and beaten a French intervention effort, they set about reconstructing the country. Railroad building and new industries sprang up alongside older activities such as mining and textile manufacturing, but little of the new prosperity touched the workers of the factories, the mines, and the railroads. The urban day laborers and the peons and Indians of the countryside continued in the same

[1] Roberto de la Cerda Silva, *El movimiento obrero en México* (Mexico, 1961), p. 62.

miserable circumstances. There was the same institutionalized exploitation of workers through the company store, impossibly low wages, and the long work day. Stratification was made more rigid by use of foreigners as skilled workers, technicians, and managers. Foreign entrepreneurs were in the forefront of the expansion of industry, railroads, and modern communications in Mexico.

New demands were articulated in early organizational and strike efforts of workers, and treatment of unions emerged as an issue. After the Revolution against Díaz came the recognition of the new demands in fundamental law. Article 123 of the Constitution of 1917 crystallized basic policy goals for labor as central to the purpose of the new regime and the renovated political system. Foremost among labor's constitutional goal values were such considerations as rules concerning hours of work, conditions of work, and machinery of enforcement.

Reactions to perennial abuses in many aspects of employer-employee relationships were evidenced in Article 123. In the sphere of compensation there were provisions against contractual obligations for employee purchases at company stores, infrequent wage payments that might cause workers to borrow from employers against future wages, requirements for the payment of wages in legal tender, minimum wage levels (set up at the state level), and double pay for overtime. Conditions of work for women and children were regulated; for them there was to be no more work under unhealthful conditions or in specified types of enterprises. The number of hours was set for all workers. There was to be an eight-hour day with shorter periods for night work. Overtime was limited in general and prohibited entirely for women and children.

Large-scale employers were assigned a number of specific obligations in addition to those included in the above provisions. Among the most important were requirements for construction of housing and provision of schools and hospitals when these were lacking within a reasonable range of the factory or mine. Also indicative of efforts to remedy past abuses were the provisions that the employer provide safe and hygienic conditions of work. Employers were bound to pay compensation in case of industrial accidents. Employees were given the right to organize, strike, and bring cases before arbitration boards for the settlement of disputes. Machinery for enforcement and settlement of disputes was to center around local, state, and national boards, called boards of conciliation and arbitration.

For some years after the promulgation of Article 123 little in the way of legislative initiative for implementing the forward-looking constitutional provisions of 1917 was forthcoming. The conciliation and arbitration boards, major labor decision-making machinery envisaged by the Constitution, did not receive their recognition as true courts from the Supreme Court until the mid-1920's. By 1930 two-thirds of the states had passed comprehensive labor laws which were at great variance with one another. The Federal Labor Law, badly needed to bring order to the situation, did not emerge until 1931 after an amendment to Article 123 placed all legislative authority for labor matters in the federal government.

The labor law of 1931 with amendments is still the code in force. Under it, organized Mexican workers have been awarded privileges and benefits their forefathers never would have believed possible. In order to protect Mexicans against foreign technicians, employment preferences go to Mexicans up to 90 per cent in all skilled categories. Union members, as well as capable former employees, also have preference. Wage payment cannot be postponed merely on the owner's wish; it must come no less frequently than once a week. Collective contracts can and usually do include a closed shop clause — that the employer must hire only union members. Compensation, first aid services, and, in some cases, hospitalization, are provided in case of injury. Employers can rescind a work contract only in the most unusual cases.[2] Employers must continue to pay wages while the worker is on strike when the strike is ruled "legal" by the board of conciliation and arbitration having jurisdiction.

Since 1931 these benefits, as well as many others, have been placed in operation under federal labor law. In 1933, labor affairs were located in an autonomous agency, the Department of Labor; in 1940 labor administration began to operate at the ministerial level. Elaborate inspection and general control machinery has developed in the Ministry of Labor in addition to boards of conciliation and arbitration at municipal, state, and national levels. Government appointees to these boards hold the decision-making balance over labor and management board members; however, in recent years this has perhaps been less advantageous for labor in conflicts with management. This is because government officials are not clearly pro-labor as was the case in the time, for example, of Lázaro Cárdenas. In the overall view, however, time adds to the reservoir of skill and experience upon which to draw in staffing the labor ministry and the government positions on the boards, so that labor problems receive more professional and impartial treatment as the years pass.

[2] Benefits in practice are more likely to correspond with legal provisions in the larger firms. Smaller firms receive less attention as a rule from enforcing officials.

Major Policy Areas

Social Security

A working social security program is a basic element in any general policy oriented toward the improvement of conditions for wage earners. In 1942, during the presidency of Manuel Ávila Camacho, conferences were organized to discuss and propose ways and means of establishing a social security program. In January, 1943, came the legislation which provided the basis for a system of social security which has been expanding in coverage and benefits ever since. The law of 1943 created the administrative machinery for carrying out a social security program. The new agency was called the Mexican Institute of Social Security (IMSS) and a director general was appointed by the President. The IMSS was given the status of a "decentralized agency" as distinct from a "state participation enterprise," regular line department or regulatory commission. Thus, IMSS was treated from the outset as an agency performing a public or social service function with autonomous status designed to protect it to some extent from maneuvers of a purely political type, e.g., interpersonal or intergroup conflicts which might obstruct its intended mission.

By 1944 coverage began in the Federal District and by the first part of January, 1947, a number of important cities such as Monterrey, Puebla, Guadalajara, and Orizaba had social security coverage available with 631,099 persons participating in the program.[3] In 1946, two years after the IMSS began its operations, there were only 246,547 persons participating as pensioners with an annual cost of a little over $110,000.

During this initial two-year period there was a great effort to select talented and skilled people to form the core of the IMSS staff. The goal was to form a pool of talent which would acquire a high proficiency over the years in handling social security problems. IMSS staff salaries went up 90.88 per cent from 1943 to 1946 in an effort to attract the best people. Courses in social security began to be taught in the National University (UNAM) in 1950. The efforts to attract capable people were successful. The IMSS is generally respected as one of the best — if not the best administered agency of Mexican government. A wage dispute involving doctors working for IMSS in 1965 did not alter the favorable picture.

During the presidential term of Miguel Alemán, 1946–1952, the IMSS greatly expanded its functions. Its program included not only

[3] Miguel García Cruz, "La seguridad social," in *México: cincuenta años de revolución* (Mexico, 1961), II, p. 524.

construction of hospitals, clinics, aid stations, and factory first aid, but also varied responsibilities to pensioners. Those covered under the IMSS program and their beneficiaries grew to number 1,140,883 persons. A network of modern hospitals and clinics sprang from drawing boards and became reality. Every type of medical assistance doubled or trebled. Mexicans for the first time had access in large numbers to the benefits of antibiotics. Amounts granted in pensions rose from a little over 200,000 pesos in 1947 to above 4,500,000 in 1952. In addition to coverage in Nuevo León, Puebla, Jalisco, Veracruz, and the Federal District, the IMSS began operations in Tlaxcala, Tamaulipas, the state of Mexico, and Oaxaca. The Fourth Inter-American Conference on Social Security was held in Mexico City in 1952, and Mexico was assigned the chairmanship of the Permanent Inter-American Committee on Social Security. It was a period of great strides forward for the social welfare represented by IMSS, but it was also extremely costly. Contributions of those in the program had to be raised from 6 to 8 per cent of wages and salaries. Employee payments are matched by employers.

In December, 1952, Antonio Ortiz Mena took over the reins of the IMSS, and Adolfo Ruiz Cortines began his six-year presidential term. The new director stressed rigid observance of budgets, constant reorganization of services to achieve greater effective uses, continued expansion of coverage into more states and into the countryside, and further expansion of the number of IMSS installations, i.e., hospitals, clinics, administrative buildings, and so forth. Operations of the IMSS greatly expanded over the following six years. Expenditures were 841,211,049 pesos in 1958 while they had been only 260,479,041 pesos in 1952. Income was 1,110,676,898 pesos in 1958 and had been only 298,672,254 pesos in 1952. With sound management, reserves which stood at 383,250,568 in 1952 rose above 1,257,963,997.[4] Expenditures for medicine increased 40 per cent, from 73,481,315 pesos in 1953 to 102,558,075 pesos in 1958.

Operations were expanded so that there was some form of IMSS program in twenty-nine states. The number of clinics was increased from 42 to 226, 139 urban and 87 rural. From 19 hospital units with 1,698 beds in 1952, the system expanded to include 105 hospitals with 7,410 beds in 1958. The number of pensions went up 80 per cent while the amount of money outlay increased 40 per cent. To teach improvement of living style to peasants, 6,168 small model dwellings were built in the countryside, with immediate benefit to 30,840 persons at a cost of 204,797,842 pesos. On the negative side there were in

[4] Instituto Mexicano del Seguro Social, Subdirección General Técnica, *Población Amparada por El Seguro Social: Cifras Estadisticas, 1944–62.*

1958 only 99,542 rural persons with social security coverage — about 7.5 per cent of all persons covered.[5] Clubs, or so-called Houses of the Insured (*Casas de las aseguradas*) were organized throughout the country to provide women with elementary instruction in hygiene and family administration. Throughout the IMSS system the policy of keeping a minimum of highly effective, highly paid staff members was reflected in the fact that, while the number of personnel in the system went up 50 per cent from 1952 until 1958, salary levels climbed 250 per cent. The number of doctors in the system had grown to 3,977 and nurses to 5,147.[6]

When the presidency of Ruiz Cortines ended in 1958, Benito Coquet was chosen to head the IMSS during the presidency of Adolfo López Mateos. Coquet promised a continued effort to improve technical and administrative organization especially with regard to medical services. In addition, a major aim was the expansion of the social security program in the countryside. There was further expansion of the building program for hospitals, clinics, and other basic installations; and there was a renewed effort to improve liaison among employers, labor, and government to extend the progress of the social security program.

During the period from 1958 to 1964, the average annual increase in the number of persons covered under the social security program was 628,000. By 1964 the program was functioning in 510 *municipios,* 331 more than in 1948. From 1958 to 1964, 135 additional hospitals, clinics, and smaller medical aid facilities were placed in operation, 84 of these in the countryside. In addition to the medical facilities, there were 764 administrative centers, clubhouses, classrooms, and meeting rooms of various sizes built in 30 federal entities. Coverage for peasants was substantially increased, though the great majority of country people still remained uncovered.[7]

The overall view showed increased reserve funds as well as expanded services and types of coverage. The IMSS was becoming an important stockholder in both private and quasi-public enterprises. Social security was, as Coquet described it, a "goal unreached," but the efforts to approximate the goal were clearly expanding. In this area of affairs, as much as or more than in others, millions of Mexicans could experience the fruits of the promise of the Revolution. Especially for organized urban labor, the IMSS had come to mark progress toward a better life.

[5] García Cruz, p. 540.
[6] García Cruz, pp. 543 and 552–553. A strike of doctors in Mexico early in 1965 indicated that IMSS had been unable to meet salary standards in this area despite all efforts to do so.
[7] Adolfo López Mateos, *Último Informe* (September, 1964).

Profit Sharing

In 1962 a decision was made which was calculated to resolve at least temporarily one of the major issues which had grown from increasing labor demands over the years of the 1950's. This issue had to do with the role which labor might play in enterprise. There had been some thought in the past that labor leaders or labor councils might participate in the governing of an enterprise, and there was also a more modest hope that labor might participate, somehow, in the gains to which it contributed. It was this latter aspiration that was written into law in 1962 embodying the idea that workers should participate in the profits of the enterprise in which they were engaged.

Under the so-called *Reparto de utilidades* workers receive a portion of a given amount separated from overall earnings of the firm as stipulated by the National Commission for the Division of Profits (*Comisión Nacional para el Reparto de Utilidades*, CNRU). The CNRU is to carry out investigations and make studies in order to reach a decision as to how profit sharing should work in particular industries in relation to the problem of economic development. The key provision here is that capital should receive "reasonable interest" or "reasonable return" on its investment. The findings in this connection are always subject to review by the CNRU. Whatever percentage the CNRU decides should be set apart for profit sharing constitutes the workers' share in the profits of a particular enterprise. The income on which profit sharing is be computed should be the same as that reported to the Ministry of the Treasury. Workers or their representatives can object to the estimate of income presented to the Ministry of the Treasury by the firm. Under the provisions of law the ownership or management of the firm must inform the workers or their organization what the firm's statement of earnings is within ten days after it is submitted to the Ministry of the Treasury. Within thirty days of that time the heads of the union who speak for the workers in the factory, or the majority of the workers themselves constituted as an *ad hoc* group, must send their statement of approval or disapproval to the Ministry of the Treasury. The Ministry of the Treasury makes the final decision on the question of whether or not the firm has submitted the correct returns, and this cannot be appealed by the workers. Distribution of the profits to be shared among the workers is supposed to take place within sixty days after the deadline for payment of taxes on the submitted estimate of earnings by the firm.

The pool of money to be divided is separated into two kinds of funds. One type of fund is divided equally among all workers on the basis of the number of days they worked in a year. Another kind of fund is divided on the basis of proportion of gain; that is, on the basis of the highness or lowness of their salaries over the year. The salary of the worker in connection with the last type of division of profits is determined strictly on the basis of his daily wage; special benefits are not included, and the daily salary is actually an average of all daily wages earned throughout the year.

An initial determination as to the money going to particular workers in a given factory is made by a commission organized at the factory level composed of an equal number of workers' representatives and management. If this commission cannot reach an agreement, then an inspector from the Ministry of Labor makes the decision, and the workers, in turn, if they are dissatisfied with this, can submit their own opinion to the Ministry of the Treasury and the Ministry of Labor. If there is a year of loss, this year of loss in which the workers get no return from the division of profits cannot be made up from the profits of a good year. Moreover, salaries cannot be figured on the basis of various indemnities which might come to workers because of injuries or some other kind of peripheral benefit payment. Finally, the law explicitly states that the right of workers to share in profits does not imply in any way capacity on their part to participate in the direction or administration of the enterprise.

Certain enterprises are excluded from the profit-sharing plan. Any enterprise that is in its first two years of operation or any enterprise with an entirely new product in its first four years of operation is excluded. The novelty of the product will be determined by criteria already entered in Mexican law. A period of exploration for materials in an extractive industry will not be subject to the profit-sharing plan. Neither private foundation operations which exist for humanitarian purposes rather than profits, nor the Mexican Social Security Institute (IMSS) are subject to profit sharing. Certain enterprises capitalized at a very small amount are not included. Within the enterprise the top management people are excluded from the profit-sharing plan, as also are apprentices. Part-time laborers participate only if they have worked at least sixty days for the enterprise during the year.[8]

Unquestionably a piece of legal machinery can be improved from time to time from the standpoint of various groups. However, no legal machinery works well without the element of good faith. The establishment of such a psychological climate must be accomplished. A second major problem is that of administration. Under the existing arrangement, there are signs that there will be difficulties in both areas. In the initial years of profit sharing it appears that it has been difficult to get

[8] *Diario Oficial,* December 31, 1962.

an understanding among laboring groups as to the nature of the formula by which money is set aside to be divided among the workers. A representative of the CTM, Juan Moises Calleja, pointed this out in an effort to avoid future difficulties. Calleja said that workers tend to believe that the amount to be divided is 20 per cent of the gross income of the enterprise, which is not the case.[9] The great majority of firms gross less than 300,000 pesos per year before taxes, and a typical firm would be one with a gross of 200,000 pesos per year. In such a case the initial basis for calculation would be probable net income of 17 per cent of the gross income before taxes, which would be 34,000. Specified types of taxes are collected from this amount. The sum left is 30,700. An additional 30 per cent, or 9,200 of this, would go for interest and reinvestment of capital. In the above terms, the net profit as a basis for distribution would be 21,490 pesos. Out of this 21,490 pesos, 20 per cent would be distributable for the workers; or, in other words, 4,298 pesos. Thus, where workers might assume that of the original 200,000 pesos there would be 40,000 pesos available for distribution, there would be in fact only a little over one-tenth of that amount.

Another question involves the inclusion in the profit-sharing plan of enterprises among government operated decentralized firms. Here, Fidel Velázquez, leader of the CTM, has proposed that all of the decentralized enterprises of any size such as the electrical enterprises and the firms such as Altos Hornos (steel) should be included. Velázquez said that nearly all enterprises, public or private, should be included in profit sharing and that where firms attempt to avoid their obligation it "will be necessary for the unions to act energetically."[10]

The problem of labor-management misunderstanding, in part a problem of establishing good faith, was well expressed in the comments of outstanding labor leaders. The veteran secretary of the Federation of Workers of the Federal District (CTM), Jesús Yurén, pointed out that while some employers were following the formula of the CNRU to the letter, others were doing their best to avoid their proper obligations under the profit-sharing law. Yurén was especially concerned with the unwillingness of a number of enterprises to make known the amount of their profits which he declared to be definitely a violation of the provision of the original law to the effect that the statement of profits should be available to the workers at the time that it was sent to the Ministry of the Treasury.

Another problem had to do with fiscal arrangements. The accounting of some enterprises for the fiscal year has made it difficult to de-

[9] *Excelsior,* June 27, 1964.
[10] *Excelsior,* June 27, 1964.

termine at a particular moment the effect of profits from which the profit-sharing pool should be drawn. Labor leaders argue that even if employers claim there have been no profits they ought to submit a statement of their accounts for examination by the unions. Moreover, it is pointed out that the unions are in a position to know whether or not employers are falsifying their reports because labor leaders can determine the amount of raw material going into the plant and estimate from this the cost of manufacturing and the sales price as well as the number of units sold. These estimates give a rough idea of the profit and loss position of management. Particularly, it is stressed that the Ministry of Treasury should take care to provide a hearing including points of view other than those of management on the profit statement. Labor argues that at least some enterprises should be subject to a special audit on the part of the Ministry of the Treasury.

Another labor complaint has to do with the size of profit shares in small factories, where it is said that profit shares given to laborers in some cases are ridiculously small. Bottling plants are held up as an example; labor leaders claim that shares in some of these plants drop as low as twenty pesos. Leaders have been presenting these cases and others to the President of the Republic and the Ministries of Labor and Treasury.

Labor-management differences in estimates on profit sharing are sometimes dramatically highlighted by individual cases. In one major case involving an electricians' union (SME) and the publicly owned Companía de Luz y Fuerza del Centro, S.A., the estimate of the management and of the union leaders as to the amount to be distributed among workers differed nearly 100 per cent. The company was willing to distribute 2,500,000 pesos, whereas the union felt that a proper accounting would indicate at least an additional 2,500,000 pesos.[11]

Even though management in some smaller enterprises apparently has attempted to avoid obligations entirely with regard to distribution of profits, and even though management in some of the larger enterprises has presented calculations of profits which have not met with labor support or labor approval, management in general has not appeared desirous of obstructing the new legislation. Certainly leading business organs have not manifested great alarm with regard to the

[11] Fidel Velázquez, head of the CTM, pointed out that about 4,000 enterprises must operate under the profit-sharing law, and he felt that only about 3,000 were really attempting to carry out their responsibilities. Velázquez demanded that the government initiate proceedings against those companies which were acting in such a way as to attempt to avoid their obligations. There have been examples of success, however, and perhaps one of the most successful of the efforts to distribute the profits has taken place in connection with the Mexican oil monopoly, Pemex. *Excelsior,* June 6, 1964.

implications of the profit-sharing legislation from the standpoint of their own operations.

The National Chamber of Manufacturers (CNIT) has taken the position that there are four critical points with regard to the administration of the law. These involve the incentive which a law may give to productivity of labor, the problem of accounting in connection with the new income which workers should receive in relation to increased productivity, the determination of the percentage of profits susceptible of distribution in relation to the capital of the enterprise, and the establishment of a "reasonable return" (*interés razonable*) which is recognized by the law itself as an important factor in stimulating investment.

The CNIT has held many round-table discussions throughout the country, has kept its members informed, and has hired a team of specialists in fiscal and statistical matters to evaluate proposals coming from the membership. In general the CNIT would propose that an establishment which showed extraordinary profits should take the worker into account in this respect as an element in the success of the enterprise and give him something beyond what ordinarily would be the case under the existing arrangements for profit sharing. The chamber believes that the amount of money available should vary according to the success of the enterprise and also according to the type of enterprise. However, it is emphasized that workers should not feel they have some voice in the management because they are sharing in profits, and the CNIT is adamant about this latter point. At the same time, the chamber believes it very important for management itself not to feel that a profit-sharing plan eliminates the need to adjust base salaries in accord with the standard of living. From the chamber's point of view, these are the most important points related to the law itself.

In general, the law for participation in profits seems to present an important legal milestone in satisfying demands and meeting major issues raised by the aspiration of organized workers in the industrial sector.

Although the major demand for profit sharing has been met in terms of government policy, there will be many smaller demands and lesser issues to resolve in connection with the overall implementation of the policy. Aside from the views of the CNIT, other widely articulated points among spokesmen for Mexican business touch on several areas that are of vital importance in connection with the further administration and elaboration of the law. There is the question of the attitude of foreign investors in connection with this law; here again it appears that while some groups are rather alarmed at the prospects, in general this is not regarded as a revolutionary plan that will upset the usual relationships in the Mexican type of capitalistic system, or perhaps one should say mixed socialistic-capitalistic system. One Mexican official was quoted as saying that on the average he estimated profit sharing would amount to less than two weeks' pay for employees the year around, while W. S. Jones, a hotel operator, said that "this will be another needle in our side, but it won't put anyone out of business."[12]

The important fact to remember from the standpoints both of foreign and domestic firms is that the law makes allowances for taxes which the company must pay and also for opportunities for reinvestment on the part of the company. The Mexicans stress that one of the major reasons why such plans have failed or have not done well in Venezuela, Peru, Colombia, Chile, and Argentina is that the importance of reinvestment needs has not been recognized in the legislation in those countries. Clearly, Mexican policy-makers expect to take some of the pressure off themselves through this law, feeling that it is just one less thing which Communists can offer in the way of distribution of wealth. Mexican industrialists themselves, such as José Riojas, Jr., manager of Industrias Riojas, S.A., manufacturer and distributor of Wurlitzer products in Mexico, have said that even though they originally resented the profit-sharing plan, they now recognize that government has a point in providing workers with some additional income. They recognize that at least the whole thing has a certain psychological appeal for the wage earner. At the same time, management, as indicated above, is protected through the reinvestment and tax quota provisions, so that here, at least, is a possibility for maximizing satisfaction on all sides.

A major problem with regard to profit sharing goes to the heart of the whole series of other problems recognized by most top Mexican leaders and politicians. In Mexico's drive toward further industrialization and modernization there is a growing discrepancy between the benefits received by those in urban areas and those who remain in the countryside, particularly those who work for wages in the country. Over half the Mexican population is classified as rural, and yet available records and census data are extremely inadequate. There are recorded, for example, as workers in various rural-type occupations (agriculture, forestry, and related matters), only 6,144,930.[13] Clearly, there are many others who are part-time workers and who do not fall into the occupational categories used in this census. There are other problems with the census which bear on application of profit-sharing legislation to the countryside. Some of the people mentioned in the

---

[12] *Wall Street Journal,* December 5, 1963.
[13] Dirección General de Estadística, *VIII Censo General de Población, 1960: Resumen General* (Mexico, 1962), Cuadro 26, p. 417.

census are those who live on *ejidos,* and there are an estimated 18,000 *ejidos,* with about 1,443,692 *ejidatarios.* This census figure from the General Statistical Office (DGE) is somewhat different from that given by the Ministry of Agriculture (SAG) which places the number of people on *ejidos* at 2,200,000 or a little over; while the Department of Agrarian and Colonization Affairs (DAAC) adds several thousand to this latter estimate of the SAG.

Unquestionably many *ejidatarios* employ rural workers either on a permanent or part-time basis, as do cattle ranchers and people engaged in the exploitation of forestry preserves. This also takes place to a certain extent in the fishing industry. The accounting of such employers is often very skimpy. It is very difficult to come to any conclusions as to just what their profits are, and what share of the profits should go to their workers. As the former Minister of the SAG, Julián Rodríguez Adame, said: "Agriculture is really a way of life more than it is a business, and the whole accounting problem is much different." Added to the above considerations is the fact that there is no census of agricultural cattle or sheep-raising entrepreneurs, nor is there a census of persons exploiting forest resources. Under such circumstances it is next to impossible to find out who are the entrepreneurs and how many people they hire. Thus, as one official commented to the writer, "in its complexity, it would be real work for Romans," to apply the law of profit sharing in the countryside.

The implications of this situation were spelled out in a report by Federico Sánchez Fogarty of the CONCAMIN, which was sent to the President of the CNRU, Hugo B. Margáin. The core of the message was that the gap between the purchasing power of the organized working groups in the urban situation and of those who are laborers in the country grows greater all the time. Fogarty argued that the profit distribution plan would work to increase this gap. He also pointed out that the growing discrepancy means a decreasing internal market. Thus, regardless of the manner in which difficulties are ironed out in the administration of the profit-sharing law, and regardless of the conflicts between labor and management in the industrial, commercial and transport sectors, the problem of bringing the law to the countryside continues to be one of the most pressing in connection with this type of legislation as well as other types of legislation designed to improve the lot of the less affluent in the Mexican society.

Labor-Management Relations in Publicly Owned Enterprises

One of the major problems for organization and achievement of harmonious relationships within the Mexican labor movement and between the labor movement and other organized sectors of the society involves labor-management relations in the quasi-public or publicly owned enterprises. One of the oldest enterprises of this type is Pemex, the government-controlled oil monopoly which dates from the latter 1930's. Recently formed public enterprises include the formerly private electric utilities taken over in the last few years by the Mexican government from, for the most part, foreign private interests. An enterprise falling in between young and old public firms would be the government-owned airways, Aeronaves de México. Of course, the very oldest of all groups involved in work for the government comes under the heading or the category of bureaucrats who have their own union, which is known as the FSTSE.

Government in dealing with the organized bureaucrats and with other unions in the public sector finds itself in the role of management while labor finds itself affected with the public interest. Under these circumstances difficult problems can arise, and both sides have to move rather gently and very tactfully in dealing with each other. This is particularly true in that area where benefits involving costs of the enterprise or costs of government are concerned. Medical benefits, housing opportunities, working conditions and, obviously, wage levels are all involved here. These are the principal subjects when workers start negotiating with management of public enterprises. The problem is doubly difficult because the managers themselves are placed there by those who are the controlling policy-makers of Mexican government. In the end, all owe their jobs to the President of the Republic. Thus management must never be defied openly because to do so is to defy, in fact, those who are the governors of the Mexican people. Defiance of management easily can be construed as an act of defiance, not only toward government but toward the people as a whole — the system. Thus, a stand against management takes on overtones of subversion, and can escalate to the status of an act of high treason — an act against the Revolution itself or against the "revolutionary" regime.

Because of the ramifications in such a labor-management situation, language has to be worked out using certain forms by means of which the workers can present demands without appearing to challenge the precepts of the government. Under these circumstances a number of modes of praise are invoked in connection with any request or any public statement by a leader or a group of leaders concerned with employee demands. These modes of praise are highly formalized to indicate the greatest possible respect and admiration for those who are in the top policy-making positions. As a matter of fact, these modes of respect are designed to legitimize top decision-makers as trustees of the revolutionary tradition who are doing the best possible job within the framework of the norms and the goals set forth by the "revolutionary" regime.

For example, workers in the Ministry of Water Resources (SRH) wanted to add new categories of employees with regard to pension plans and vacation plans. They encountered great opposition from the Assistant Minister of the Treasury, in spite of their claims of support by their own Minister of Water Resources. It was necessary in presenting this situation to the higher authorities to proceed through a number of formalities. Thus the President of the Republic was extolled for all of the things that he had done for the workers in the various government agencies, including Water Resources. So also was the Minister of Water Resources praised for his support of these demands by the workers.[14] The demands or the requests that were being made were then stated, and the nature of the problem with the official of the Ministry of the Treasury was clearly described. The final stage in this appeal, as in the case of any other appeal of the same nature, included a statement of complete loyalty, confidence, and admiration for the President of the Republic and for his collaborator with whom the SRH workers were so closely connected: namely, the Minister of Water Resources.

Similarly, in the process of renegotiating their contract with management, leaders of the Pemex workers invoked revolutionary tradition and the act of expropriation which had taken the oil from foreign hands and placed it in the hands of the Mexican government. Former president, Lázaro Cárdenas, was also highly praised as the man who carried out the expropriation. Succeeding Presidents, and particularly the President of the moment, Adolfo López Mateos, were highly praised — so also was Gutiérrez Roldán, whom López Mateos appointed to run Pemex. These people were lauded as persons acting in accord with the tradition of the Revolution and of Cárdenas and other heroes of the *Petroleros*. Particularly the workers' pronouncements stressed the helpful attitude of the President in renegotiating collective bargaining contracts throughout his years in office and mentioned the various improvements that had been made in relation to the standard of living of the workers during this period. Especially mentioned were the small industries and retail outlets which had been sponsored with government capital in order to provide certain necessities for the workers at its lower cost. On the other hand, the difficulties which the workers had had in finding an adequate and an understandable procedure in the financing of houses for themselves and their families were mentioned. Also mentioned were the actions of some contractors in

[14] In addition there was recognition of the constructive role of the head of the bureaucrats' union (FSTSE), Jesús Robles Martínez.

adulterating materials of the houses under contract to the workers. The overall orientation, however, was toward labor-management cooperation within the framework of the norms and heroes of the "revolutionary" regime with the petitions for change and redress well cloaked in ceremonial style.

Clearly, any group that expects to achieve certain demands, when there are others who also have competing demands in a situation where resources are limited, must operate from a position of strength. How, then, does a union of workers in a government-owned industry go about acquiring support and presenting itself as being in a position of strength if that strength cannot be expressed in fast and sharp and informative gestures, and if the appeals cannot be stated in sharp and informative terms? The answer is that one mobilizes one's strength, if one is a leader of a particular union, by looking around to discover which other unions might find it worth while to form an alliance that would provide some sort of mutual advantage.

Wage earners in electrical utilities installations recently taken over by the Mexican government constitute an excellent example of a labor group which finds itself in a favorable position to form alliances and gather support from other unions and other sectors of the economy. Perhaps as much as any single group of workers, people involved in these enterprises are in a position to bring the entire industrialized sector of Mexico's economy to a halt. Moreover, the quality of their work and the enthusiasm which they show, as well as their capacity or their desire to improve themselves, has a great deal to do with the improvement of electrical services necessary to the continued expansion of the Mexican industrial plant. The electrical workers are vital to the fields closely related to industrial activity, e.g., communications and transportation. They are also important to the comfort of many individual families, since they stand at the source of power for private homes.

There are two unions of real importance in the electrical field. One of them is the Mexican Electrical Workers Union (SME). The other is the Union of Electrical Workers of the Mexican Republic (STERM). When the SME undertook the renegotiation of its contract in the spring of 1964, it was dealing entirely with government officials. Instead of its traditional appeal to aspects of the Revolution which might place government on one side over against private enterprise, it was necessary to take a different approach to argue the point that the workers should have certain advantages even though government ownership had theoretically set aside implications of class warfare. The appeal followed the usual lines with praise for the President of the Republic, his appointees on the new Federal Electrification Commission, and the Minister of Labor, Salomón González Blanco. However, the SME clearly saw that the peripheral benefits and higher wage levels for which it was asking would need a good deal more than the standard formal praise for the policy-makers and a few indications in subdued language of the aspirations of the workers themselves. As a result talks were undertaken with various leading labor and peasant confederations in the Mexican political system. An impressive array of statements of support was obtained. In addition to all the unions from the anti-BUO bloc, endorsements came also from the National Peasants' Confederation (CNC) and the CTM, the leading confederation of the BUO bloc. Perhaps the reason that the SME was able to line up support in both labor blocs was that both could hope for the affiliation of the SME, although the anti-BUO bloc has had its affiliation in nominal terms.[15]

The negotiations were under way throughout March and the first part of April, 1964, but the outcome was fairly certain after the endorsements of the SME position began to pour in. The final settlement came on April 8. The arrangement involved fringe benefits such as housing improvements, additional sick leave, and more vacation time. The President of the Republic received the leaders of the SME at his official residence, Los Pinos, and complimented them on their success in the negotiations. However, it is important that he added a sobering note, admonishing the leaders concerning their responsibility for providing ever higher quality of service in the Mexican industrialization effort. The leaders indicated also their own determination to help bring this about. The formal presentation for the SME was made by the leader, Luis Aguilar Palomino. Both the President's statement to the workers' representatives and the statement of the leader of the SME were in very formal terms indicating goals, aspirations, and mutual respect.[16] In a very similar pattern the other major union of electrical workers, the STERM, threatened to strike against the fifty-four electrical utilities operating under the Federal Electrification Commission. Most of the demands of the leaders were granted, and the strike was forestalled.[17]

The final difficult area for negotiations and the harmonization of conflict involves the existence of captive unions (*sindicatos blancos*)

[15] For a discussion of the different blocs and their member organizations see Chapter 3.

[16] *Excelsior,* April 1–8. Unions which are not so strategically placed cannot ordinarily expect such a successful outcome in their negotiation of a collective contract, if for no other reason, simply because the amount of goods available in the Mexican system is yet exceedingly limited.

[17] *Excelsior,* June 26, 1964.

and a related factor of corrupt union leadership. Such situations represent enough difficulties for workers in the case of unions operating in private enterprises; in the private firm these conditions can be recognized for what they are and efforts can be made to change them through the election of other union committees and affiliation with rival confederations.[18] Where workers in government enterprises or in government ministries are concerned, the problem is more difficult. Under such circumstances, only the most outstanding and well entrenched leaders of the employees can speak out — and then often with difficulty. There were revealing statements made in this connection at the Casa del Agrarista in June, 1964. Arturo López Portillo, employees' leader for the Ministry of the Treasury, went through the usual forms. He endorsed the Revolution as the basis for workers' rights and spoke of the leaders and top policy-makers as persons respecting these rights. However, he also pointed out that the Federation of Workers' Unions in the Service of the State (FSTSE) was certainly no supporter of company unions — unions unconditionally committed to keeping order among employees and enforcing management demands. On the issues of corruption, he emphasized that the bureaucrats, i.e., the employees, have a perfect right to dismiss a union leader who does not fulfill his obligations to them. López Portillo made the point that pressure should not exist from the top to keep the rank and file in line. He argued that employees should be allowed to displace a leader who fails to represent them as they feel they should be represented. Another bureaucrat leader, Francisco López Serrano, head of the employees' union of the agrarian department (DAAC), while emphasizing the importance of union democracy (*libertad sindical*), also emphasized that whenever a high functionary was using his post for his own personal gain, it should be "the obligation of the bureaucracy to denounce such corrupt officials."

A whole new philosophy and style of action in labor-management relations has to be worked out in systems that attempt to maintain some freedom while at the same time controlling a large portion of the economy through public rather than private investment. In the publicly owned industries major problems include the manner in which employees mobilize their strength, the manner in which they deal with their union leaders, and the manner in which the union leaders themselves deal with representatives of management. The language which is used in these cases — the whole style of the proceeding — will have to be smoothed out and made even more effective as the years go on because industrialization does not represent an easy process of

[18] See Chapter 3, the case of La Covadonga.

adjustment for many Mexicans. Where the old philosophy and the old style of action connected with the notion of class warfare are no longer applicable, new methods of expressing discontent and of reconciling conflict will have to be even more clearly adaptable to avoid dissatisfaction with social structures which do not admit use of the old ways. Failure in this respect can only lead to greater frustration and provide an invitation to violence.

The Discontented Middle Stratum

The problem of arranging new approaches to old problems within the shifting context of a society undergoing rapid change is pointed up in a study by Professor Joseph A. Kahl.[19] Kahl focused on three types of employees in a highly modernized factory setting just outside of Mexico City. Men in these three categories were semi-skilled workers, foremen, and engineers or professionally trained directors of the plant. Fault might be found with the Kahl article because of the small number of people studied. There were twenty-four semi-skilled workers, nineteen foremen, and only six engineers. On this basis generalization may be difficult, but there is an insight here which has utility in the absence of studies of broader scope. It is that "Mexico does not yet appear to have institutionalized an accepted career for middle ranks of industrial workers."[20]

In his study, Kahl reported that the workers he interviewed were literate but had come from varied backgrounds, including farm families, rural petty merchants, and blue-collar labor. Foremen at the plant were predominantly born in cities; several had finished secondary training, and some had even started university courses. In contrast among the semi-skilled group of ordinary workers none had gone beyond sixth grade. Many foremen had fathers who were small urban businessmen or white-collar workers. Only one had a father who was a small-scale farmer.

The third and highest status group were the engineers and engineer-managers. The engineers all had university degrees. Four of the six came from professional or executive families, while two had climbed from skilled worker backgrounds where fathers were highly ambitious for their sons. All had families that emphasized high motivation, and the engineers themselves showed a marked high degree of professional attitude, believing in promotion on the basis of excellence rather than seniority or connections.

[19] Joseph A. Kahl, "Three Types of Mexican Industrial Workers," *Economic Development and Culture Change,* 8, (January, 1960), pp. 164–169.
[20] Kahl, p. 169.

Kahl found some disconcerting patterns with regard to mobility and job satisfaction. First of all, he found there was almost no movement between the three groups, that is, he found only one case in which a semi-skilled worker became foreman, and the standard belief in the third and highest stratum seemed to be that workers were not educated or sophisticated enough to hold a foreman's job. The foremen, themselves, saw no chance of their becoming engineers through further practical experience in the factory. The line between the professional and the non-professional was absolutely clear, and it was drawn in terms of the professional degree. In terms of satisfaction, the engineers saw their job as an opportunity to advance to even better jobs. The lowest category, the workers, saw their position as a good lifetime position in a modern factory with modern personnel methods representing great improvement over work experiences they had known in the fields and in the small towns. The foremen, however, were not satisfied; they had been unable to reach their own initial goals of a higher education and degree as engineer or something similar. The ambiguity and the undesirability of the position of foreman was indicated even in questions to the workers. When questioned, the ambitious workers indicated some hope that their sons might some day become engineers, but no one hoped for his son to become a foreman.

There is a problem here concerning mobility and the development of a middle role in industry which is understandable in terms of the increasing value which middle sectors place upon the university degree. Educational opportunities at the university level are extremely limited and as many as 50 per cent who aspire to a professional degree never get it. Thus, many able young Mexicans are placed at once outside the mainstream of opportunity. It is a special problem for those for whom insufficient funds or lack of physical stamina make achieving an engineering degree impossible. These are the ones who find open to them only the non-prestigious foreman's position or an equivalent. In these circumstances we can see why the peasant from the country finds the well-organized factory an improvement, but we can also see that an urban middle-class person or youngster may become a frustrated and aggressive individual if he has the misfortune of dropping into the group that is not quite good enough to take a place with those who have the degree at the top of the career pyramid. This urban group that falls short is a potentially significant discontented stratum in Mexico's industrializing society.

The related problems of mobility and job satisfaction among levels of employees indicate how incomplete is the proposition that division of labor becomes more complex as industry advances. Mexicans need to know more about complexity. They must learn how to convert the fact of growing complexity into development of social arrangements that adequately take into account values and aspirations of different groups of men. Industrialization tends to bring together two major structures — the structure of social hierarchy of the local community, and the occupational hierarchy of the work world. The link between these two structures is education, and it is the degree that makes the difference in the man's position. The man with a few years of primary schooling and a peasant background, who comes into a semi-skilled factory labor job, feels that he is lucky to have that kind of a job; whereas a man from an urban middle-class background who comes into the intermediate ranks of industry as a foreman, having failed to realize his primary goal of achieving a university degree, feels that he is deprived of opportunity and cannot advance. The urban middle-class person who receives an engineering degree can look forward to a satisfying career and anticipates steadily increasing rewards. The fact that so many who start out with the notion that they are going to get a professional degree are disappointed indicates that the unenviable middle category is likely to be an expanding one.

In a public industry the problem of this growing middle category is bound to be even greater than in a private one. The disappointed degree-seekers are forced to attempt adjustment within an industrial and social framework which attempts to stratify jobs as well as social positions according to the formal level of education. This confronts public industry with real difficulty, since ordinary manifestations of discontent against management are frowned upon. It is not that manifestations are impossible; demonstrations of employee discontent are a settled part of the Mexican scene even in the public sector. However, the problem of a permanently frustrated stratum of discontent among employees of the public sector certainly places a premium upon a tactful and highly institutionalized framework of ceremonial politeness in the style of dealing with disputes. Employees must continue to pay proper tribute to the top authorities in government and in management while at the same time requesting, and to a certain extent, manipulating the order of things in order to enforce a demand for better working conditions. In the future, very probably, there will be necessary in terms of social pressure a more serious consideration than ever before of the possibilities of advancement from one work category to another on the basis of competitive examination — not solely possession of the university degree. As the public sector expands this pressure will grow. It will have to be given an outlet if public enterprises are to expand their efficiency in order to provide better services for the entire Mexican people.

✤ 8 ✤

Agrarian Policy

Historical Background of Agrarian Reform

A basic factor in the Mexican Revolution of 1910 was the desire for agrarian reform. In fact, Mexican agrarian reform can be regarded as a direct consequence of the role of the peasant movement in the armed struggle: Mexican agrarian reform, that is, was a consequence of revolution and not of evolutionary planning. Its postulates and its form emerged as a response to the predominant usages and abuses evident during the first decade of the twentieth century and for some time prior to that period.

Nearly all authors who discuss the agrarian movement and agrarian politics point to the high concentration of land ownership in the rural areas of Mexico and the poor distribution of wealth as a backdrop for the Revolution of 1910 and the agrarian reform. It should be noted, however, that this pattern of high concentration of rural property characterized the Mexican countryside since early colonial times. It developed as a direct consequence of the Conquest and domination of the Indians by the Spaniards in a situation in which the conqueror established himself among organized Indian villages and carried out the first of many land grabs that were to follow. In some sense, then, the roots of the agrarian reform are to be found in the deterioration of the land tenancy system among the primitive peoples through the efforts of those who undertook the Conquest.

Initial grants by the crown to the conquerors on a large scale were later followed by an institution called the *encomienda*. The *encomienda* was a device by which the King of Spain assigned a given number of Indians for a stipulated period to a white landowner in order that the landowner might protect them and instruct them in the ways of Spanish culture and religion. In return for this help, the Indians were to pay tribute, either in labor or in kind.

185

The general picture of land distribution which characterized the colonial arrangement was one of large private holdings for Spaniards and *criollos,* large Church holdings, and some communal property assigned to Indian villages. It is possible to view the poor distribution of land under this arrangement as one of the causes, if not a principal cause, of the War of Independence. At least it may be noted that Father Hidalgo issued an agrarian decree as early as December, 1810, which commanded some distribution of land among the poor people. Attention to the concentration of land was also given by José María Morelos who succeeded Hidalgo as the leader of the movement against the Spanish.

These early considerations of the land problem were not given a place in the final settlement guaranteeing the independence of Mexico. Instead, following independence, if there was any pattern at all, it was change toward even further concentration of rural property in fewer hands. The Reform, and the Wars of the Reform, were again fought in part over the land problem, specifically over the question of the amassing of land by agents of the Church.

The great clerical properties were broken up by the leaders of the Reform era. However, as everyone knows, the efforts of the Reform did not break up the concentration of rural lands. Instead, some of the great *latifundia* changed hands. In other cases men were able to create new large holdings. The pattern of unequal distribution — a few rich and a great many poor — continued to be the dominant feature of the Mexican countryside.

The concentration of great amounts of land in the hands of a few was particularly evident during the decades reaching from the triumph of the Reform to the Revolution of 1910. By 1910 approximately 97 per cent of the total arable land of the country had fallen into the hands of approximately 835 families. The remainder was divided between village properties and small property owners.

There were four basic dimensions in the amassing of land during this period between the time of the Reform and the Revolution of 1910. Probably the most notorious activities centered around the boundary surveying and colonizing companies.[1] Almost as bad was the maneuvering to extract communal property from Indian villages. There were also payments of land by the state to private individuals as compensation for some types of debts or reward for some services. Finally, an important factor in land concentration was the absence of legislation setting a maximum limit upon property holding.

[1] Victor Manzanilla Schäffer, "La reforma agraria," in *México: cincuenta años de revolución* (Mexico, 1961), III, p. 232.

Most of the great farms ran from 10,000 to 100,000 hectares. Some, however, became as large as several hundred thousand hectares, as in the case of the Hacienda San Blas in the state of Coahuila or the holdings of the Terrazas in Chihuahua. The great farms were regarded as self-sufficient economic units having rich agricultural lands, lands for grazing, forests for providing wood and water resources. On these lands there would sometimes be many villages, the inhabitants of which worked for the *hacendado*.

There were two types of peons — workers by the job (*peones de tarea*) and workers by the year (*peones acasillados*). Both received wages, though the job workers received only about half of the usual thirty-one centavos daily gained by the *peones acasillados*. A major factor in keeping workers on the *hacienda* was the *tienda de raya*, a kind of company store that sold goods to the peon and his family. These stores also made special loans for occasions such as the Holy Week celebration. Accounting was done by the *hacendado's* clerical help and the debt was deducted from wages. Often the peon mortgaged not only himself but his children to pay for goods sold him by the *hacendado's* storekeeper. If peons fled from the *hacienda*, the federal rural police (*rurales*) would hunt them down.

The *haciendas* were in every sense feudal baronies or earldoms. Their unqualified support from political circles made their situation practically indestructible. Small property owners had the worst of the situation in competition with the great land holdings. *Latifundia* were frequently exempt from payment of taxes, workers were kept in a state of semi-slavery, and expenditures in salaries were recovered by the owner through the company stores. Historians are not in agreement about the effectiveness of the *hacienda* as a productive unit for surplus produce going to the cities, but the general picture seems to have been lack of efficiency in utilization of land.

Without a thought to these conditions, the regime of Porfirio Díaz remained aloof from the hardships of the masses of the people and considered only policies for resolution of problems pertaining to the favored classes and the friends of the regime. When the Revolution of 1910 did break out, its first great leader, Francisco I. Madero, lost the support of many devoted revolutionaries, such as Emiliano Zapata, because of his unwillingness to promise reform on a large scale of the land tenure conditions in Mexico. After Madero lost power, those who wished to take his place at the head of the Revolution — Zapata, Villa, and Carranza — all issued pronouncements favoring the dissolution of the great properties. The Agrarian Reform decree issued by Carranza on January 6, 1915, is generally taken as the beginning point of

Mexico's practical agrarian reform experiences. That decree formed the basis for Article 27 of the Constitution of 1917, which in turn provides the legal basis for agrarian reform legislation of today.

The Beginnings of Agrarian Reform

In his decree of January 6, 1915, Venustiano Carranza as "First Chief of the Revolution" siphoned off much of the political support long enjoyed by another competing revolutionary leader, Emiliano Zapata. Essentially the decree of 1915 proclaimed that land which had been illegally taken from a large number of villages of various political categories, e.g., *pueblos, congregaciones, rancherías,* should be returned to them. This was to be accomplished either through "restitution" of lands on the basis of demonstrated evidence of title or through grant or "dotation" if for some reason the village was unable to show documentation of its claims. The decree referred specifically to legislation of the Reform which it pointed out had been misapplied under the Porfirian regime.

The legal machinery for putting the decree into effect was to be found in the provision for a National Agrarian Commission, as well as agrarian commissions at the state and local levels. Provisionally, land redistribution took place through action of the state governors, state agrarian commissions and local executive committees. Decisions made at the state level were then reviewed by the National Agrarian Commission, and final title to the land was granted by a decision of the President of the Republic upon the recommendation of the National Agrarian Commission.

The decree of 1915 placed principal emphasis upon restitution of land to villages and reflected little serious consideration of the use of outright grants, i.e., dotation on any considerable scale. Only villages having what was called political status (*categoría política*), were eligible under the decree. This meant that a multitude of small communities resident on the *haciendas* known as *acasillado* communities had no status in the reform situation.

The decree was drawn in such a way as to put the initiative for taking action upon the villages themselves, not upon state and national officials. Relief from land distribution proceedings was available through the ordinary courts to the landholders so that proceedings could be held up for a great length of time under the existing court situation of the day through the writ of *amparo*.[2]

Carranza was in power a little less than five years after the promulgation of the decree of January, 1915. During that time only 190

[2] *Amparo* is sought against federal officials who can be shown in the courts to have exceeded their authority. See Chapter 6 above.

villages received definitive possession of land. The total amount of land distributed amounted to about 180,000 hectares benefiting some 48,000 *ejidatarios*.[3]

When Alvaro Obregón took power in 1920, his original legislative efforts had little effect other than to indicate enthusiasm for revitalization of the agrarian reform, but in April, 1922, a more thorough law was passed spelling out more clearly what kinds of villages would be eligible to receive land and the amounts of land they could receive. The legislation of 1922 formed a more solid basis on which further legislation could be enacted over the ensuing years. Thus, a tendency was set in motion to widen and extend the rights of the villages and increasingly to narrow rights of landlords. In this legislation the procedural rules for action by the National Agrarian Commission, governors, state agrarian commissions, and village executive committees were more clearly spelled out than was previously the case.

The legislative and administrative action of the Obregón government brought about a quickening of the agrarian reform. From 1921 to 1924, 624 villages and 139,320 heads of families received about 1.2 million hectares of land. This more than tripled the number of villages receiving land under Carranza's government. By the end of 1924 about 814 villages and 187,702 heads of families altogether had been beneficiaries receiving 1.4 million hectares of land.[4]

Following Obregón's administration, the administration of Plutarco E. Calles enacted the law of April 23, 1927. The legislation of 1927 dealt with several key problems. First, it adjusted the legal position of villages relating to the classification known as "political category."[5] The courts had become filled with cases in which villages were petitioning to have their "political category" changed so that they could ask for land. The 1927 law greatly simplified the different "political category" classifications making it possible for nearly all types of rural communities to apply for land. In addition, the law of 1927 attempted to clarify further the procedural rules of the various committees in the land distribution program. Procedure for initiating a petition was simplified, and in so doing landholders were prevented from selling off part of their land in order to avoid expropriation. On the other hand, the position of the landowners was strengthened and clarified by providing a 150-hectare limit below which land was not susceptible of being affected by the reform.

Calles was in a better position to see the agrarian reform experience

[3] Eyler N. Simpson, *The Ejido: Mexico's Way Out* (Chapel Hill, N.C., 1937), p. 79.

[4] Simpson, p. 87.

[5] Frank Tannenbaum, *Peace by Revolution* (New York, 1933), p. 204.

in perspective than his predecessors had been; he realized that it was necessary to provide new institutions for financing the reform programs in order for productivity and the rural standard of living to be raised. Thus, under Calles there were a number of decrees which provided for agrarian bonds and a National Bank of Agricultural Credit.

Other Calles legislation touched on the problem of irrigation and of the colonization of new lands. Not only did Calles improve the legal situation with regard to the agrarian reform, he also provided concrete evidence of the commitment of "revolutionary" governments to implementation of the reform by distributing 3.2 million hectares over the period, January, 1925–December, 1928, to the benefit of 1,576 villages and 307,607 *ejidatarios*, better than a twofold improvement over the whole period of the reform from the date of the 1915 decree to the time that Calles took office.[6]

Emilio Portes Gil became interim president of Mexico after president-elect Alvaro Obregón was assassinated in the summer of 1928. Portes Gil took office in December of 1928, and the year 1929 under his leadership marked a high point in the distribution of land over a one-year period. During that year 693 villages and 108,846 *ejidatarios* received more than a million hectares of land. Gil also sponsored legislation further restricting the area of maneuver remaining to large landowners, and a new water law definitely gave the nation inalienable control of all factors pertaining to the water supply.

When Portes Gil was succeeded by Pascual Ortiz Rubio, the major trends that had developed in agrarian reform, i.e., facilitating petitions for land and restricting landowners in their capacity to resist the reform, were interrupted and for the moment reversed. In May, 1930, Ortiz signed an official resolution addressed to the president of the National Agrarian Commission which set a period of sixty days for all communities planning to petition for land to present their case, after which there would be no further appeal. This so-called "stop law" was to apply to the state of Aguascalientes to begin with, but in the next year and a half similar presidential orders affected twelve other states. The results were sudden and concrete: land distributed in 1930 dropped from over 1,000,000 in 1929 to 744,091 hectares, and in 1931 to 610,304 hectares. In 1932, only 384,401 hectares were distributed. However, a positive step in favor of agrarian reform was taken while Ortiz was President in that the capacity of the landowners to use *amparo* to obstruct land reform petitions was ended by legislation of December, 1931. Under the latter legislation landowners in restitution or dotation proceedings no longer were allowed recourse to the *amparo* writ.[7]

[6] Simpson, pp. 94–97.
[7] Simpson, pp. 111–120.

Opposition from various sources within the circle of revolutionary leadership led Ortiz Rubio to resign in September, 1932, and he was succeeded on the designation of Congress by General Abelardo L. Rodríguez. In July, 1933, after he had been in office about ten months, President Rodríguez issued a decree which quietly put an end to the so-called "stop laws" of Ortiz by abolishing all time limits set on village petitions for land. State agrarian commissions which had been dissolved were then quietly reconstituted. Thus the agrarian reform was put back on the track in accord with the tendencies developed through the governments of Obregón, Calles, and Portes Gil.

In December, 1933, the first complete agrarian code was put into effect by President Rodríguez. A new Agrarian Department was provided to facilitate the handling of petitions for land at the national level. The state agrarian commissions became "mixed" agrarian commissions, and their functions were spelled out more clearly. Governors of states continued to play a major part at the state level, and there were in addition agrarian executive committees and commissariats of *ejidos*. Though the procedural roles which these bodies were to play were still not clarified in such a fashion as to end all difficulties, the provisions were more clear as to what lands were susceptible of distribution and what were not. Moreover, rights of individuals and *ejidos* with regard to water and other resources of the countryside were more clearly defined. Dotation, or outright grant as a way of distributing land was for the first time clearly treated as the larger part of the agrarian reform. The code was in fact the most important statement of goals and procedures outside of Article 27 itself.

In addition to the refinements evidenced in the code there was a related yet distinct area of concern treated by the Rodríguez government — credit. As pointed out above, the Calles government pioneered in this area by setting up the National Bank of Agricultural Credit. Under Rodríguez there was issued a Law of Agricultural Credit on January 24, 1934. The law of January 24, 1934, provided at long last some operating funds for loans through the National Bank of Agricultural Credit to go to the *ejidatarios* meeting criteria of worthiness.[8] At the same time opportunities for loans to individual agriculturalists of certain classes were provided with preference being given in competitive cases to *ejidatarios*. Moreover, the rights of resident peons (*peones acasillados*) were clarified.[9]

In spite of the new legislation, however, a very substantial segment of opinion led by Calles himself believed that the basis of agrarian reform should be the small, privately owned property rather than the

[8] Lucio Mendieta y Nuñez, *El problema agrario de México* (Mexico, 1937), p. 300.

[9] Nathan L. Whetten, *Rural Mexico* (Chicago, 1948), p. 132.

ejido. Much of the discussion over the six-year plan that was proposed in the December convention of the Revolutionary Party in 1933 as well as the maneuvering with regard to the naming of a candidate centered around the question of whether or not the basis of the agrarian program should be founded on small property purchased by the peasantry, or upon the idea of the *ejido*. There were other issues, but certainly this was one of the most crucial.

Agrarian Reform Under Cárdenas and Subsequent Developments

Out of the convention of December, 1933, came the candidacy of General Lázaro Cárdenas. Cárdenas made several changes in the Agrarian Code of 1934. One of the most important affected the resident peons (*acasillados*) in their capacity to petition for land. Although the code of 1934 was first to give such persons any right to share in the redistribution of lands, it nevertheless limited the right considerably. The limitations were removed by a decree of Cárdenas in August, 1937, making it possible for these resident peons to exercise the same agrarian rights as other segments of the rural population. The act greatly increased the number of *haciendas* subject to subdivision. Perhaps the resident peon provision more than any other single provision was basic to the great expansion of agrarian land distribution under the Cárdenas government.

During the first year of Cárdenas' presidency, 2,900,226 hectares were distributed, better than twice the amount for any particular year up to that time. The amount was increased in the second year of his presidency, 1936. In no single year were less than 1,700,000 hectares distributed, and in one year (1937) the number of hectares distributed surpassed 5,000,000. Altogether in the six years of Cárdenas' presidency, 1934–1940, there were approximately 17,890,577 hectares distributed among the Mexican people.[10]

With the coming of Manuel Ávila Camacho to office in December, 1940, the pace of land distribution slowed somewhat, although there was by no means a radical withdrawal from the land distribution program. In 1941, land distributed by Ávila Camacho was less than one million hectares, but it went considerably over one million in 1942 and stayed in the neighborhood of a million hectares of land per year until the last year of his administration. Altogether Ávila Camacho distributed 6.6 million hectares — not the same pace as set by Cárdenas — yet more than any of Cárdenas' predecessors.[11]

[10] Whetten, p. 125.
[11] Howard F. Cline, *Mexico, Revolution to Evolution, 1940–1960* (London, 1962), p. 213.

The rate of land distribution declined still more after Ávila Camacho, although it must be acknowledged that distribution did not come to a standstill. Thus President Miguel Alemán in the years 1946 to 1952 distributed over five million hectares.

Legislation of the Alemán presidency has formed an important basis as well as limiting framework for subsequent agrarian policy. Of particular importance are two Alemán measures. First of all, there is the amendment to Article 27 of the Constitution which went into effect on February 12, 1947, shortly after Alemán became President. This amendment revived in part the *amparo* proceedings which were eliminated during the presidency of Ortiz Rubio. Under the Alemán amendment any owner or possessor of an agricultural or livestock holding who had been granted a certificate of inaffectability, or might be granted one in the future, was given the capacity to initiate injunction proceedings — *amparo* — to prevent the taking of his lands and waters for expropriation under the land reform program. The reopening of the resort to *amparo* was designed to prevent attacks upon small property holders by landless agrarians led by unscrupulous agrarian politicians.[12] Large landholders not eligible for certificates of inaffectability were not given this recourse.

In December, 1949, a series of alterations appeared in the Agrarian Code which again acted to slow up land distribution or put limitations upon those seeking land but at the same time added rationality to the overall distribution procedure. Under the provisions added to the code in this year of Alemán's presidency the minimum *ejido* grant was raised to 10 hectares of irrigated land or 20 of seasonal land. The result intended was reduction of the incidence of small uneconomic plots, sometimes referred to as *minifundia*. The importance of the private holdings was recognized in provisions for certificates of inaffectability to exempt from future expropriation holders of 100 hectares of irrigated land or 200 of seasonal land or pasture. The *amparo* proceedings mentioned previously were written into the code as additional assurance against raids by landless agrarians led by demogogic leaders — the so-called *paracaídista* "parachutist" types before whom small holdings were particularly vulnerable. Small landholders rarely were in possession of men and arms necessary to fight off the determined groups of peasants who simply staked off chunks of property and began to sow their own crops.

Some large holdings involving badly needed crops such as bananas, coffee, and sugar cane, were covered under the inaffectability procedures, and the code provided that in the case of cattle raising, lands

[12] The *paracaídista* (groups of landless peasants) raids of the latter 1950's presented exaggerated examples of this problem.

could be extensive enough to graze up to 500 head or their equivalent in other livestock. Special cases were recognized in which as many as 50,000 acres of pasturage could be made inaffectable for twenty-five years. No change was made in the prohibition against foreigners holding real estate within 100 kilometers of land boundaries or 50 from the seacoast.

In all, many more restrictions were placed upon land distribution, and there were corresponding advantages evident for landholders. Yet, as has been pointed out above, the amount of land distributed during the Alemán government was by no means negligible. The new procedures, while protecting private holdings in some respects and giving perhaps greater order to the agrarian distribution program, did not by any means end it.

Alemán's successor, Adolfo Ruiz Cortines, distributed 3.5 million hectares. In his last year of government, 1958, Ruiz Cortines informed the Congress in his State of the Union message that land to be redistributed was becoming very scarce.[13] He also emphasized the importance of the small private holding. The small private holding side by side with the *ejido* was to be regarded as the other pillar of Mexican agriculture. On the basis of this policy orientation, plans were to go forward to raise the social and economic levels of the countryside. A decision was made to focus on creation of new resources and utilization of unexploited ones rather than proceed with further division of lands under cultivation. This decision, too, was related to the determination to avoid multiplication of smaller uneconomic units. A more secure status was given the small private holding and was spelled out in terms of the growing colonization program on the one hand and the decision to create new kinds of *ejidos* on the other. Thus, under the agrarian code, persons unable to obtain land in their own areas became eligible for grants on new lands opened up through irrigation or reclamation projects. As of 1958 there were about 924 such colonies occupying 6.2 million hectares of land.

Agrarian Reform Under López Mateos

President Adolfo López Mateos in his early speeches and policy decisions indicated that land distribution was still to be considered a major concern of "revolutionary" governments, and he promised that his

---

[13] Cline, *Mexico, Revolution to Evolution,* pp. 213–214. The pressure to acquire land continues. In 1965 the state of Tlaxcala bought 1,500 hectares of land on which to settle *paracaídistas* who were persuaded to leave the lands they had invaded. At the same time the federal government was asked to depose the governor of the state of Colima because he was obstructing the expropriation and distribution of large *haciendas* in that state.

government would view as "affectable" for distribution any land falling into relevant legal categories. Many large farms and pastoral operations enjoying certificates of inaffectability were to see their certificates revoked during the ensuing years. Within two years of taking office there had already been distributed 3.2 million hectares of land.

The government of López Mateos gave a greater impetus to the distribution of land than any government since Lázaro Cárdenas. As López Mateos said in his final State of the Union message: "It had been affirmed for years that lands susceptible of distribution in accord with law no longer existed or were on the point of disappearing. My government, in six years, has distributed more than a third of the lands distributed during the forty-four years that the Agrarian Code has been enforced. . . ."[14]

Official statistics indicated that between January 6, 1915, when Carranza issued his famous agrarian reform decree, and December, 1958, when López Mateos took office, land distributed amounted to 43.5 million hectares. To this amount the government of López Mateos added roughly 16 million hectares. This brought the grand total of land distributed by the end of 1964 to 59.5 million hectares. In his last year of government alone, López Mateos distributed 3.9 million hectares. This revitalization of reform, in addition to helping many landless persons, testified once again that the attachment to the revolutionary symbol of land distribution was capable of being revived and revitalized at any time under a "revolutionary" government.

Determination to use public lands to provide land for the landless was reflected in the distribution of 2.9 million hectares of public lands by the López Mateos government. Also, restitution was clearly not dead, since 2.3 million hectares were given in this manner over the full period, 1958–1964. Greater attention to the Indian was reflected in the establishment of an Office of Communal Lands in the Department of Agrarian Affairs and Colonization (DAAC).

Over the six-year period, 119,801 certificates of agrarian rights were issued in an effort to promote colonization. Twenty-eight new population centers were constructed in the Panuco region, 7 in the Alto Candelaria in Campeche, 12 in Quintana Roo, 45 in the south zone of Veracruz, 60 in Oaxaca. Thousands of persons were moving into these new population centers and surrounding lands prepared by the government. Under the population resettlement program, people abandoned old and exhausted lands in Zacatecas, Jalisco, Guanajuato, Mexico, and the Laguna region, as well as other areas of the country where poor land and/or small plots had made farming unprofitable.

[14] *Último Informe* (September, 1964).

In addition, the government sought to cut down on the conflicts among *ejidatarios* and their offspring as new generations sought land on which to build homes, set up small gardens, and begin poultry raising activities for purposes of family support. The government put through organization of urban zones within many *ejidos* with the goal being urban zones in all *ejidos* of the republic. Nearly 3,000 urban zones were organized over the six-year period. Many urban zone certificates were for the so-called *solar urbano,* which provided, in addition to living space, small plots for poultry and truck garden vegetables to improve the family diet.

Still another aspect of the agrarian program of the López Mateos government was the development of model *ejidos* in order to achieve the "integral" improvement of *ejidos* in the various regions of the country. These model *ejidos* (*ejidos tipo*) it was hoped, would influence *ejidos* in the zones surrounding them and bring about new patterns of living and farming in the countryside. Over the six-year period seventy of these model *ejidos* were established. It was possible under law also for *ejidatarios* to request the government to help them renovate their existing *ejido* arrangement in order to develop a model *ejido.*

Eighty-six livestock raising *ejidos* were established. The government took steps to correct a longstanding abuse of the *ejido* arrangement which involves abandonment of *ejido* plots or illegal renting out to a large holding cultivated by some private agriculturalist. Thus the government issued 75,207 judgments depriving persons of *ejidal* rights by reason of their abandonment or abuse of their *ejidal* holdings. One malfunction of agrarian leadership was attacked when a number of private rental contracts made by agrarian leaders with private interests were cancelled. The contracts had had the effect of placing *ejido* land temporarily under private control.

Where private property was involved, the López Mateos government was at times very lenient and at others very strict. With respect to inaffectability of livestock raising properties, the government was strict. Forty-six certificates of inaffectability were rescinded and none issued over the six-year period. On the other hand, 40,260 certificates of inaffectability were issued to small agricultural properties over the six-year period.

With the advent of the López Mateos administration, a new realization of the inadequacy of the existing agrarian program swept Mexico. Many young theorists set out to provide outlines for new policy.[15]

---

[15] See Marco Antonio Durán, "Agrarismo y desarrollo agrícola," *Investigación Económica,* XXIII, 92 (Cuarto trimestre de 1963), pp. 677–708; Marco Antonio Durán, "Las funciones de la propriedad de la tierra en la reforma agraria mexicana," *El Trimestre Económico,* XXXI, 122 (Abril-Junio de 1964), pp. 228–242; Ramón y Ricardo Acosta, Fernández y Fer-

Increasingly, writers and policy-makers spoke of the new ideal in agrarian reform which they called "integral" agrarian reform (*reforma agraria integral*). The principal tendency in this writing was to stress the importance of treating the problem of the *ejidatario* and small property owner in a fashion integral to the social and economic problems of the rest of the country. Thus, the existing procedures of dotation, restitution, and amplification were to be revitalized while at the same time making way for a new approach to deal with situations in which there was a lack of land for distribution under the old programs. Particularly important was the accelerated program for the creation of new centers of population. By these various means, the government was able to achieve a distribution figure of over 200,000 hectares of land monthly.

Particular targets were the remaining *latifundios* and land monopolies of various kinds along with the certificates of inaffectibility that had been granted many persons in the livestock business. There was a renewed determination to bring into use stretches of national territory which had been unproductive in preceding years. New administrative devices were worked out to assure that only authentic peasants as distinct from land speculators masquerading as peasants would receive benefits under the existing irrigation and construction programs. An effort was made to expand the *ejido* concept by establishing, in addition to the agricultural *ejido,* numerous livestock and forestry *ejidos.* Renewed interest was taken in those *ejidos* established on a communal basis. Under a decree of April 23, 1959, new regulations concerning the planning, control, and supervision of investments of communal *ejido* farms proposed to guarantee the conservation and increasing capital of these farms. A new interest was taken in the problem of social solidarity among the *ejidatarios* themselves. The internal government of many *ejidos* came under close scrutiny, and a renewed effort was made to assure the respect of the deliberations and resolutions passed by general assemblies of *ejidatarios*. The major purpose at this point was the avowed proposal to do away with *caciquismo* at the *ejido* level and to this end an effort was made to remove and replace all *ejido* authorities who had finished their stipulated terms.

Both theoreticians and officials began to stress the importance of the *ejido* as an "economic unit of production" (*unidad económica de producción*). The idea was to secure recognition of the fact that under dotation many units were not sufficient because of their small size, and that there would have to be a greatly expanded use of technology and

nández, *Política agrícola* (Mexico, 1961); and Victor Manzanilla Schäffer, "La reforma agraria," in *México: cincuenta años de revolución* (Mexico, 1961), III, pp. 227–263.

fertilizers in order to make them productive. It was widely suggested that one way of achieving this objective would be to provide some form of guidance to the *ejidatarios* so that they could learn not only more about methods, but also expand their knowledge of productive activities. For example, the government set out to encourage *ejidatarios* to become more self-sufficient through diversifying their crops. As indicated above, an effort was made to propagate the idea of small-family model farms which would feature crop diversification. *Ejidatarios* were also encouraged to keep bees and learn more about poultry raising.

Over and over the theme was stressed that the agricultural *ejido* must cease to be a mere subsistence operation. This emphasis was in contrast to the concept of some earlier writers which pictured the *ejido* as sufficient unto itself, producing whatever it might consume. The theorists under López Mateos pointed out that this was merely a microcosmic version of the old *hacienda porfiriana* with its closed economy and that to consider seriously such a concept was to consider the segregation of the *ejido* system from the general economy of the country with all of the pernicious results inherent in such a situation. The new emphasis was to be upon the incorporation of the *ejido* in the total economic system of production, circulation, and consumption of goods.

Basic to the López Mateos concept of the *ejido* was its broadened function — it was not to be merely an agricultural *ejido*. The *ejidatario* was to be encouraged to develop skills and acquire equipment that would enable him to perform the initial stages of manufacture or process of *ejidal* products. Here the theorists and the government set about trying to disseminate the concept of small-family industry while at the same time seeking to encourage the development of rural artisans through appropriate legislation. The goal was a narrowing of the gap between the manufacturing activity of the cities and the agricultural activity of the countryside. Various procedures involving interministerial cooperation for achieving the integral improvement of the peasant family along these lines were worked out. Spokesmen for the government envisaged a total transformation in the countryside to the point that the rural areas would become the habitat of middle-class producers and consumers.[16]

Along with its expropriation of *latifundios,* cancellation of simulated or fake certificates of inaffectibility and elimination of *ejidal caciques,* the government sought to avoid upsetting the equilibrium of Mexican agriculture. It especially sought to avoid destroying the confidence of private owners. Production figures indicated that it was successful.

No aspect of the agrarian problem was overlooked, although re-

[16] For the first time efforts were made to begin rural social security coverage.

forms certainly did not eliminate existing problems. There were still the formidable obstacles of the vast inertia of the populace with its deep sociological and economic roots and a severe lack of training personnel. However, progress was made along many lines. An effort was made to give more emphasis to Indian affairs as well as to enlist more persons with technological know-how in the campaign to conserve soil and fight off the dangerous advances of erosion. The establishment of forestry *ejidos* was a new device for giving the peasants a stake in their forests and thus promoting conservation policies.[17]

The government placed a new emphasis upon clearing up boundary difficulties plaguing *ejido* properties and also stepped up efforts to avoid boundary difficulties in the new population centers to which peasants from worn-out or overpopulated lands were being transported. The agrarian department (DAAC) undertook a new drive to clarify the boundary limits of communal lands and quiet the conflicts which frequently had remained for years without resolution.

In another area of agrarian affairs badly needing attention, the DAAC undertook a program to expand the number of skilled agricultural advisers and technicians through establishment of a new training program. The chief emphasis of the program was upon skills basic to community development in the countryside. The techniques taught involved not only understanding of machinery, fertilizers, and basic agricultural practices, but also rudiments of good financial practice and social skills calculated to produce stepped-up interaction and interpersonal confidence in the community.

López Mateos said of the collective efforts of officials and analysts alike:

Action has been focused upon compliance with the juridical principles sustained by Mexican agrarianism and the maintenance of peasant unity. We consider that, if we act according to law and protect within constitutional norms both the *ejido* and the small property, we will have order and tranquility. The latter are the bases of productive work which will permit achieving the standard of living needed to accomplish the great tasks confronting the country.[18]

In spite of the vital interest awakened in the problems of the rural areas during the López Mateos government and measures taken to

[17] The agrarians of the López Mateos administration prided themselves on their pragmatism and openly denounced extremists who tried to make the pressing problems of the countryside into a vehicle for political ambitions, the point of reference being particularly the CCI (see Chapter 4).

[18] Departamento de Asuntos Agrarios y Colonización, *Seis Años de Política Agraria del Presidente Adolfo López Mateos, 1958–1964* (Mexico, 1964), p. 79.

resolve some of these problems, many difficulties remained to plague the succeeding administration of Gustavo Díaz Ordaz. Aside from the perennial shortage of land, perhaps the single most persistent problem was the exceedingly small landholding, whether an *ejido* parcel or privately owned plot. The magnitude of the problem was pointed out by Francisco Hernández y Hernández early in the López Mateos administration. With *ejidatarios* added to private property holders the smallest holdings, one to five hectares, numbered well over two million plots on approximately ten million hectares, while holdings above 51 hectares numbered only a little over 25,000, and accounted for over six and a half million hectares of land. Holdings of a more medium character, six to fifty hectares, came to something over 160,000 and accounted for a little over three million hectares of land.[19] Clarence Senior found the same pattern of too many people on inadequate holdings in the Laguna region.[20]

The hard facts appear to be that small, economically unworkable plots — *minifundia* — predominate. In *ejidos* the vast majority are holders of small parcels, and the average annual per capita income for over a million private owners of *minifundia*-sized plots stands at less than 400 pesos. On the other extreme, 7 per cent of private owners can expect an average annual income of about one million pesos while farming on the average about 2,000 hectares per proprietor. This tiny group accounts for 35 per cent of total agricultural income. This pattern holds true when one views the concentration of property on irrigated land alone. (See Table 4.) Thus, the great holdings with a small number of proprietors can utilize the latest techniques and fruits of the industrial economy to obtain high yields for high valued crops, while a vast number of very small-scale private proprietors or *ejidatarios* have to confine their activities to low value crops, with consequent meager incomes. Major problems will continue to focus

[19] Francisco Hernández y Hernández, "El movimiento campesino," in *México: cincuenta años de revolución* (Mexico, 1960), II, pp. 231–233.

[20] "The area of irrigated land per capita in 1950 of the two major land-tenure systems was . . . : Ejidos — 4.4 hectares; private properties — 25.7 hectares. The average for the private properties does not show two phenomena of importance: (a) the fact that 5 per cent of the owners held 26 per cent of the private land and 14 per cent owned 55 per cent, and (b) that even these data underestimate the amount of concentration because they do not reflect the simulated sales which took place widely on the eve of and immediately following the expropriations.

"Furthermore, it should be noted that 66 per cent of the land possessed by the private owners was irrigable land while only 37 per cent of that of the *ejidos* was so rated." Clarence Senior, *Land Reform and Democracy* (Gainesville, Fla.; 1958), pp. 95–96.

Table 4

Concentration of Property: The Distribution of Property in Irrigation Districts in 1958

Size of property	No. of persons	% of users	Area (hectares)	% of area
0 to 20 Has.	249,929	92.2	1,033,625	52.2
20.1– 50	15,711	5.8	449,937	22.7
50.1–100	4,491	1.7	356,207	18.0
More than 100	694	0.3	141,567	7.1
Total	270,825	100.0	1,981,336	100.0

Source: Adolfo Orive Alba, "Las obras de irrigación," in *México: cincuenta años de revolución* (Mexico, 1960), I, p. 367.

on the landless *ejidatarios* and the low incomes of the *ejidatarios* on the uneconomical plots.

Díaz Ordaz will be confronted by another major problem in addition to the related questions of *minifundia* and concentration of land. This is the problem of credit. Credit has been a perplexing area ever since Calles established the first government agricultural credit institution in the mid-1920's. The problem centers on insufficient funds and also involves corruption and poor management of the credit institutions from time to time. The opening shot in the battle revolving around agrarian credit was fired when the Díaz Ordaz administration brought forward a proposal for a new credit institution, *Banco Nacional Agropecuario,* with combatants taking sides according to their respective preferences for generous lending policies for *ejidatarios* or for private property. No one seemed to believe there could be an equally good policy for both types of borrowers. The problems of Díaz Ordaz would not be settled easily. The countryside is Mexico's greatest headache.

✤ 9 ✤

Modernization

Mexico is a rapidly changing, rapidly developing country which has hurdled many obstacles in the process of abandoning the traditional society. Since the key organizations and institutions of Mexico's political system are closely linked to the modernization process, it seems appropriate to treat some aspects of this process in concluding this discussion of Mexican politics.

Modernization is a term which refers to a multitude of social concerns much too extensive for exhaustive examination within our available limits of time and space. However, an effort will be made to call attention to several variables which are generally assigned high priority. For purposes of this study it seems best to have a look at four main areas — industrial growth, transportation, commercial development, and educational progress.

In discussing modernization, distortion of the general picture may be partially avoided through some mention of shortcomings and failures, areas of life where modernization has not reached. Thus it is necessary to call attention to the fact that there exists a "marginal" Mexico which is not enjoying the benefits of new growth and change. There are political implications in this situation that must not be overlooked. Finally, in this chapter there is a concluding glance at the big picture and a focus of attention once again on the politics of modernizing Mexico which have been in fact the central concern of this book.

Industrialization

Hopes for the industrialization of Mexico reach back long before the Revolution. In spite of the mercantilist policies of Spain during the colonial period there were a handful of persons who, even at that time, argued for diversification of the economy and industrialization. However, Spanish policy-makers never took these arguments seriously.

After independence those who looked appreciatively toward the comprehensive industrial techniques that were being developed in England found that many political and economic obstacles were in the path before Mexico could take a similar road. In this immediate post-independence period the only efforts to introduce a new industrial activity took place in connection with the founding of textile mills near Orizaba, Veracruz.

With the emergence of the Reform generation in the middle 1850's there were a few businessmen who thought in terms of breaking the hold of the Church on the rural economy and on credit facilities as well as the solution of other pressing problems. Such persons joined with the new group to carry out the Reform, but the laws of the Reform and the edicts of its leaders, while they made inroads against the power of the Church, the higher military clique, and some landowners with commercial interests, failed to bring about the changes necessary. Mexico did not develop a pattern of balanced agricultural and industrial growth similar to that in the United States and Western Europe. By 1876, when Porfirio Díaz became President, the pattern of great land holdings, while generally removed from the hands of the Church, still remained. Industrialization, for its part, could show only the rudimentary beginnings of railroad and telegraph systems, a few textile factories, a little milling, and some "cottage-type" industries.

The motto of the Díaz regime (which lasted until 1910) was "Order and progress" and there was enough of both of these to give Mexico an industrial base for take-off into sustained growth. However, the Revolution of 1910 brought most of the industrial activity to a standstill. There was widespread destruction of capital equipment, and a net loss for the industrialization process resulted.

When the revolutionary fighting had ceased and the real process of consolidation began under Obregón in 1920–21, a number of factors combined to favor renewed development. Businessmen who had been prominent in pre-revolutionary days returned to the country from exile. A new group of enterprising younger men emerged to stimulate a forward movement in the industrialization process. Still another group of able business leaders appeared in the 1930's. These capitalists of the 1920's and 1930's prospered and expanded their enterprises under President Calles and later under President Cárdenas in the latter 1930's. Foreign capital unwilling to cooperate with Mexican government investment plans was not tolerated by Cárdenas. Simultaneously, Mexican industrialists who showed that they could combine public spirit with profit motive were encouraged.

World War II made an important contribution to the Mexican industrialization process. Average increases in industrial output were over 9 per cent a year in the period 1940–1945, and Mexico actually began to export manufactured goods. The end of the war, however, created problems for burgeoning Mexican industry. Once foreign producers were in a position to fill long suppressed domestic needs they began to seek foreign markets. Mexicans found themselves in a difficult position not only with regard to the relatively small export trade they had built up but in their domestic markets as well.

Various devices were used by government to improve the position of the Mexican producer in the immediate postwar years. The peso was devalued to give Mexican products a competitive advantage in price levels. Tariffs were raised, and import controls were established. Public services such as transportation and power affecting cost levels for enterprises were improved. By the end of the 1940's Mexican industrial production was again on the increase. In fact, during the six years of Miguel Alemán's presidency (1946–1952) steel output doubled, and many new consumer products, such as electric washing machines and refrigerators, were manufactured for the first time in Mexico.

Once again an event with far-reaching international consequences, the Korean War, affected Mexico's economic situation. The war years were prosperous, but as the fighting drew to a close, the output of products basic to Mexico's economic situation in most cases stood still or declined. However, by 1955 favorable government policies and great determination on the part of local entrepreneurs had the industrialization process moving forward again. Some older industries such as textiles began widespread modernization. Basic industries such as steel expanded, and the manufacture of pharmaceuticals got a foothold. For the presidential period, 1952–1958, basic industries established new records for production. Insofar as basic industry was concerned Mexican policy appeared firmly established in favor of further expansion.

When Adolfo López Mateos became President in 1958 the full effort of the Mexican state was placed behind the drive for greater steel and electric power production. Basic industries owned by the government were expanded, and all major aspects of Mexican basic industry showed increases ranging up to 20 per cent. After a brief recession in 1961, industrial growth recovered its forward momentum, and when the new President, Gustavo Díaz Ordaz, took over his duties in December, 1964, the manufacturing and basic industry of the Mexican economy appeared ready for another forward push based on abundant resources of industrial raw materials as well as managerial drive and know-how both in the private and public sectors of the economy.

There are several areas which are basic to an examination of

Mexico's industrial growth. Let us turn now to a brief discussion of each of these.

Petroleum

Production of petroleum began in Mexico in 1901, when an American, Edward L. Doheny, brought in his first well near Tampico in the state of Tamaulipas. Subsequently the British began operations in the Tehuantepec region. From 1901 to 1921 total production in Mexico increased every year until the country became the number two oil producer of the world. This phase ended about 1921, and oil production declined a little every year from 1922 through 1932. Government policy toward the oil companies, development of saline deposits in some major fields, and of course, world depression all brought reduced production.

As the years of the 1920's and 1930's passed there were repeated crises between the government and the oil companies. Conflict centered around interpretations of Article 27 of the Mexican Constitution which vests sub-soil rights in the state, and the difficulties finally reached a point which prohibited reconciliation. First came a labor-management dispute which the government was unable to resolve. There followed a dispute between the government and the companies themselves which resulted in an impasse as the companies refused to obey a government directive. When the companies questioned the word of President Lázaro Cárdenas the expropriation order went out on March 18, 1938.[1] Following the expropriation, the government formed a new agency entitled Petroleos Mexicanos (Pemex). The petroleum industry of Mexico has been under the supervision of this autonomous governmental agency ever since. The responsibilities of the new organ were spelled out in a constitutional amendment in 1940. Under that amendment it was provided that only the state could carry on exploitation in the petroleum fields.[2]

The early years were very difficult for Pemex; abroad the industry faced the hostility of the great foreign oil companies with their control of tanker service on the world's seaways, while at home government oil executives confronted excessive demands by labor, expectations of graft on the part of subordinates, and unrealistic pricing policies

[1] See Chapter 1 for a more complete statement of the oil expropriation episode.

[2] The role of the petroleum industry in Mexico's economic development is covered by Padilla Aragón, "La industria petrolera y su influencia en el desarrollo industrial," in *La industria petrolera mexicana* (Mexico, 1958), pp. 45–67.

developed at the presidential level to keep the price of fuel oil and gasoline uniform across the country.

Outstanding in putting the Mexican oil monopoly on an effective operating basis was the service of Antonio Bermúdez under Presidents Alemán and Ruiz Cortines. Improvement continued during the López Mateos presidency. At the beginning of the presidency of Gustavo Díaz Ordaz there had already been eight years of regular growth with yearly production surpassing the figure of 116,400,000 (159-liter barrels).[3] Mexico has tripled its refining capacity, more than quadrupled its proven oil reserves, and quadrupled the length of oil lines. Moreover, the country has now moved into the area of petro-chemicals with eighteen plants projected at various locations across the country. Mexico, an importer of natural gas when Pemex began to function in 1938, has actually become an exporter of this valuable fuel resource today.

There are many criticisms which can be leveled at Pemex in terms of the manner of its operation, but probably the most devastating criticisms of a socio-political nature come from Brandenburg, who points out that the products of Pemex are often carried in trucks which are the property of politicians, that the policy of allowing Pemex stations to remain in private hands has permitted virtual monopolies for those lucky enough to get franchises with the usual political implications, that the distribution of natural gas — although handled by several companies — appears to be very lucrative and related to possession of political influence, and that the few petro-chemical plants projected for "private" ownership seem to have fallen into the hands of prominent politicians.[4]

Electric Power

The generation of electric power in Mexico began with private companies in mining and textiles who needed electricity. Electrical utilities as such emerged as early as 1881, providing street lighting for a small section of Mexico City, and with the appearance of European and American firms on the scene in the early 1900's, electrical generating capacity expanded rapidly. The major company was Mexican Light and Power Company, dominated by a Belgian group and known as Mexlight. It was this company that was given the exclusive right to service Mexico City for the period, 1906–1926.

By 1926 there was considerable stirring in government circles over the question of public ownership of the electric-power industry. As

[3] Frank Brandenburg, *The Making of Modern Mexico* (Englewood Cliffs, N.J.), p. 275.

[4] Brandenburg, p. 275.

of January, 1934, sentiment had progressed to the point that the government went on record in favor of the establishment of a national commission on electricity to promote the expansion of generating and distributing capacity. Under the six-year plan which was approved by the governing party (then called PNR) and Calles, the man who at that time was the head of the Revolutionary Coalition, criteria were spelled out for the development of the industry. There were two major points. First, supply of electric power should not be tied to the profit considerations of the companies. Instead, the central criterion should be maximum use by agricultural and industrial enterprises. The second criterion called for a wider distribution of power throughout the various regions of Mexico.

The body established to carry out these goals was the Federal Electricity Commission (CFE). With the beginning of the operation of the CFE in 1937, new limitations were placed upon foreign ownership. Incentive on the part of the private companies to invest declined, and generating capacity grew very little in the years between 1937 and 1945. Meanwhile Mexlight had been joined by a subsidiary of Electric Bond and Share, known as American and Foreign Power.

In the years following World War II the CFE began to invest an increasing amount of capital in the electric power industry. It was recognized that the situation of the latter 1930's and the war years had put Mexico in the dangerous position of being unable to supply the electrical service necessary to support projected economic development. A major effort was therefore made in the years after 1945, and the fact that consumption increased nearly 11 per cent a year, almost doubling the increase in gross national product in the period 1945 to 1960, points up the success of the effort to expand production of electricity. A major change took place in the pattern of allocation of electrical power. About 70 per cent of electrical production going to the industrial sector was used for the manufacture of consumer goods in 1945, with the remainder going for the manufacture of capital goods. These proportions were reversed by 1960.

The relations between the state and the private companies were relatively calm during the years of Miguel Alemán's administration (1946–1952), although there were difficulties even at this time. However, the real increase in the electrical industry probably was due less to better relations between the government and business than to the determination of the government itself to expand generating and distributing capacity regardless of the cost. With the advent of the Ruiz Cortines administration in December, 1952, it was felt that a new look was necessary at the relations of government and business in the electrical field. A special committee was organized to study the necessities of the electric power industry, but its recommendations were for the most part never acted upon.

During the 1950's the big holdings of Mexlight and of American and Foreign Power came under ever more serious government fire. Especially serious were the controversies over rate-setting; there was also continuous violation of private concessions by the Federal Electricity Commission. The private companies had drawn up new expansion plans, but as the future grew dimmer the plans lay dormant. The companies began drawing more and more on energy generated by CFE installations. On various key issues the state and the foreign-owned companies reached an impasse. More and more Mexlight and American and Foreign Power began to think of selling out to the Mexican government. Finally, in April, 1960, the government acquired American and Foreign Power Company, with all its properties, for a price of $65,000,000. In the late summer of 1960, Mexlight went to the government for a cost of $52,000,000.[5] In addition, the government assumed the medium and long term debt of the company, amounting to $78,000,000. In many quarters Mexicans hailed the purchase of the two power companies as an achievement ranking with the 1938 expropriation of the petroleum industry for the cause of Mexicanization of the country. Mexicans had acquired nearly complete control of a vital and expanding industry. In installed capacity, for instance, there had been 1,400,000 kilowatts in 1951. By 1961 this installed capacity had grown to 3,275,000 kilowatts, an increase of 13 per cent during the ten years.[6]

With the nationalization of the two big companies and a number of small ones the Mexican government came into control of 98 per cent of the installed capacity for public electricity service. In addition there are privately owned generating plants in industries such as mining with generating capacity strictly for the consumption of the enterprise. These have a capacity of 6,140,000 kilowatts which is equivalent to 18.8 per cent of the total national installed capacity. The proportion of electricity generated thermally to that generated hydraulically runs at about 60–40.[7]

Major hydroelectric plants include the new dam on the Balsas River, called the Little Hell or *Infiernillo*, with about 600,000 kilowatts of installed capacity. There is also the dam at Acapulco with about 208,000 kilowatts and several other lesser dams, such as those on the

---

[5] For a thorough discussion of the Mexicanization of electric power see Miguel S. Wionczek, "Electric Power," in *Public Policy and Private Enterprise in Mexico,* Raymond Vernon, ed. (Cambridge, Mass., 1964), pp. 91–106.

[6] Banco Nacional de Comercio Exterior, S.A., *Mexico, 1963,* pp. 27–28.

[7] Banco Nacional de Comercio Exterior, *Mexico, 1963,* p. 136.

Panuco, the Tepalcatepec, the Grijalva, and the Papaloapan Rivers.[8]

Generally, it can be said that the electrical power industry is fulfilling the needs of industrialization in Mexico. However, industrialization makes great demands in terms of ever higher investments for electric power installations, and Mexico will have to obtain loans from the World Bank, the Export-Import Bank, and other foreign lending agencies to expand production at the necessary rate. An important problem for the future centers on the poverty of the rural areas where a low standard of living and low productivity are pointed up by the fact that 50 per cent of Mexico's electric consumption as of 1964 was located in five federal entities — the Federal District, Puebla, Veracruz, Michoacán, and the state of Mexico.[9]

The Steel Industry

Modernization and its basic element, industrialization, are greatly handicapped without the presence of a steel industry. Basic to a steel industry is a domestic iron ore supply. Also important are coal supplies. Fortunately for Mexico there are iron ore reserves on the order of 600,000,000 metric tons. Perhaps most promising of known deposits is that recently discovered at Peña Colorada in the state of Colima. Other important deposits are located in the states of Durango and Michoacán. Iron production in Mexico has been keeping pace with demand. With the yearly production standing at about 1,600,000 metric tons the steel industry of Mexico ranks second among the countries of Latin America.[10] Mexico's major mills are the Fundidora de Fierro y Acero de Monterrey, which was founded in 1903, and the Altos Hornos de Mexico, which began operating in Monclova, Coahuila, in 1944.

Steel production and production of iron ore keep rising but continue to fall short of consumption. However, the imports of steel which occur are mostly in specialty steels which are not produced in Mexico. In spite of the continued need to import, the steel industry has made remarkable strides: production in 1960 was ten times higher than that of 1940. The proportion of steel consumption which had to be covered by imports was about 55 per cent in 1940, and in 1960 it was only 20 per cent.[11]

[8] Banco Nacional de Comercio Exterior, *Mexico, 1963,* p. 138.

[9] Efforts in this connection are illustrated by the continuing expansion of electrical facilities in the sparsely populated territory of Baja California de Sur where the government is spending over 39,000,000 pesos to bring electricity to over 85 per cent of the widely scattered population by the end of the 1960's. *Excelsior,* January 31, 1965.

[10] Only two Latin American countries, Mexico and Brazil, had an integrated steel mill before the 1950's.

[11] Brandenburg, p. 277.

Major weaknesses in the steel industry involve the large amount of steel that is produced from scrap iron rather than from iron ore. This practice involves import costs that might otherwise be avoided by relying upon the available reserves of iron, manganese, and other materials. Another major difficulty has been the low ratio of output to installed capacity, the result of low efficiency. It appears, however, that this problem is beginning to be alleviated.

In Mexico the government has become the major promoter of the steel industry. Not only is the majority equity for Altos Hornos de Mexico in the hands of the government, but since 1962 the government has held majority shares in La Consolidada, which has been integrated with Altos Hornos. In addition to this public ownership there has been generous financial assistance for a number of privately owned "steel producing" and "steel elaboration" concerns. Also the government has been the largest single steel consumer so that the government has provided ownership, financing for private ownership, and a major market for production. Government officials have high hopes for the steel industry, not only in terms of its domestic demand but also in terms of the possibility of exporting crude steel. Plans for the steel industry in the period, 1961–1965, called for production to reach the 3,875,000 metric ton mark with a per capita consumption of 100 kilograms by 1965 as opposed to 57.7 kilograms in 1960.[12]

Cement Industry

Basic to the expansion of plant construction, of a highway network, and of modern building construction in general is the presence of a cement industry. Unlike some other basic industries in Mexico, cement has remained largely the province of private enterprise. Furthermore, private enterprise in cement manufacture has met the challenge of industrial growth, something which has not happened in the electrical power industry, which has been nationalized. Indeed, success has been so outstanding that it appears there is no pressure anywhere to bring Mexican government into this field. Many items are made from cement which are basic to Mexico's modernization. Street light posts and telephone poles, for example, are made from cement. There are, of course, the usual uses for cement in building of all types, especially office buildings and manufacturing plants. Cement is also used for dams, for bridges, for highways, for streets, and for countless other facilities and trappings of modern material development.

Cement production began in Mexico in 1906 but was nearly wiped out by the decade of Revolution from 1910 to 1920. In the 1920's, however, growth began at a moderate rate, and new plants began to

[12] Banco Nacional de Comercio Exterior, *Mexico, 1963,* p. 150.

make their appearance. Appearance of new plants continued during the 1930's, and by 1940 there were eight cement plants operating in Mexico. There was manifest need for increased production. Demand further outstripped supply during the war years, but following the war cement plants began to spring up in various parts of Mexico. As things stood in 1965 the Mexican cement industry not only was keeping pace with Mexican economic development but was actually producing a surplus for export.[13]

One of the healthy aspects of the cement industry is that there is plenty of competition, which results in a variety of cements being produced and keeps prices in line, reducing marginal high cost plants. Another important contribution of the cement industry is its decentralization, providing provincial areas with new industrial activity around which still further activities can be built. Of the twenty-two plants operating in Mexico, over half are outside the densely populated central market zone. It is these considerations which make the future of the cement industry in Mexico brighter than that of the economy as a whole.[14]

Chemical Industries

An important characteristic of the modernization-industrialization process is the development of chemical industries. In Mexico the chemical industries continue to be one of the most dynamic branches of the national economy with great interest being shown in further expansion both by private investors and the government. Most major branches of chemical production are involved. Caustic soda is produced as well as coal tar derivatives. There is also production of chemical fibres. The production of sulphuric acid has increased steadily since 1950 to the point that it nearly satisfies all internal consumption needs of the chemical and steel industries — a very large order indeed. There are eleven firms with thirteen plants having a combined installed capacity of 300,000 metric tons for production of sulphuric acid. Production of caustic soda is keeping up with existing plant having a daily capacity of three metric tons. Mexico has eleven caustic soda plants in production.[15] In the synthetic fibre industry the biggest company is Celanese Mexicana, established in 1947.[16] Chemical fertilizers

[13] An outstanding achievement of the Mexican cement industry has been to capture the markets in the so-called free zones along the country's northern borders where one would expect that cement brought by ocean carriers would undercut the domestic products.

[14] Brandenburg, p. 286.

[15] Banco Nacional de Comercio Exterior, *Mexico, 1963,* pp. 161–162.

[16] Textiles are one of Mexico's oldest industries, having begun in 1830. In their present condition they are not one of the most noteworthy aspects of Mexican modernization. Many of the plants have been using obsolete

and insecticides are also showing an upward production trend, and the foundation and expansion of petrochemicals gives the whole field of chemical industries a new breadth and importance for the future.

Production of Transportation Vehicles

Mexico has had automotive assembly plants since 1925. Characteristically societies in the process of modernizing first have assembly plants and later develop their own domestic construction plants. This appears to be the route along which Mexico also is traveling.[17] Since 1950 the Mexican government has encouraged in various ways the sale of cars assembled with a maximum amount of Mexican-made parts, and the government itself has become involved to some extent in the auto assembly business. Since 1952, when it put up a plant for manufacturing small automobiles and diesel trucks using patents of the Italian Fiat Corporation and later Renault, the general emphasis of government policy has been toward narrowing the opportunities for import of deluxe models and already assembled autos. In 1964 provision was made for further cutting the number of foreign-made parts allowed in any automobile assembled in Mexico.

Another aspect of transportation has been the production of railway boxcars, an increasingly important development in recent years. The center for the manufacture of boxcars is the National Railroad Construction Company located at Ciudad Sahagún, about 65 miles from Mexico City. The plant went into operation in December, 1954, and has been turning out a yearly 1,600 units, principally freight cars, boxcars, and gondolas. It was estimated that by 1964 there were 13,000 made-in-Mexico railroad cars on the tracks. The use of foreign parts in the manufacture of these cars has dropped from 82 to 20 per cent. Some of the freight cars are moving into export trade.[18]

Transportation

Expanding transportation facilities are essential to material progress. The condition of the transportation system or systems, as it may be, is a key indicator of the modernization achievement of a particular country. Mexico has both rail and highway nets as well as air transportation.

---

machinery and in general have had inefficient practices which the industry is now trying to overcome.

[17] The General Motors plant at Toluca, state of Mexico, opened early in 1965, and has a maximum capacity of 20,000 units per year. This represents a new and immensely important step forward in the development of a Mexican automotive industry. With the opening of this plant Mexico is in a position to export on a significant scale.

[18] Brandenburg, p. 295.

Railroads

Railroad building on a small scale began early in Mexico, and by 1875 there were 357 miles of railroads. Railway construction expanded greatly after that time, but in many cases there was a duplication of service and competition for export business rather than emphasis upon linking various regions of the country with a view to providing for the internal market. Before the fall of Porfirio Díaz (1919) the government had bought a majority interest in the three largest railroad lines, and Mexico's railway system had been formed with 12,257 miles of railroads, almost as many as Mexico had in 1964. In recent years the government has concentrated less on expanding the track mileage than on improving track bed. There are long stretches of track which now are broad gauge where there used to be narrow gauge track (over 90 per cent of the track is now broad gauge), and there is frequent use of the so-called "elastic" track — long sections of soldered track resting on concrete ties. In addition to improvements in roadbed an effort is being made to modernize the fleet of locomotives by bringing in new diesel engine units (about half the locomotives are diesel-powered). Other signs of progress include more modern railroad stations and railroad repair shops. The construction of boxcars and other freight units mentioned above also has helped improve the Mexican railway situation and it is generally agreed that both passenger and freight service represent many improvements over the situation twenty years ago.

Mexican rails are government-owned.[19] Major administrative criticisms revolve around failure to pass on the gains in the railroad industry more rapidly to shippers and failure to utilize all available cargo space from the shipping point. Accounting in the case of government-owned and operated industry is always difficult, but it is noteworthy that Mexico's credit with the Export-Import Bank in connection with the purchase of railroad equipment has been excellent. The Exim Bank made its thirteenth major railway equipment loan to Mexico for the purchase of thirty diesel locomotives in 1965. Altogether in 1965 Mexico had borrowed $228,500,000 from the Exim Bank for railway equipment and had repaid all but $79,500,000. No payments or interest were overdue.

[19] The exceptions are four privately owned and operated rail lines, the longest of which runs for 77 kilometers between Tijuana and Tecate in Baja California. In all, total private service covers only 186 kilometers, clearly a very small percentage of the total network .

Highways

Development of modern highways in Mexico dates from about 1925, when a commission known as the National Road Commission was set up to sponsor a highway building program. Under this group highways were built out from Mexico City to Puebla, to Pachuca in the state of Hidalgo, and to Cuernavaca in the state of Morelos. With the lessons learned from the foreign engineers in the building of these roads, the Mexicans set about building a highway net that would connect all major points of the country. One of the major roads in this effort was the Pan American Highway constructed during the administration of President Lázaro Cárdenas. Important programs both of major highway expansion and in the expansion of "feeder" roads occurred during the latter 1940's and 1950's. Counting both public highways and toll roads, Mexico was expected to have 35,000 miles of permanent transit highways by 1965.[20]

Highway development has been made possible through a tax on gasoline, through the use of tax monies from various national and state government funds, and, in part, through foreign loans. Motor transportation in Mexico is complicated by the fact that the traveller often has to slow to ten miles an hour trying to negotiate the primitive cobblestone streets of some small town that stands as a barrier along the main artery of highway travel. Even at such a slow pace the holes in the street surface constitute a major hazard to automobiles, as does the narrowness of the streets themselves. Both conditions are better today than they used to be, but other problems are developing in the large cities. This is particularly true of Mexico City, where automobile traffic has increased to such an extent that the streets in many parts of the capital are clogged with vehicles.

Aviation

The history of aviation in Mexico dates from the second decade of the twentieth century, but the first truly commercial airline did not get under way until 1924. Gradually the number of commercial airlines operating in Mexico has grown to over 300, with thirty-four lines offering regularly scheduled flights. There are 900 airports, thirteen of which serve international traffic. Mexico has three airlines of her own which fly international routes. Various plans have been brought forward to make the overseas flights profitable, but as yet no satisfactory plan has been hit upon. One difficulty involves the

[20] See Paul Lamartine Yates, *El desarrollo regional de México* (Mexico, 1961), pp. 73–74.

nineteen foreign-owned airlines flying the airways to and from Mexico.[21]

Commerce

Commerce has many aspects which might be discussed in connection with modernization. In some sense transportation and communication, already mentioned, fit in here, as do many types of food processing, warehousing of all kinds of goods, and the entire gamut of retail activity. What we are particularly concerned with is the change in the way goods have been put into the hands of consumers in Mexico in the years since World War II. The traditional patterns which prevailed in Mexico in 1945 were reminiscent of the United States at the turn of the century. In the better stores glass counters covered most of the items; seldom was there an open rack or an open counter which would give people an opportunity to examine the merchandise closely. Credit buying, of course, was practically nonexistent and generally imported goods were preferred to Mexican-made goods. In the streets the masses purchased basic necessities from vendors who provided a narrow choice of low-quality items. Frequently the corn for tortillas was ground in the home; slaughterhouses were usually unsanitary; adulteration of milk was frequent; and an established price for goods was unknown. Bargaining over prices was an integral part of the

[21] Although space does not permit discussion of Mexico's communications net, one should point out that there is a well developed postal service with over 4,500 post offices throughout the country; the telegraph has been operating in Mexico since 1852, and remains a basic communications medium, with 29,500 miles of line and 14,000 telegraph stations. There are 635,000 installed telephones in the country. The latter probably has the poorest service of all communications. However, as 1965 began, steps were under way to change this situation. An expenditure of 525 million pesos was planned for the year with a proposed expenditure of 2.5 billion pesos by 1968. The telephone companies are privately owned. In radio broadcasting Mexico has about 420 stations of which 385 in 1965 were commercial stations. Competitive production in the world market and in Mexico's domestic market among electronics manufacturers makes it relatively inexpensive to own radios in Mexico. There were over 6,000,000 radios in 1965, and Mexico on this point rated higher than any other Latin American country. In television, at the present rate of growth it appeared that there would be close to 2,000,000 sets by 1970. Motion pictures as a medium of communication in Mexico are extremely important in that the Mexican public has yet relatively few television sets and consumer prices are set by the government at a very low rate. Going to movies is one of the average Mexican's favorite entertainments. Mexico has its own movie industry. Mexicans seem to prefer American and other foreign films, though the government is working to change this.

merchandising process. In contrast to these arrangements, Mexico of today knows the hallmarks of modern sales practices. This means that quality and prices are frequently standardized, and that credit buying is widespread. Clothes are accessible for consumer examination as are many other types of goods. Shops are loaded with Mexican-made products which are often preferred to foreign makes, although it must be admitted that tariff barriers have something to do with the price levels that make Mexican goods competitive.

The dairy industry, and in general the handling of milk products, is much better policed than formerly. The old monopoly in the handling of fish which frequently resulted in unsanitary products has been abolished. New practices in the raising and handling of fowl have made this product generally safe instead of generally unsafe. Slaughter-houses are more often clean than dirty.

Food packaging has been particularly important in the new ware-housing methods which have brought continuous supply in the food industries, where before there were often shortages because of lack of methods of storage and packaging. Indeed, the packaging industry can be said to have kept up very well with the challenge of moderniza-tion and the movement away from traditional methods of merchan-dising.

In the manufacture of consumer goods there are important Mexican business combinations in canned foods, packaged bakery goods, pack-aged coffee, carbonated beverages, beer, textiles, kitchen appliances, and porcelain, although foreign firms continue important in refriger-ators and stoves, sewing machines, soaps and detergents. The Mexicans together with the foreign groups provide these and other items. The backbone of the consumer goods industry is made up of a combination of domestic and foreign capital.

In retail sales, both of food and dry goods, as in other categories of consumer products, Mexicans have taken gigantic strides in the past twenty years. For example, there are now self-service food super-markets. There are also giant discount house-supermarket establish-ments operating in chains just as they do in the United States. There are also chains of smaller grocery stores both in Mexico City and throughout the states.

One of the major innovators on the Mexican scene has been Sears Roebuck. The Sears operation began in Mexico in 1947 and was probably the most important force in taking Mexico away from tradi-tional merchandising practices. Sears has also been immensely im-portant in stimulating Mexican consumer goods manufactures. Both large industries and small manufacturing establishments have come into being largely on the basis of demand from Sears retail sales. The new approach has been successful, and Sears has become one of the largest private businesses in Mexico. It is also one of the most modern both in its sales methods and its handling of personnel, having paved the way in both fields.

Particularly outstanding among Mexicans in the consumer goods field both as manufacturer and retailer has been the Salinas Rocha complex, which is led by sons of the founders, both of whom were trained at the Wharton School of Finance and Commerce in the United States. Still another group in Mexico which once was a leader in merchandising is sometimes referred to as the "French Group," and has been connected with such important stores in Mexico City as El Puerto de Liverpool and Palacio de Hierro along with a strong complex of textile manufacturing plants. This group has been pushing to get in the forefront of innovation and modernization.

The Mexican government has also been responsible for developing new ways of merchandising. Indeed, private entrepreneurs have developed more modern techniques in response to new government legislation regarding slaughterhouses and food and drug processing. The government has also established a modern plant for meat processing and canning. Particularly important has been the role of the government agency known as CONASUPO, which attempts, in the fields of purchasing and retailing, to keep down the price level of basic commodities. CONASUPO includes another government agency, previously alone in the field, known as CEIMSA. CEIMSA still operates, but within the framework of CONASUPO. The purpose is to provide a direct link between producer and consumer, cutting out the extra charges that go with middlemen practices in many areas. It is possible through the action of this agency, which buys and sells many basic foodstuffs, to control to some extent the prices of private stores by setting a lower price and forcing others to meet the competition. One device that has been developed in connection with the operation of CONASUPO is the mobile grocery store in which trailers pulled by diesels visit slum neighborhoods in Mexico City selling basic grocery items. Thus the state, which has moved into basic industry and transportation, has also been moving into the consumer goods field. If, however, Mexico can develop fast enough to boost consumer power, it is unlikely that the government will become as important in this area as it has in others. This is essentially because the Mexican government is pragmatic rather than socialistic in its orientation and generally does not become involved where private enterprise is fulfilling a useful social role.

Education

Education stands near the center of the modernization process. Without it the technical skills so essential to modernization are likely to remain unmastered. And without education the communication process, which requires sharing of values on a wide scale, remains undeveloped, since symbols known to and used by leaders and followers alike do not exist. Moreover, it is nearly impossible to have effective popular participation without wide dissemination of the basic learning skills, the three R's.

Clearly, literacy by itself does not bring more democratic practices in the sense of wide effective participation among the populace, but, as many have pointed out, more democratic practices are not likely to come without literacy. Both psychologically and materially the collective effort needed to provide the driving force for the process of modernization is severely handicapped without a literate population possessing a variety of technical and social skills. Thus, nearly all twentieth-century revolutions have brought forward the promise to expand existing educational facilities and bring basic learning skills to all members of the population.

No one knows just the degree of illiteracy in Mexico prior to the Revolution of 1910, but it seems fair to estimate that the average for the country was about 80 per cent with the illiteracy rate in some areas running several points higher.[22] Education provides hope for improvement — for a better life — and is a tool to create a stronger and more unified nation. The aspirations involved were reflected in slogans of the Revolution such as "Land and Books," or "To Educate is to Redeem," and it is significant that the third article of the revolutionary Constitution of 1917 was concerned with education.

The emphasis assigned to education in the Constitution, in subsequent laws, and in the budgets of many administrations since 1917 has not been sufficient to meet Mexico's needs. The obstacles to educational goals have been great. First of all, Mexico has had one of the highest birth rates in the world.[23] There has also been a vast amount of inertia in rural areas, and in some parts of the country there have been complex linguistic and culture patterns. The difficulties of educating have been much greater in some regions than in others. There are many communities which still have no schools; there are many others where schools offer no more than one or two grades. In

[22] Eighty per cent is the minimum figure. Some writers estimate 90 per cent or over.

[23] Gilberto Loyo, *Población y desarrollo económico* (Mexico, 1963), p. 46.

the majority of elementary schools students continue to be enrolled only in the first two grades.

In the usual Latin American pattern, Mexicans who can afford to do so send their children to private schools, but the number of those thus well situated is relatively small, so that the main burden of educating the nation falls to government. While some of the existing private schools are overtly Catholic and demand the learning of catechism and attendance at mass, many private schools overlook these matters. Generally, the Roman Church has lacked the financial and personnel resources necessary to make it an effective educational force on a large scale. Moreover, constitutional provisions and the general trend of government policy have obstructed clerical efforts in the educational field. One of the most notable exceptions is the Jesuit Universidad Ibero-Americana in Mexico City.

Educational efforts have hardly been an unqualified success, but they certainly have not been an unqualified failure in "revolutionary" Mexico. The rate of achievement is pointed out in Table 5. With scarce material resources the Mexicans set out to innovate to meet the challenges of their environment. They learned how to establish schools in rural areas; they trained personnel to teach in Indian schools; they developed a device known as the "cultural mission" and another known as the "rural normal school." Anti-illiteracy campaigns were inaugurated in the 1920's and 1930's, and in the 1940's a sweeping effort to have "each one teach one" produced observable results.

In general, the percentage of government budgets devoted to education rose during the 1930's and 1940's. However, in the latter 1940's emphasis on other programs began to cut down the relative expendi-

Table 5

School Enrollments (1910–1960)

Years	General population	Primary population	Children not enrolled (%)
1910	15,160,369	3,486,910	74.6
1925	14,334,780	2,945,519	67.9
1940	19,653,552	3,952,512	41.4
1960	34,625,000	7,660,514	34.38*

* Note difference in percentage, 1940–1960, compared to 1925–1940.

Source: Víctor Gallo M., "La educación preescolar y primaria," in *México: cincuenta años de revolución* (Mexico, 1962), IV, p. 70.

tures on education. The pattern of diminishing expenditures changed when Adolfo López Mateos took office in 1958; at that time the percentage of the budget devoted to education began to increase. Under López Mateos, a National Commission on Education was organized to set up a long-term plan for the development of education at all levels and particularly at the primary level throughout Mexico. The result of the commission's deliberations was an Eleven Year Plan which went into effect in 1960. The education budget in 1960 went over 18 per cent of the general budget for the first time since the 1940's. The total sum planned for expenditure over an eleven-year period was approximately five billion pesos. Under the Eleven Year Plan, 27,440 classrooms are to be constructed in rural areas. These are to operate on a single session basis. In the cities there are to be constructed 11,825 new classrooms to operate on a double session basis. Another phase of the plan involves repair for 36,735 rural schools and 11,238 houses for rural teachers, as well as repair for 2,518 urban schools. Still another aspect of the plan calls for training 61,200 new teachers at the rate of 5,600 teachers a year from 1960 through 1966, and 6,000 teachers a year from 1967 through 1970. Included also in the planning is the reorganization of the Federal Institute of Teacher Preparation (IFCM). On a broader scale the reorganization of the entire national normal school system is also called for, and in this connection the construction of four new regional normal schools is planned.[24]

An important phase of the Eleven Year Plan calls for the presentation or donation of teaching material. This distribution of material comes under the "free textbook" program which was inaugurated by López Mateos shortly after taking office. Experience showed that many children were unable to pay the required prices for texts, a difficulty which was aggravated by the fact that the schools often lacked library facilities. Much time was spent, therefore, while the teacher dictated lesson material so that it could be copied into notebooks; this material was frequently memorized for examination purposes. Under the free textbook program all students in the first four grades are given the same government-issue textbooks. The goal is to include all six primary grades in the distribution of this free textbook material. The free textbook program is under the control of the National Commission of Free Textbooks (*Comisión Nacional de los Libros de Textos Gratuitos*). The program was inaugurated in 1959. By 1960, 17 million volumes were being printed and by the mid-1960's, well over 20 million volumes were being distributed.

[24] Celerino Cano, "Análisis de la acción educativa," in *Mexico: cincuenta años de revolución* (Mexico, 1962), IV, p. 30.

At mid-year of 1965 the Minister of Education, Agustín Yáñez, emerged from a conference with the President and made a presentation to the press which clearly indicated the determination of the Díaz Ordaz government to comply with the goals of the Eleven Year Plan formulated under former President Adolfo López Mateos. Plans were under way for contracts with the government in building classrooms. Sixteen states had already signed contracts, and on this basis 3,526 classrooms were projected. Money had also been allotted for 3,970 more primary teachers, 3,874 literacy instructors and 3,671 secondary teachers. The free textbook program was holding its own with the population increase. In the first half of 1965 17,343,277 books were distributed. For the entire year of 1965 the government expected to have completed a total of 1,057 educational plants capable of providing secondary instruction to 55,800 students. The entire prospect looked bright enough to prompt the Minister of Education to remark that 1965 was well over 100 per cent of the average annual increase which had been planned in order to solve the problem of affording schooling opportunities for all Mexico's children by 1970.[25]

Neither what the minister said nor what he omitted were most important in this press conference. His willingness to state precisely a number of goals reflected a seriousness toward this problem on the part of the government that augured well for the Eleven Year Plan. Explicit commitment to concrete goals should be distinguished in this case from a general oratorical pronouncement on the desirability of furthering education.

One of the points on which the success of the Eleven Year Plan will depend is the proposal to strengthen the operation of the Federal Institute of Teacher Preparation (IFCM). This agency helps to train professors who have not yet received their teacher's degrees. Enrolled with the IFCM are over 27,000 student professors. They reflect the pressure upon Mexican educators to reduce the number of non-degree people in teaching positions. Until the Eleven Year Plan was adopted, only about 3,000 teachers were receiving degrees every year from the country's normal schools. The object is to increase this number considerably. As has been pointed out above, personnel is being added to the eleven regional sub-offices of the IFCM as well as to the thirty-two state coordinating agencies. Arrangements have been made for distribution of free textbooks to the student teachers, and lessons by correspondence are broadcast over seventy radio stations.

There are, however, a number of obstacles which the Eleven Year Plan encounters. For example, there are a large number of small com-

---

[25] *El Día,* June 10, 1965.

munities in which it is difficult to establish primary schools that fit normally within the system. The government has used cultural missions to help with this problem. The cultural mission is a team of technicians who go out to the villages to try to bring some of the elements of modern living. The cultural mission reflects recognition that the proper community attitude must exist if the children are to learn their lessons. The mission undertakes the basic education of the whole population of the local community.

Preparation of the community, i.e., its social development, is related to the work of personnel from a number of ministries and not just the Ministry of Public Education. Other types of personnel include agricultural specialists, experts in problems of small industries, doctors, nurses, and social workers. The cultural mission helps to cultivate a closer connection among the representatives of the agencies that are serving rural communities. Clearly the agencies have different rules, but their purposes are congruent. In addition to the Department of Agrarian and Colonization Affairs at least three other ministries are frequently involved — the Ministries of Agriculture, Health, and Education. They all have different approaches, but theirs is the same goal.

It is clear that the cultural mission occupies a central role in the social development of rural villages and that this is closely tied to economic development and modernization in general. Some cultural missions are motorized, many others are not, or are only partially motorized. Motorized missions will frequently have as many as three units which carry small libraries, audio-visual equipment, and small workshops. Motorized missions support the programs of non-motorized missions and help to coordinate them. More and more cultural missions are becoming motorized under the Eleven Year Plan. Over twenty of the seventy-eight non-motorized cultural missions in operation now have some motorized equipment as distinct from the situation at the beginning of the Eleven Year Plan. Besides cultural missions, there are also reading rooms which are kept open in many of the more backward areas. Another device is the instructional "brigade" which teaches fundamental agricultural techniques, but at the same time attempts to inspire a more general thirst for learning.

Use of the cultural missions is based upon the fact that education may be served in many ways other than the teaching of the three R's. Various aspects of modernization, when they reach a village, improve the climate for learning in school. A public sanitation plant, for example, or a system providing public drinking water may bring a sense of progress and an urgency to participate in the new kind of life; so do irrigation works and small industries. The construction of modern dwellings and the distribution of information on new techniques of agriculture and the mechanic arts as well as new ways of living all produce a climate more favorable to the educational process itself.

In spite of the Eleven Year Plan, with its projected expansion of classrooms and numbers of teachers, its free textbooks, and its strengthening of cultural missions, the pressure on Mexican policy-makers to produce adequate educational facilities will continue for some time. The nature of the problem is pointed out to some extent by the following considerations. In 1958–1959 all the primary schools of the republic — federal, state, municipal, and private — enrolled 4,436,651 children. Of these children 2,437,539 were in schools supported by the federal government. The number of students in schools supported by the federal government increased by 1961 to 3,171,768 and continued to increase at a rate of nearly 500,000 per year.[26] Clearly, under such circumstances the challenge in terms of expanding existing plant and producing the necessary teachers is great indeed.[27]

There is no question that, even though provision of primary education constitutes a fundamental commitment of the regime, fulfillment of that commitment in itself would not take care of the educational needs of the country. Technicians and engineers of all kinds are necessary, and these must be trained beyond the primary level, otherwise there can be little innovation, and the drive for modernization will lose its force.

The existing secondary system of public school education in Mexico began with four installations in the Federal District in 1926. There were about 3,860 pupils. The system has grown to the point that there are now 350 secondary schools with others in stages of completion

[26] There are no available figures on the distribution of students among schools other than federal ones. It is thus difficult to say what part of the burden is borne by state, municipal, and private schools. Municipal schools are few and are supported with scarce municipal funds and some private money. State schools rely on a combination of federal and state funds. Purely private schools, of course, are dependent on tuition and donations.

[27] Jaime Torres Bodet, "Perspectives de la educación," in *México: cincuenta años de revolución* (Mexico, 1962), IV, p. 4. The basic structure of education in Mexico provides a number of avenues to post-primary accomplishment other than the standard pattern, which is one of primary six years, secondary three years, preparatory two years, and university three to seven years. Thus, instead of entering secondary after primary, students may enter a five-year preparatory school, or they may enter a six-year normal school. Also, after primary, students may go to a school of commerce or attend some school of pre-vocational studies. Some vocational schools, as in the case of agricultural training or training in the mechanic arts, may operate at the level of preparatory and normally lead into specialized technical fields of the type offered in the National Polytechnic Institute. See George F. Kneller, *The Education of the Mexican Nation* (New York, 1951), p. 13.

being brought along all the time. There are over 120,000 pupils, and this figure does not take into account various types of secondary education being dispensed in the private schools, in the preparatory schools attached to the universities, and in pre-vocational schools. In fact, the number of students who are getting some kind of education beyond the primary level is increasing rapidly, but facilities and teachers must be further increased to meet the needs of those who now seek this opportunity. A new tactic by which the government now attempts to meet the challenge centers on encouragement of various types of private and quasi-public enterprises to support schools from their earnings in order to ease the government burden. Incentives relied upon are not altogether clear.

One important side of the battle to expand secondary education in Mexico involves the need to replace the traditional attitude that a secondary education is simply a matter of manufacturing candidates for schools of the university. Progress has been made at this point by dividing the original five-year period of preparatory education for the university into three years of secondary and two years of some other kind of training. It is also done by cutting down on the number of subjects taught to secondary students, setting these at a new minimum, including history, the sciences, mathematics, foreign language, and civics.

The Eleven Year Plan and directives relating to it stress the importance of training for civics both in terms of social action and in terms of academic work. The object is to provide not only a student who will aid the modernization process, but also one who understands the reasons for supporting the *patria*.[28]

In lesser number than the secondary schools are the forty-one federal schools with over 24,000 students which the Mexicans call special training schools (called now technical, industrial, and commercial schools). These include studies oriented toward industrial work and artisanry. One of the objectives is to expand the facilities of these schools, diversifying them and accentuating in them the character of elementary industrial preparation without overlooking the formative aspect so important in a school attended by adolescents. The students in such schools are predominantly in elementary technical preparation (56.7 per cent), in commerce (28.8 per cent), and in sewing, cooking and other aspects of home economics (14.5 per cent).[29]

Relatively few young people matriculate in Mexico's universities. Even so, the costs are high. Officials point out in public announcements

[28] Bulletin of the Directive Committee of the National Technical Council of Education (CDECMTE). January, 1960.
[29] Torres Bodet, pp. 9–14.

that, even though constitutional imperatives command education to be given by the state free of charge, there is no fundamental rule saying that the government must undertake the gigantic task of seeing to it that all educational functions from primary grades through the university must be performed. Thus, unions, private enterprises of various kinds, and even public enterprises as well as civic work organizations are asked to consider that there is incumbent upon them an increasing and undeniable responsibility to help provide various types of education in Mexico.

A major problem of higher education in Mexico is the centralization of facilities and the mushrooming of enrollments in the Federal District. One reason for this situation has to do with the tendency of Mexican industrialists and financiers to overlook the importance of philanthropic giving to education. Support comes, with a very few notable exceptions, from federal and state funds, and these tend to be unbalanced in favor of the facilities in the Federal District, since events in the capital are most in the eye of policy-makers.

One of the major problems with regard to concentration of resources in the Federal District rests on the fact that the greater part of the professional people, including teachers, locate in Mexico City. Mexicans say a majority of the professionals are recruited from outside the population of the capital. Young people born in the provinces travel to the capital, and only infrequently return after graduation to the region where they spent their youth. This is the unfortunate phenomenon of an educational "macrocephalia" which greatly limits technological know-how and social skills of all kinds needed to promote cultural and economic life of the provinces. Politically the result is unsatisfactory not only because the focus of these professionals continues to be on the capital rather than on their home areas, but also because they find great frustration in this focus. Social values and social influence thus accumulate in the capital, and so also do facts of value such as information concerning access to those in political power. The capital becomes overcrowded with legions of competitors often without hope and frustrated in their aims, bitter in their failure.

In recent years Mexican officials have been encouraging the universities of the states to provide a more even development of educational facilities at the university level throughout the country. The plan is to have state universities arrange with others to provide only certain schools, resulting in a division of labor which is less costly than the situation in which each state university tries to cover the full range of professional subjects. The scheme which has caught the imagination of Mexico's educational leaders at the university level is one in which three to five state universities work out agreements for a division of labor spanning a number of different kinds of training. Such agreements, it is said, would produce a series of regional universities offering as a unit an education equaling that of the National University of Mexico (UNAM).

Finally, in addition to the issues of private participation and the combination of state facilities, there is the concern with an orientation which goes beyond mere dissemination of higher learning. The universities must produce not only skilled leaders but responsible leaders, it is argued. Their function must be viewed by the leadership of the universities as well as by the students in the light of the social contribution which the university as an institution can make, not only through its presence but through the work of its students after they graduate. The goal, as Jaime Torres Bodet pointed out to the National Technical Council of Education (CNTE) on July 29, 1959, is "to combine sensitivity, character, imagination, and creativity with an understanding of democracy not only as a legal structure but also as a system of life dedicated to economic, social, and cultural improvement of the whole people." Schools must produce not only an opportunity for the individual to improve himself but also inculcate in the students dedication to progress for the entire country. He said, "[we need] students who know how to work hard, have technical competence, but also have, above all, a spirit of justice and a love for the *patria*."[30] Mexico cannot wait for these things to happen simply through the process of time. Mexican officials must encourage this kind of development through constant lectures and speeches and, hopefully, example itself.

Meanwhile the problem of winning the idealism of the students in support of the regime continues. Carlos A. Madrazo, president of the PRI, called this to the attention of his own generation of politicians — men who got their start about 1930 — when Madrazo alone among the country's leading politicians supported a student maneuver in favor of the drivers on one of Mexico City's bus lines in the spring of 1965. The drivers struck for higher wages, were ignored by management and by all relevant government agencies, and finally turned to the politically conscious students for help. The students kidnapped sixteen buses and parked them in a lot on the national university campus. While most officials in government and party leaders characterized the students as extremists, leftists and Castroists, Madrazo came out in support of the student effort. He warned the men of his generation that they might lose the university students entirely if care was not exercised. Madrazo clearly saw such events as much more vital

[30] Torres Bodet, p. 16.

than phrases like "love of fatherland" and speeches prepared by skilled orators.

The constitutional and social norm of the Mexican educational system is the obligation to expand the essential base of the public school system of education so that no one lacks that indispensable cultural minimum which is the completion of primary school — first through sixth grades. The problem raises the question of the expense for the construction of classrooms, the payments of salaries, and the training of teachers. It also raises the question of motivation for many Mexican youths who suffered economic deprivation in order to attend even the primary grades. Also involved is the question of leadership from the secondary and normal school levels of training in order that the entire educational training system may go forward. Leadership from the secondary, normal school, and ultimately the university levels of training must be expanded continually if the entire educational system, and with it modernization as a process, is to advance.

Awareness of the problem presented in education of the Mexican people was reflected at the top level of political leadership in a speech by the presidential candidate López Mateos in the city of Durango in 1958:

> [The Mexican educational system] presents in many aspects a too theoretical tone. . . . man needs to know what he ought to do, intellectual preparation ought to take place along with technical preparation. . . . The national educational system ought to represent less a pyramid at the base of which is found the mass that only studies the ABC's and at the peak of which is found the minority which is graduated in the professions and specializes in the sciences. . . . It is indispensable that the greater number of the population receive a better quality of knowledge in order to take advantage of the technology of the era in which we live for their own benefit and for the benefit of the collectivity.[31]

Soon after Gustavo Díaz Ordaz became President he served notice that education was to be one of his major concerns. A new National Literacy Campaign was started with great fanfare and official speech-making throughout the country. At the same time Augustín Yáñez, the Minister of Education, attended a meeting at which the official line incorporated the goal of schooling for every child by 1970.

Certainly education and a literate population are fundamental goals of the Revolution. Failure to achieve them cannot be overlooked by governments who claim a place in the revolutionary tradition. This is

[31] Torres Bodet, p. 15.

precisely where the Eleven Year Plan with its projected accomplishments for 1970 becomes a vital factor in the whole picture. For the fact is that the Mexican Revolution has fallen short in many ways and education is one of these. Moreover, the specific importance of education seems to intertwine with other revolutionary goals of modernization which have not been fulfilled for many Mexicans.

Modernization and Marginalism

The problem confronting Mexico with regard to education is in many ways a problem of the discrepancy between opportunities made available to the urban population and those available to the rural population. A significantly larger number of the urban population, approximately 76 per cent, can read and write while only about 48 per cent of the rural population can do so.

This discrepancy is relevant to the general picture of modernization in Mexico because criteria relating to social change have the same tendency as does the difference in educational level. For example, it is estimated that only 13 per cent of the urban population do not eat bread made from wheat (*pan de trigo*), while over 50 per cent of the rural population fall in this category. Some of the figures collected in connection with the 1960 census provide an estimate that over twenty-five million persons, age one or over, ate some meat, fish, milk, or eggs while over eight million ate none of these. The distribution of benefits between the urban and rural populations once again followed the examples given above, with about 87 per cent of the urban population eating one or more of these types of foods while more than 50 per cent of the rural population ate none of these. The use of shoes is also taken as a criterion of development. About 84 per cent of the urban population of Mexico use shoes, but only about 40 per cent of the rural population do so.[32]

It has been suggested that the above-mentioned indicators form a pattern. Illiteracy, the absence of wheat products, meat, fish, milk, eggs in the diet, the use of sandals or simply walking barefooted all seem to go together; that is, if a person fits in one category the probabilities are high that he will fit in most of the others as well. Most of the people in these categories are rural people. Thus there is what might be termed a second world in Mexico, a marginal world. One might refer to this phenomenon as "marginalism."[33] One of the

[32] Pablo González Casanova, *La democracia en México* (Mexico, 1965), pp. 63–64.

[33] González Casanova, p. 64. Pablo González Casanova has been director of the *Escuela Nacional de Ciencias Políticas y Sociales* of the *Universidad Nacional Autónima de México* for the past ten years and has devoted most

dark sides of Mexican development is that the quantity of the rural
population which falls within this marginal category seems to have
increased over the past decades, a fact which is obscured by the propor-
tional decrease of the same group. The apparent paradox can only be
explained in terms of Mexico's population explosion, which involves
an increase of about one million inhabitants per year.

As indicated above, one of the significant considerations which makes
deprivation in the countryside more important is that the number of
rural dwellers has increased. This is a fact which tends to be obscured
by the proportionate increase of the urban population over the rural
population. It is enough to make one stop to reflect, however, when
one considers that the rural population was estimated at approximately
eleven million in 1910 and a little over seventeen million in 1960. The
hunger for land and the general low level of living in the country are
more understandable in these terms. Given this kind of picture, it is
possible that there will still be at least ten million illiterates, three
million of school age without the opportunity to attend school, ten
million who cannot afford to eat wheat products, and as many as
fourteen million who cannot afford shoes in 1970.[34]

At the bottom of the marginal group is the Mexican Indian. Once
again it has been pointed out in government statements and by scholars
that the Indian proportionately has become less a factor in Mexican
life. But again the proportions obscure the effect of the population
increase and the fact that Indians or people with an Indian way of life
have been increasing in absolute numbers. In fact it is maintained
that the last census reflects both a relative and absolute increase in
the number of persons speaking solely an Indian language or dialect
and an absolute increase in the group speaking Indian as well as
Spanish languages.[35] There are projections which show a continuation
in this pattern.

The importance of the Indian in Mexican life lies in the fact that
his treatment tends to pull down the general level of living in the region
where he is found. Characteristic of these regions are predominantly
subsistence economies, a minimum monetary level, low quality products, depleted lands, low quality seeds, poorly bred work animals, and
pre-Hispanic or colonial methods of land exploitation. In general,
predominantly Indian regions tend to have a lower standard of living

---

of his research and analytical effort to the study of marginalism and its
effects.

[34] If the Eleven Year Plan in education is successfully carried through by
the Díaz Ordaz government, many deprivations of the marginal Mexico
which we are describing in this section will decrease significantly.

[35] González Casanova, p. 71.

than do other agricultural regions. The state of Oaxaca is a classic example of such a poor region. All kinds of indicators point this up — the high infant mortality rate, illiteracy, absence of such services as schools, hospitals, sewage and electricity, a high degree of alcoholism, aggressiveness of one community toward another, great reliance upon magic, economic manipulation and political manipulation of most people in the region by those few who have capital and political resources at their disposal.[36]

It appears that where the Indian and the *ladino*[37] live side by side, political exploitation of the Indian seems to be the rule and this in turn sets norms in Mexican politics which are not the most desirable. The *ladino* through his contacts with higher authorities manages to keep the Indian in a situation of tutelage. It is always the *ladino* who staffs the formal or constitutional institutions of government. The anthropological accounts of Indian life in Mexico are replete with events involving injustice toward Indians on the part of the *ladino* government authorities, humiliation of all kinds, violence, even to the point of military attack and acts which run all the way from mere caprice to the planned robbery of Indian lands and the elimination of Indian leaders.[38]

The *ladino* official develops an image of the Indian which seems to carry over into other areas of political life. The behavior pattern established not infrequently is applied even when Indians are not concerned. The Indian is approached as an inferior being who is lazy and given to lying and stealing and who deserves little from the authorities. This image is based upon a heightened sense of superiority toward the subject of authority. The treatment of the Indian tends to ramify to reach all people in the marginal category. It creates on their part a sense of conformity, of withdrawal from any conflict, of the acceptance of paternalism, of skepticism. This is the kind of person who does not understand the institutions described in this book, and the usual accompanying condition of illiteracy or semi-illiteracy means that the person knows little or nothing of the revolutionary heritage

[36] Edmundo Valadés has given great insight into the nature of political and economic manipulation in the country in "La muerte tiene permiso," *Antologiá contemporánea del cuento mexicano* (Mexico, 1963), pp. 83–88.

[37] The *ladino* is the more modernized, latinized, Spanish-speaking man — usually in these circumstances a *mestizo* or person of mixed Indian and Caucasian strain.

[38] Julio de la Fuente, "Población indígena" (unpublished): Jorge A. Vivó, "Aspectos económicos fundamentales del problema indígena," in *Revista América Indígena,* 3 (January, 1947), pp. 121–126; Gonzalo Aguirre Beltrán y Ricardo Pozas, *Instituciones indígenas y México actual* (Mexico, 1954), pp. 278–279.

described earlier in the book as the basis of legitimacy for the present system. To the marginal Mexican the law and the courts are of little use. The formal institutions are not expected to provide justice. There is only acceptance and supplication. In the most unusual of circumstances there is for the marginal man the resort to violence, but the significant point is that there exists no middle ground.[39]

Participating Mexicans

But what about the Mexico with which most of this book has been concerned? On the basis of many standard criteria Mexico is developing and has demonstrated great progress toward its development goals. Per capita product has gone up. During the last twenty-two years the gross national product has tripled. During the same time per capita income has doubled. The country stands out according to these and other indices as one of the most advanced and most rapidly advancing in Latin America. In fact, only one other country, Venezuela, can approach the rate of economic growth which Mexico has achieved. In spite of the great inequalities — social, economic and cultural — which even the most casual observer is bound to note, the success which the country has had in meeting its problems of growth has tended to create a psychology of optimism among Mexicans of high and low status. Thus, while there are those who point out the social discrepancies within the country, there are many others who point to its advances.

It is difficult to know just whom to believe. There is the Mexican "conservative" who is irritated by what he calls the demagoguery of the Mexican Revolution. There is the "politician" connected with government who lauds the acts and works of the "revolutionary regime," and there is the impatient "radical" who looks toward a new socialist revolution which he feels will achieve finally the goals of the 1917 Revolution that have not been reached. Those who take the positive view of accomplishments of the regime have a great deal on their side. They can point to the vast expansion over the past fifteen years in the distribution of electricity. They can point to the absolute increase in the number of schools, and show that while illiteracy stood at 66 per cent in 1930, it had dropped to 37 per cent in 1960. New roads are opened and new dams are placed in operation almost every week. Leaders talk in rational terms about the needs of the country and explain in detail the next steps which they intend to take in order to meet those needs. And that part of Mexico which has advanced beyond

[39] Pablo González Casanova estimates that there may be as many as 50 per cent of the Mexicans of today who fall in this category (p. 81). The author believes this estimate too high.

232 MODERNIZATION

the marginal situation for the most part believes what the technicians and politicians say that they will do for the country.

The prevailing climate of opinion in Mexico is optimistic. In general people believe that the system permits the individual to work out his personal and family problems and that there is social mobility. This psychology on the part of those Mexicans who are participating in the fruits of the country's development is based on many factors. Not only do people know that per capita income has increased, they also know that vast changes have been made which have benefited millions of people. Such a change is to be found in the agrarian reform in which 43 million hectares of land have been distributed to some 2,200,000 heads of families. Roads have made it possible for people to leave a rural situation that has become intolerable and move to urban centers with the hope of a better life in the new milieu. There is also regional movement from poorer areas to more prosperous ones.[40] Increasing numbers of Mexicans are moving out of the lowest paid jobs in agriculture to take more remunerative work in industry, commerce, and services. It is very important for this kind of mobility to take place. Much of Mexican optimism is based on the undeniable fact that nearly every Mexican knows someone who has been able to improve his economic and social condition within his lifetime. All investigators who have attempted to scrutinize the stratification arrangement and the problem of vertical mobility seem to be in general agreement that the tendency is to move from lower to higher levels.[41]

These changes from rural to urban, from agriculture to industrial, from less well-paid occupations to better paid work, from a rural person with no property to one who has a small property or is an *ejidatario,* and the movement from poor regions to those which offer more opportunity all tend to satisfy rising Mexican expectations and channel activity into moderate and peaceful pursuits.

The participating Mexicans — the ones who are enjoying to some extent the fruits of economic development — understand certain basic rules which pertain to political action in Mexico. They understand, for example, that the present system is a complex mixture of legal, rational, and modern forms of administration and decision-making operating along with older traditional ways. They understand that much has to

[40] Yates, p. 105.

[41] Cf. Howard F. Cline, *From Revolution to Evolution, 1940–1960* (London, 1962), p. 123; Ifigenia Martínez de Navarrete, *La distributión del ingreso y el desarrollo económico de México* (Mexico, 1960), pp. 74–75; Ana Maria Flores, *Investigación nacional de la vivienda mexicana, 1961–1962* (Mexico, 1963), pp. 51–57; Gino Germani, "Clases populares y democracia representativa en América Latina," en *Desarrollo económico,* 2 (Julio, 1962), p. 29.

be accomplished through personal relationships which are themselves tied closely to the legal, constitutional institutions of government. They accept the notion of the well-connected intermediary in government circles who acts as their representative at election time, presenting their protests, formulating their demands, and in general acting for them as a kind of "lobbyist" with peculiarly Mexican characteristics. It is understood that working through the intermediary and the organization he may have formed is a way of participating in the government of the country, and a way of obtaining concessions from new governments. The intermediary and his organization are to be found on the labor scene, in the National Peasants Confederation, in the National Popular Organizations, and in the PRI itself to which all these other organizations are affiliated.

To some extent also the opposition parties act as intermediaries and speak for dissident persons and groups that cannot find a place within the official party apparatus. Outside all these channels one finds at times intermediaries among priests, lawyers, and doctors who in some way have developed close contact with government circles. The masses in Mexico who are the participators have learned to use the intermediary to gain access to authority along with the labor, peasant, and party organizations. The participators have become accustomed to pressure group tactics which function with more or less efficiency within the framework of the constitutional rules themselves, the presidency, the congress, the courts, the state and local governments, the parties, the peasant, labor, and professional organizations, and the chambers of industry and commerce. This is the system the description of which has been the object of this book.

The author closes with this word of warning. There remains a Mexico which is not organized, which is politically quiescent, and which understands none of the new and peaceful ways of achieving goals. For this Mexico there is no middle ground between servile conformity and resort to force. This is the Mexico which must be incorporated into the modernizing national culture if violence in the countryside is not to disrupt the new way of life which is developing.

BIBLIOGRAPHY

The sources in this bibliography represent only those materials which were found to be of particular use in writing the book. The bibliography is therefore selective and does not pretend to include all possible references.

BOOKS AND PAMPHLETS IN ENGLISH

Alexander, Robert J. *Communism in Latin America*. New Brunswick, N.J.: Rutgers University Press, 1957.

Almond, Gabriel A., and James S. Coleman, eds. *The Politics of the Developing Areas*. Princeton, N.J.: Princeton University Press, 1960.

Almond, Gabriel A., and Sidney Verba. *The Civic Culture*. Boston: Little, Brown and Company, 1963.

Bernstein, Harry. *Modern and Contemporary Latin America*. Philadelphia: J. B. Lippincott Co., 1952.

Brandenburg, Frank R. *Mexico: An Experiment in One-Party Democracy*. Unpublished dissertation, University of Pennsylvania, 1955.

Brandenburg, Frank. *The Making of Modern Mexico*. Englewood Cliffs, N.J.: Prentice-Hall, Inc., 1964.

Clark, Marjorie R. *Organized Labor in Mexico*. Chapel Hill, N.C.: The University of North Carolina Press, 1934.

Cline, Howard F. *Mexico, Revolution to Evolution, 1940–1960*. London: Oxford University Press, 1962.

Cline, Howard F. *The United States and Mexico*. Cambridge, Mass.: Harvard University Press, 1953.

Dahl, Robert A. *Modern Political Analysis*. Englewood Cliffs, N.J.: Prentice-Hall, Inc., 1963.

Emerson, Rupert. *Political Modernization: The Single-Party System*. Denver: The Social Science Foundation and Department of International Relations Monograph Series in World Affairs, University of Denver, 1963.

Glade, William P., Jr., and Charles W. Anderson. *The Political Economy of Mexico*. Madison, Wis.: The University of Wisconsin Press, 1963.

Goldkind, Victor. "Another View of Social Stratification in Chan Kom: Conflict and Cacique." Unpublished manuscript, San Diego State College, 1965.

Hyman, Herbert H. *Political Socialization*. Glencoe, Ill.: The Free Press, 1959.

James, Daniel. *Mexico and the Americans*. New York: Frederick A. Praeger, 1963.

Kling, Merle. *A Mexican Interest Group in Action.* Englewood Cliffs, N.J.: Prentice-Hall, Inc., 1961.

Kneller, George F. *The Education of the Mexican Nation.* New York: Columbia University Press, 1951.

Lewis, Oscar. *Five Families.* New York: John Wiley & Sons, 1959.

Lewis, Oscar. *The Children of Sánchez.* New York: Random House, 1961.

Mosk, Sanford A. *Industrial Revolution in Mexico.* Berkeley, Calif.: The University of California Press, 1950.

Padgett, L. Vincent. *Popular Participation in the Mexican 'One-Party' System.* Unpublished dissertation, Northwestern University, Evanston, Ill., 1955.

Parkes, Henry Bamford. *A History of Mexico.* Boston: Houghton Mifflin Company, 1938.

Parsons, Elsie Clews. *Mitla — Town of Souls.* Chicago: University of Chicago Press, 1936.

Paz, Octavio. *The Labyrinth of Solitude.* Trans. Lysander Kemp. New York: Grove Press, Inc., 1960.

Scott, Robert E. *Mexican Government in Transition.* Urbana, Ill.: University of Illinois Press, 1959.

Senior, Clarence. *Land Reform and Democracy.* Gainesville, Fla.: The University of Florida Press, 1958.

Simpson, Eyler N. *The Ejido: Mexico's Way Out.* Chapel Hill, N.C.: The University of North Carolina Press, 1937.

Tannenbaum, Frank. *Mexico, The Struggle for Peace and Bread.* New York: Alfred A. Knopf, 1951.

Tannenbaum, Frank. *Peace by Revolution.* New York: Columbia University Press, 1933.

Tucker, William P. *The Mexican Government Today.* Minneapolis, Minn.: University of Minnesota Press, 1957.

Vernon, Raymond. *The Dilemma of Mexico's Development.* Cambridge, Mass.: Harvard University Press, 1963.

Whetten, Nathan L. *Rural Mexico.* Chicago: The University of Chicago Press, 1948.

Wionczek, Miguel S. "Electric Power," pp. 91–106 in *Public Policy and Private Enterprise in Mexico,* ed., Raymond Vernon. Cambridge, Mass.: Harvard University Press, 1964.

Wyckoff de Carlos, Ann. *Mexico's National Liberation Movement — The MLN.* Institute of Hispanic American and Luso-Brazilian Studies, Stanford University, 1963. Unpublished.

BOOKS AND PAMPHLETS IN SPANISH

Aguirre, Beltrán, Gonzalo y Ricardo Pozas. *Instituciones indígenas en el México actual.* Mexico: Instituto Nacional Indigenista, 1954.

Álvarez del Castillo L., Enrique, Miguel de la Madrid Hurtado y Raúl Cordero Knocker. "La legislación obrera," pp. 195–222 in *México: cincuenta años de revolución*. III. La Política. Mexico: Fondo de Cultura Económica, 1961.

Anon. *Mi libro de tercer año*. Mexico: Comisión Nacional de los Libros de Texto Gratuitos, 1960.

Aragón, Padilla. "La industria petrolera y su influencia en el desarrollo industrial," in *La industria petrolera mexicana*. Mexico: Fondo de Cultura Económica, 1958.

Banco Nacional de Comercio Exterior. *Comercio Exterior*. Mexico, 1963.

Banco Nacional de Comercio Exterior. *México, 1963*. Mexico, 1963.

Barrón de Morán, Concepción. *Mi libro de cuarto año*. Mexico: Comisión Nacional de los Libros de Texto Gratuitos, 1960.

Cano, Celerino. "Análisis de acción educativo," pp. 23–32 in *México: cincuenta años de revolución*. IV. La Cultura. Mexico: Fondo de Cultura Económica, 1961.

Castañeda, Jorge. "México y el exterior," pp. 267–287 in *México: cincuenta años de revolución*. III. La Política. Mexico: Fondo de Cultura Económica, 1961.

Confederación Nacional de Organizaciones Populares. *Bases constitutivas, declaración de principios y estatutos*. Mexico, 1947.

Confederación Revolucionaria de Obreros y Campesinos. *Declaración de principios, programa de acción y estatutos*. Mexico, 1952.

de la Cerda Silva, Roberto. *El movimiento obrero en México*. Mexico: Instituto de Investigaciones Sociales, U.N.A.M., 1961.

de la Fuente, Julio. "Poblacion indígena" (unpublished).

Departamento de Asuntos Agrarios y Colonización. *Seis años de política agraria del Presidente Adolfo López Mateos, 1958–1964*. Mexico, 1964.

de Pina, Rafael. *Curso de Derecho Procesal del Trabajo*. Mexico: Ediciones Botas, 1952.

Diario Oficial de la Federación. 1960–1964.

Dirección General de Estadística, *VIII Censo General de Población, 1960: Resumen General*. Mexico, 1962.

Echánove Trujillo, Carlos A. *Sociología mexicana*. Mexico: Editorial Porrua, 1963.

Fernández y Fernández, Ramón. *Economía agrícola y reforma agraria*. Mexico: Centro de Estudios Monetarios Latinoamericanos, 1962.

Fernández y Fernández, Ramón y Ricardo Acosta. *Política agrícola*. Mexico: Fondo de Cultura Económica, 1961.

Flores, Ana Maria. *Investigación nacional de la vivienda Mexicana, 1961–1962*. Mexico: Instituto Nacional de la Vivienda, 1963.

Flores, Edmundo. *Tratado de economía agrícola*. Mexico: Fondo de Cultura Económica, 1961.

Fuentes Díaz, Vicente. "Partidos y corrientes políticas," pp. 375–399 in *México: cincuenta años de revolución*. III. La Política. Mexico: Fondo de Cultura Económica, 1961.

Galicia Ciprés, Paula. *Mi libro de segundo año*. Mexico: Comisión Nacional de los Libros de Texto Gratuitos, 1960.

Gallo M., Victor. "La educación preescolar y primaria," pp. 43–103 in *México: cincuenta años de revolución.* IV. La Cultura. Mexico: Fondo de Cultura Económica, 1962.

García Cruz, Miguel. "La seguridad social," pp. 501–570 in *México: cincuenta años de revolución.* II. La Vida Social. Mexico: Fondo de Cultura Económica, 1961.

González Casanova, Pablo. *La democracia en México.* Mexico: Ediciones Era, S.A., 1965.

González Casanova, Pablo. La opinión pública," pp. 403–421 in *México: cincuenta años de revolución.* III. La Política. Mexico: Fondo de Cultura Económica, 1961.

Hernández y Hernández, Francisco. "El Movimiento Campesino," pp. 205–247 in *México: cincuenta años de revolución.* II. La Vida Social. Mexico: Fondo de Cultura Económica, 1961.

Herzog, Jesús Silva. *Inquietud sin tregua.* Mexico: Cuadernos Americanos, 1965.

Instituto Mexicano del Seguro Social Subdirección General Técnica. *Población Amparada por El Seguro Social: Cifras Estadísticas, 1944–1962.*

Iturriaga, José E. *La estructura social y cultural de México.* II. Mexico: Fondo de Cultura Económica, 1951.

López Aparicio, Alfonso. *El movimiento obrero en México.* Mexico: Editorial Jus, 1952.

López Mateos, Adolfo. *Último Informe* (September, 1964).

Loredo Goytorúa, Joaquín. "Producción y productividad agrícolas," pp. 99–164 in *México: cincuenta años de revolución.* I. La Economía. Mexico: Fondo de Cultura Económica, 1960.

Loyo, Gilberto. *Población y desarrollo económico.* Mexico: Selección de Estudios Latinoamericanos, 1962.

Manzanilla Schäffer, Víctor. "La reforma agraria," pp. 227–263 in *México: cincuenta años de revolución.* III. La Política. Mexico: Fondo de Cultura Económica, 1961.

Martínez de Navarette, Ifigenia. *La distribution del ingreso y el desarrollo económico de México.* Mexico: Instituto de Investigaciones Económicas, UNAM, 1960.

Mendieta y Núñez, Lucio. *Efectos sociales de la reforma agraria en tres comunidades ejidales de la república mexicana.* Mexico: Universidad Nacional Autónoma de México, 1960.

Mendieta y Núñez, Lucio. *El problema agrario de México.* Mexico: Ediciones Porrua, 1937.

Molina Enríquez, Andrés. *Los grandes problemas nacionales.* Mexico: Imprenta de A. Carranza e Hijos, 1909.

Organo de la Liga Agraria Estatal de Baja California, CCI. *Brecha: México es primero.* No. 4. Mexicali, Baja California, 1964.

Orive Alba, Adolfo. "Las obras de irrigación," pp. 337–381 in *México: cincuenta años de revolución.* I. La Economía. Mexico: Fondo de Cultura Económica, 1960.

Pani, Alberto J., ed. *Una envuesta sobre la cuestión democrática de México.* Mexico: Editorial Cultura, 1948.

Partido Revolucionario Institutional. *Ley para la Elección de Diputados y Senadores del Congresso de la Unión y Presidente de la República.* A pamphlet containing the electoral law of 1945 and subsequent changes through 1949. Mexico, 1949.

Ramírez Reyes, Manuel. "El desarrollo histórico de los partidos políticos mexicanos," La Sociedad Mexicana de Geografía y Estadística, Sesión Académica Ordinaria (October 8, 1963), unpublished.

Rivera Marín, Guadalupe. "El movimiento obrero," pp. 251–286 in *México: cincuenta años de revolución.* II. La Vida Social. Mexico: Fondo de Cultura Económica, 1961.

Sánchez Mireles, Rómulo. "El movimiento burocrático," pp. 289–305 in *México: cincuenta años de revolución.* II. La Vida Social. Mexico: Fondo de Cultura Económica, 1961.

Secretaría de Gobernación. *Ley Electoral Federal.* Mexico, 1951. [Amendments through 1964.]

Sierra, Justo. *Evolución política del pueblo mexicano.* Mexico: Fondo de Cultura Económica, 1955.

Solís Quiroga, Héctor. *Los partidos políticos en México.* Mexico: Editorial Orion, 1961.

Torres Bodet, Jaime, "Perspectivas de la educación," pp. 3–20 in *México: cincuenta años de revolución.* IV. La Cultura. Mexico: Fondo de Cultura Económica, 1962.

Valadéz, Edmundo. "La muerte tiene permiso," pp. 83–88 in *Antología contemporánea del cuento mexicano.* Mexico: Instituto Latinoamericano de Vinculación Cultural, 1963.

Yates, Paul Lamartine. *El desarrollo regional de México.* Mexico: Fondo de Cultura Económica, 1961.

Zamarripa M., Florencio. *Díaz Ordaz: Ideología y perfil de un revolucionario.* Mexico, 1964.

ARTICLES

Almond, Gabriel A. "A Developmental Approach to Political Systems," *World Politics,* 17 (January, 1965), 183–214.

Almond, Gabriel A. "Comparative Political Systems," *Journal of Politics,* 17 (August, 1956), 391–409.

Almond, Gabriel A. "Political Systems and Political Change," *American Behavioral Scientist,* 6 (June, 1963), 3–10.

Coleman, James S. "Education and the Political Scientist," *Items,* Social Science Research Council, 19 (March, 1965), 3–5.

Davis, Horace B. "Numerical Strength of Mexican Unions," *Southwestern Social Science Quarterly,* 35 (June, 1954), 48–55.

Durán, Marco Antonio. "Agrarismo y desarrollo agrícola," *Investigación Económica,* 23 (Cuarto trimestre de 1963), 677–708.

Durán, Marco Antonio. "Las funciones de la propiedad de la tierra en la reforma agraria mexicana," *El Trimestre Económico,* 31 (Abril–Junio de 1964), 228–242.

Easton, David. "An Approach to the Analysis of Political Systems," *World Politics,* 9 (April, 1947), 383–400.

Feierabend, Ivo K., Rosalind L. Feierabend and Betty A. Nesvold. "Correlates of Political Stability." Paper presented before the *American Political Science Association* (September, 1963).

Garza, David T. "Factionalism in the Mexican Left: The Frustration of the MLN," *Western Political Quarterly,* 18 (September, 1964), 447–460.

Germani, Gino. "Classes populares y democracia representation en América Latina," *Desarrollo Económica,* 2 (Julio, 1962), 20–31.

Johnson, Kenneth F. "Ideological Correlates of Right Wing Political Alienation in Mexico." Paper presented before the *Western Political Science Association* (March, 1965).

Kahin, George McK., Guy J. Pauker, and Lucien W. Pye. "Comparative Politics of Non-Western Countries," *American Political Science Review,* 51 (December, 1955), 1022–1041.

Kahl, Joseph A. "Three Types of Mexican Industrial Workers," *Economic Development and Cultural Change,* 8 (January, 1960), 164–169.

Needler, Martin C. "Changing the Guard in Mexico," *Current History,* 48 (January, 1965), 26–31.

Needler, Martin C. "The Political Development of Mexico," *American Political Science Review,* 55 (June, 1961), 308–312.

Padgett, L. Vincent. "Mexico's One-Party System: A Re-evaluation," *American Political Science Review,* 51 (December, 1957), 995–1007.

Scott, Robert E. "Budget Making in Mexico," *Inter-American Economic Affairs,* 9 (Autumn, 1955), 3–30.

Taylor, Philip B., Jr. "The Mexican Elections of 1958: Affirmation of Authoritarism?" *Western Political Quarterly,* 13 (September, 1960), 722–744.

Vivó, Jorge A. "Aspectos económicas fundamentales del problema indígena," *Revista América Indígena,* 3 (Enero, 1947), 121–126.

NEWSPAPERS AND PERIODICALS

El Dia. Mexico, D.F.
El Universal. Mexico, D.F.
Excelsior. Mexico, D.F.
Hoy. Mexico, D.F.
Siempre. Mexico, D.F.

The New York Times. New York.
The Wall Street Journal. New York.
Tiempo (Hispano Americano). Mexico, D.F.
Time. New York.

INDEX

Agrarian reform, 38–39
  under Cárdenas, 192
  historical background of, 185–191
  recent problems of, 194–201
Agrarian sector of PRI, 35, 53–55, 110–122
Alamán, Lucas, 15
Alemán Valdes, Miguel, 41
  and the CNOP, 125, 135
  and industrialization, 204
  and social security, 167
Almazán, Andreu, 64–65
Alvarez, Juan, 14
Alvarez, Luis H., 68, 69–70
Amparo, 148–149, 193
  See also Courts
Anti-BUO, 95, 103–108
Ávila Camacho, Manuel, 41
  and labor, 92–93
Aztecs: *see* Indian

Bonillas, Ignacio, 25, 26
Brandenburg, Frank, 47, 81, 141n, 156n, 206
Bravo, Nicolás, 15
Bucareli agreements, 28
BUO (Workers' Unity Bloc), 94, 104–107, 180

Cabinet, 157–160, 221–222
Cacique, 82–85
  See also Continuismo
Calles, Plutarco E., 29–35, 48–49, 189–190
Cárdenas, Lázaro, 34–71
  and the CNC, 110–111, 121
  and industrialization, 203
  and labor, 92
  See also Agrarian reform and *Ejido*
Carranza, Venustiano, 23–26, 27, 89, 187–188
Casa del Obrero Mundial, 89
CCI (Independent Farmers Confederation), 77, 120–122

CEIMSA (Mexican Export and Import Company), 217
  See also CONASUPO
Cement industry: *see* Industrialization
CGT (General Labor Confederation), 90–97, 104–106
Chamber of Deputies:
  election duties of, 79–81
  See also Congress
Chemical industries: *see* Industrialization
Clergy, 10, 13, 16, 31
Cline, Howard F., 21, 108n
CNC (National Peasants Confederation), 35, 54, 110–120, 180
CNIT (National Chamber of Manufacturing Industries), 131–135, 174
CNOP (National Confederation of Popular Organizations), 41, 54, 123–129
CNRU (National Commission for the Division of Profits), 170, 176
CNT (National Workers Confederation), 94, 104–107
Commerce, 215–217
Communists, 67–68, 77, 92, 93
Comonfort, Ignacio, 17
CONASUPO (National Popular Subsistence Corporation), 72, 217
CONCAMIN (Confederation of Chambers of Industry of Mexico), 129–135, 176
CONCANACO (Confederation of National Chambers of Commerce), 129–135
Congress, 147–148, 159
Conservative tradition, 15
Constitution of 1824, 15
Constitution of 1857, 17
Constitution of 1917, 28, 31

241